HUAL

Also by Mia Magik

IntuWitchin: Learn to Speak the Language of the Universe and Reclaim Your Inner Magik

The above is available at your local bookstore,
or may be ordered by visiting:

Hay House UK: www.hayhouse.co.uk
Hay House USA: www.hayhouse.com®
Hay House Australia: www.hayhouse.com.au
Hay House India: www.hayhouse.co.in

Praise for Mia Magik

"Living the essence of her teachings, Mia is the voice for Mother Nature. Very few people carry the kind of high magik Mia does; it doesn't get any bigger. This book will teach you how to dialogue with all life and master the art of communicating with the universe."

— **Sah D'Simone,** author of *Spiritually Sassy*

"Mia has single-handedly brought the cool factor back into witchcraft to reach an entire generation with an important arcane art. She is a woman whisperer with magic at her fingertips."

— **Regena "Mama Gena" Thomashauer,** author of *Pussy: A Reclamation*

"Mia Magik is my #1 resource for all things magic. Everyone's favorite witch on Instagram and beyond, she is a fairy-tale queen come to life. Her book is dearly needed."

— **Sahara Rose,** author of *Discover Your Dharma*

"As adults, sometimes we judge what we don't understand instead of getting curious and trying it out. This time I tapped into that inner child and let go. Thanks, Mia Magik, you've helped me so much in such a short amount of time!"

— **Ally Love,** contributor to the *TODAY* show

"Suffice to say, she's not your grandmother's witch. With her cascading brown hair, come-hither expression and upbeat demeanor, she seems more like a cross between a Victoria's Secret model and Tony Robbins."

— *Los Angeles Times*

"Mia has overcome a lot in life using manifestation, and she wants to help others do the same. Her work utilizes ancient wisdom that she adapted for her modern practices to help clients get rid of limiting beliefs that are holding them back in life, move past personal blocks, and live up to their potential.... It's easy to see why Mia is in demand."

— *Forbes*

WITCHUAL

Transformative Rituals to
Reclaim Your Powerful Magik
and Live a Fearlessly
Authentic Life

MIA MAGIK

HAY HOUSE

Carlsbad, California • New York City
London • Sydney • New Delhi

Published in the United Kingdom by:
Hay House UK Ltd, 1st Floor, Crawford Corner,
91–93 Baker Street, London W1U 6QQ
Tel: +44 (0)20 3927 7290; www.hayhouse.co.uk

Text © Mia Magik, 2025

Cover design: Kathleen Lynch • Interior design: Lisa Vega • Author photo: Sara Khan

The moral rights of the authors have been asserted.

All rights reserved. No part of this book may be reproduced by any mechanical, photographic or electronic process, or in the form of a phonographic recording; nor may it be stored in a retrieval system, transmitted or otherwise be copied for public or private use, other than for 'fair use' as brief quotations embodied in articles and reviews, without prior written permission of the publisher.

The information given in this book should not be treated as a substitute for professional medical advice; always consult a medical practitioner. Any use of information in this book is at the reader's discretion and risk. Neither the author nor the publisher can be held responsible for any loss, claim or damage arising out of the use, or misuse, of the suggestions made, the failure to take medical advice or for any material on third-party websites.

A catalogue record for this book is available from the British Library.

Tradepaper ISBN: 978-1-83782-067-2
E-book ISBN: 978-1-4019-7502-9
Audiobook ISBN: 978-1-4019-7503-6

10 9 8 7 6 5 4 3 2 1

This product uses responsibly sourced papers, including recycled materials and materials from other controlled sources. For more information, see www.hayhouse.co.uk

The authorized representative in the EU for product safety and compliance is Penguin Random House Ireland, Morrison Chambers, 32 Nassau Street, Dublin D02 YH68, Ireland. https://eu-contact.penguin.ie

Printed and bound by CPI Group (UK) Ltd, Croydon CR0 4YY

*This book is dedicated to remembering, and the
Divine Feminine in all of us. The wild, creative,
abundant magik of Nature that courses through your veins,
every element, mountain, forest, and your very breath.
To the women who are rising into this power,
remembering our sacredness, and the men who hold us,
who value these aspects in themselves and
are brave enough to heal alongside us.*

*For the Holy Mother Earth, who makes us all family.
For the wisdom keepers from every tradition and corner
of the world, who have courageously upheld the ancient practices,
ceremonies, and rituals that remedy the aching wounds in our souls
and soothe our spiritual suffering. Thank you for sharing your stories,
myths, and legendary lessons with those of us who
have been stripped of our own cultural history.*

*Thank you to my romantasy girlies, who took a break
from the fae and dragon realms to learn how to bring even
more of that magik into your life. To each and every one
of you who reads these pages, allowing yourself to be inspired
to change and serve this holy planet in even some small new way.
For the good girls and the bad ones who are finding their magik
in both shadow and in light. My greatest wish is to live in
a more magikal world where we've healed what once harmed us,
and I can't do it alone. Thank you, from the bottom of my heart,
for joining me on this journey. This book is dedicated to you.*

Contents

Introduction ✶ 1

Chapter 1:
A New World of Witchual ✶ 21

Chapter 2:
Mother and Father Nature ✶ 55

Chapter 3:
Singing for My Seven-Year-Old Self ✶ 83

Chapter 4:
Becoming Her Body ✶ 111

Chapter 5:
Anima Mundi ✶ 133

Chapter 6:
"Sleighing" the Dragon ✶ 167

Chapter 7:
The Circle of Life ✶ 195

Chapter 8:
Kitchen Witchery ✶ 219

Chapter 9:
The Imperial Secrets of Adornment ✶ 241

Conclusion ✶ 263

Acknowledgments ✶ 265

About the Author ✶ 269

Introduction

When was the last time you viscerally experienced your inherent Divinity? Inhaled awestruck wonder at your connection to something greater, whether in subtle, quiet whispers of wind or crashing thunder booming across mountaintops? Consider the moments you've marveled at the simple miracle of being alive. This is the essence of Witchual.

Once upon a time, we all honored Earth, the mother we share. Bestowing Her blessed bounty upon us, we hailed Her name in glory, singing in praise and petition to Her.

"Bring rains, abundant harvests, and healthy babies; thank you for our lives."

We listened to Her stories in birdsong and weather patterns, witnessed water's wisdom overcoming obstacles. Our harmonious, sustainable societies rested and rose with the sun's circadian rhythm. Only fire or moonlight illuminated dark nights. We knew the stars because their journeys were our wondrous entertainment, stories describing their universal travel across the indigo skies. The only blue light was daylight.

Plastic didn't exist; clothes and equipment were handmade from natural materials. We walked barefoot—sand, seaweed, mud, and stones between our toes. Every bath was a cold plunge in wild waters unless you found a hot spring. We ate seasonally and omnivorously because that's all we had access to. Our planet was a living, breathing, sentient deity whom we revered, cherished, and listened to with rapt attention. Now we emulate natural, instinctual habits as antidotes to modern mental strife.

How did we get so lost?

We lost our Witchuals.

The most fulfilling, traditional ancestral acts were forced out of practice. Earth-based spirituality and Great Mother worship were taken from us, replaced with costly "ritual," designed to extort and manipulate.

When was the last time your community called upon rain, prayed to land for growth, or thanked the sun for shining? How many of you who menstruate had a ceremony to celebrate your first bleed?

Instead of forming tribal councils to hear and consider everyone, we're building walls and writing laws of segregation.

Depending on your personality and what you desire to feel, create, and experience, Witchual is active communication with the Universe and your higher self. A now-secret language that was once common and ranges from wild, ecstatic, and unstructured to meticulously, mindfully organized, and everything in between.

If you've read my first book, *IntuWitchin*, you're one of the few who speak the Universal symbolic tongue. Luckily, it doesn't matter *how* you speak this language, only intending to receive and hear its guidance. The foundation of this exchange is understanding that everything has meaning, especially the natural world around you. Dialogue with creation consciousness is yours to craft. That's what Witchual is all about.

Today, mass rituals and "customary celebrations" are veritable rationalizations for unconscious consumerism, harmful to humanity and the planet. Sports excuse gambling, villainizing opposing teams, binging TV, drinking excessively, amassing gargantuan amounts of plastic waste and financial debt—distracting us from what really matters. We empty savings accounts for engagement rings, lavish weddings, kitchen appliances that gather dust to "keep up with the Joneses." Rather than enhancing our communities and the villages it takes to raise a child, we spend resources on material fluff anticipating baby's arrival, but hardly show up when new parents are most in need.

INTRODUCTION ☾

We've lost the original significance of our Holy Days. Most of our celebrations unconsciously or commercially, regurgitate religious words and go through motions without knowing why or caring to, forced upon us by society. Valentine's Day alone is a multibillion-dollar industry. People get trampled fighting over Black Friday electronics to prepare for honoring *a pregnancy that occurred without intercourse*. We mourn loss of life at funerals but have no other acknowledgment for the myriad symptoms of grief. Our ancestors would roll over in their graves.

No matter where you're from, your lineage was indigenous somewhere, sometime. Western culture has globally commodified, industrialized, and homogenized life's artistry. Daily Amazon deliveries replace conversations with store clerks or baskets woven together from long grasses plucked in fragrant meadows. We've sacrificed well-being, deserted ancient magik, all but severed our connection to Nature through Her destruction. We've hidden our magikal nature from ourselves.

Mass manufacturing displaced brothers building homes hand in hand. Living symbiotically with the wild brethren whose pelts we wore, stitched by grandmothers' bone needles strung with muscle sinew and tendon thread. Now, concerned only for financial profitability, we enslave more animals for consumption or entertainment than we *leave in the wild*.

Economy and *ecology* have the same root, which means "home," but we've traded our home's health for money. Economics is not a science, just a collection of equations that justify the destruction of our natural resources for profit. Gifts are more special and precious than purchases, yet we privatize all the earth gives freely, forgetting our knowledge of terrestrial and lunar cycles to optimize growth.

Parents stopped learning from their progeny, who viscerally experience the Universe responding to them. Now, most children can name fewer vegetables than they have fingers, and have an aversion to healthy, nutritious meals, preferring "sustenance" that's poisoning them. "Medicine" is made from petrochemicals and works to "alleviate" symptoms rather than root causes, while piling on numerous dangerous side effects. We lock elders in nursing homes, disregarding wisdom, human or otherwise.

Thankfully, the true treasures of existence are actually very simple and easy to recall. Sit still. Breathe. Leave your phone for hours at a time. As leaders of the New World, we get to reclaim our power from the primordial knowledge in our DNA. Restoring the link to the intelligence within and all around you regenerates a beautiful mental and physical landscape, enriching your environmental and energetic surroundings, intimate relationships, and Earth's healing.

I wrote this book to return power to people. To awaken the sleeping dragons within us who will carry us into a new reality we've only ever dreamed of. To remind you how to maintain constant conversation with cosmic creation through your direct line to the Divine. To offer you tools for revivifying your innate ancestral and wild animal intelligence. To be a lighthouse that will guide you home when our world is lost in the storm.

What we know as ritual takes from everyone. Witchual never takes from anyone; it only gives. To each one of us, to Mother Earth, and to all beings everywhere.

THE WISDOM OF RITUAL

The word *rite*, from Latin, describes ceremonial customs, *witch* means "wise," and *-ual* implies "process" or "taking action." Witchual is not just about prescribed postures and practices of other people's designation or dogma; it comes from anywhere, anytime—amplifying your powerful wisdom, illuminating how it informs your actions. My most potent transformative experiences are all just momentary inclinations I followed.

That's the deepest essence of Witchual: inspiration arisen spontaneously through your heart, born from inner compulsion to try, change, rise, grow, and evolve. Wild and sacred ideas erupt from within you, gnaw at you, pulling on your proverbial sleeve until you finally listen and attempt them. So, though there will be specific steps for you to try throughout these pages, above all, I want you to track the inklings that surface independently of my words.

Maybe you feel the urge to make a specific tea blend, take a new trail and find a special spot you can't believe you hadn't encountered sooner. Or fall in love with a season you've never experienced before, like I did in Montana's winter wonderland finishing this manuscript. Some of my most consistent Witchuals are just making wishes. On every eyelash, fluffy dandelion, and "Star light, star bright, first star I see tonight . . ." momentarily basking in the feeling of already having that desire fulfilled, my wish granted as I send it into the Universe.

We all partake in cultural or societal rituals: Sunday sermons, morning coffees, baths, weddings, bar/bat mitzvahs, baby showers, funerals, and birthdays. Unfortunately, women progressing from maidenhood to motherhood get little acknowledgment. A few gifts and some silly games. But that momentous transformation into becoming another's lifeline deserves more than a single occasion and actually discusses the magnitude of the shift in lifestyle.

Witchuals are conscious practices guided by your inner wisdom and guidance system, your IntuWItchin, in communion with Mother Earth. Infusing even the simplest acts with intention opens the door for anything to become ritualistic. Studies show that eating mindfully and blessing our food makes our bodies respond and digest more efficiently, just as spending time in Nature fortifies our immune system. Our presence, rather than society's prescription, amplifies the power of customary ceremony. We expand our consciousness and magnetism through our embodied experience.

A personalized craft reawakens intentional living's service to civilization, reintegrating sacred aspirations with inspired action. Forging a steadfast link with the Universe empowers the unlocking of our magik, multiplying our collective capacity to create change. Throughout these pages we'll explore how conscious consumption creates abundance, how ancient avatars and archetypes can activate supernatural abilities, how shadow work leads to authentic magikal powers, how inner-child communication opens the doors to make your dreams come true, and much more.

Because I wouldn't be here without Witchual.

My life took too many turns that could have proved to be imminent destruction. Witchual generated opportunities for rebirth, for creation. Without listening to those voices of Spirit and Nature that called me into the deep pools, screaming, crying, or singing, glimmers of insight that became brilliant endeavors, cosmic orgasms that coursed through me like supernovas, I would have withered away. I never would have become a powerful, courageously bold, outspoken, audacious woman. At every perfectly pivotal moment that I thought all hope was lost, Witchual kept my hope alive.

Now I am the kind of role model my inner little girl dreamed of finding. Leading a global movement of millions standing up for a greater future as a pillar of strength, inspiration, and permission to play full out.

Without it, none of this would be possible.

Frankly, my Witchual way of life saved me.

Devotion to the Goddess had become as necessary as breathing. Then, like many before me, I got into a relationship that required sacrificing my core essential nature to avoid abandonment. Meanwhile, caught up in the hustle of growing and scaling my empire, I distracted myself with illusions of needing to forfeit instinctual habits for "getting things done." One day, out of the blue, my body stopped digesting and rejected nutrients, and my hormones went haywire. I lost weight, felt exhausted each night, but just couldn't sleep.

All the test results determined the cause was stress. My life had done a 180. Instead of watching my focused inner work blossom, I had granted my external circumstances the majority of my energy and attention. I was still riding the wave of magnetizing magik and miracle manifestations, but the bigger they got, the more I shrank and played small to maintain my place in partnership. I was unconsciously rejecting the devotional way of life that had awakened my power and *brought me* my success.

I withered away. An unrecognizable hollowness took hold. The practices that had once filled my days were less and less frequent, miring my spirit in existential quicksand. Outwardly, career milestones abounded, but no outer accolade could uplift my inner torment.

I ignored my gut, and without the regular production of happy hormones (your microbiome produces serotonin, dopamine, and oxytocin), I felt irritable and melancholy, regardless of how many wins I achieved.

Then death, life's ultimate ritual, came knocking at my door and took my familiar—the most incredible creature I'd ever met, my little black cat best friend, Minerva. The grief struck me harder than I could have anticipated.

Let die the version of you who settled for crumbs of love, hid from your power, and believed that that was all you deserved.

Almost everything I identified with fell away. We lost Minerva's brother, Merlin, six months later, and I could finally let go of our relationship. I moved out of the palatial home I had created for us, and suddenly, there was nothing left to hold on to but the one thing that had always been constant before.

I dove headfirst, home, into Witchual.

I had weekly EMDR therapy, structural and somatic bodywork, yoni massages, vocal activations, acupuncture—anything that might help. I went to monthly retreats, reinstated pleasure practices, did consistent workouts, and cooked nourishing, healthy meals.

I fell in love with myself again. Through midday dance parties, morning mirror work, and community, Witchual resurrected me. I rewrote narratives and reprogrammed disempowering patterns that had kept me frozen. My life force returned. I met a true king who was inspired by my powerful magik and brought my career to soaring new heights.

Witchual brings us home to ourselves.

A NOTE ON F.E.A.R: FOR EVOLUTION AND RESILIENCE

If this anathema to spiritual suffering is so simple, why aren't we all just joyfully practicing it?

Because fear is a magikal life's greatest hindrance—the anathema to Witchual.

We shy away from creating our own ceremonial practices. Afraid they have to look a certain way, we're intimidated by "messing up" or "doing something bad/wrong/even evil." But worrying about "doing it wrong" keeps us from doing *anything*.

We discuss the Witch Wound in depth in *IntuWitchin*, but for those unfamiliar, it describes the epigenetic and energetic terror we can feel when returning to the sacred, ancestral ways we were forced to abandon.

Witch Trials annihilated millions of women (and men/non-binary folk) throughout the Middle Ages. Our inner critics or saboteurs—the amalgamation of societal/cultural/familial programming and trauma—tell us we're too much or not enough. I call the mental Witch Wound the Inner Witch Hunter. Harmful self-hatred talks us out of practicing magik or rising into our greatness, critically wreaking havoc on our sexuality, personal expression, trust in ourselves, others, Nature and more. This is residual epigenetic and inherited programming in our cells from a period of history where being ourselves could mean execution.

Healing or practicing any energetic artistry put you in danger. If you spoke up or on behalf of such a person, shared an opposing opinion to the church's narrative, or prayed the way people always had, you were locked up, or shut up, *permanently*.

Coming out of the broom closet, wanting to share your gifts or spirituality with others, the Witch Wound or Inner Witch Hunter's ugly claws can grip your back. Just picking up this book, you are rebelling against systems of oppression.

The Witch Wound often manifests in our expression, throat tightening (reminiscent from hangings), feeling like we're drowning (the accused were often tied to iron chairs and thrown into deep water), being held back (tight shoulders or back pain), or like we're being silenced, potentially as if hands were wrapped around our neck.

Fearing Nature arises because that's where we gathered medicine and prayed together. Women were told being dirty was unladylike and uncivilized; only peasants work land. Accusers or persecutors induced generational trust issues.

Fears are evolutionary opportunities to generate resilience, motivation to go bigger, spread seeds of this sacred work farther and wider.

We need to listen to actual threats to our safety, but fear mostly calls forth our courage, asking us to be brave, acting as the compass guiding us toward healing. As we learn to make new choices, we communicate to our mind, body, and soul who we are becoming:

"My altar is a sacred place I will confidently show to my in-laws."

"I trust my friends to accept my spirituality."

"I will wear my royal regalia."

"I *believe* in magik."

Taking leaps of faith invites the net to appear. If you want to expand the edges of your comfort zone, you have to step outside of them. The courage required to do so, alone, conquers many challenges.

When you feel afraid, unsure, or confused, breathe. Ask Earth for guidance. Disconnect from distracting devices; reconnect to the Great Mother, your soul's nature. The electromagnetic energy and negative ions emitted in natural environments are scientifically proven to heal you, reattuning your body to the highest vibrations.

When unfamiliar, the process can feel uncomfortable, but keep trying; make it a practice. We're much more accustomed to "zoning out" than tuning in. You might find yourself constantly reaching for devices or worrying obsessively, even about being out in the wilderness. Hone the skill of connecting by breathing through the Witch Hunter's old threatening habituated patterns. Unwinding fear from your nervous system recalibrates it with Nature's harmonic resonance.

Life gets incredibly magikal once you start dismissing damaging responses to your magik, disregarding the Inner Witch Hunter's disdain for your practice, and stop depressing your Natural power.

The intention of *Witchual* is to remedy the affliction of isolation and separation that impacts every human on Earth. Trusting yourself, the planet becomes who you instinctively turn to in moments of loss or confusion. Inquiring what you want to feel, experience, or create lets your rituals arise and unfold naturally from where you place your attention and intention.

Luckily, the single most powerful way to reignite our spiritual sparks, fan flames of hope, reunite with our inherent nature (as Nature), and realign ourselves with Divine Universal flow is in fact the oldest path of doing so.

Ritual.

Unlike dogmatic religion shaming your power or pleasure, Witchual celebrates the best and alchemizes the worst of who you are. It's the most effective way of personally communicating to the Universe: "Hi, I'm Mia, I know I'm connected to you; here's what I intend to create through that connection. Thank you for allowing me to experience it."

Combining devotional intention and attention to being the hero(ine) courageous enough to claim and live your most magikal life, *makes life magikal.* Give yourself permission and go for it.

There's no reason *not* to.

THE RECLAMATION

Fairy tales are rich repositories of ancient beliefs, safeguarding our genuine Divine potential persistently through time. Many historians have studied their intentional encoding, which has been passed on to children when it was unsafe to keep original traditions alive. In fact, legends are Earth's oldest religion, designed worldwide to help us learn. Tales were initially told orally and were therefore entirely mutable, changing between tellers, locations, and audiences. Putting them to page halted their evolution and alteration. Many stories stagnated and lost their invitation for interpretation by being frozen in writing.

The one story in particular, of a miraculous phenomenon that's been taken as fact, dismisses any other enduring folkloric records as nonsensical or downright impossible, when they're *all* depicting our divine potential. Jesus's tale is in fact an allegory of initiation from far older solar deities like Osiris from Egypt or Dumuzi from Sumeria and describes the alchemical and spiritual processes of awakening to Christ Consciousness through metaphorical rites like baptism for purification.

Paul, in the first Biblical teachings, described Jesus as an avatar, not an actual historical person. In fact, there is no such place as Nazareth; this is a mistranslation of the word *Nazarene*, which meant "spiritual initiate."

Carl Jung argued Gods and Goddesses mythologically depicted humans with greater powers and heightened senses, describing neurological processes and spiritual capacity: "A single archetype may appear in a variety of symbols. Such images are more than subjective fantasies. They are the psyche's vocabulary through which Initiates can communicate with their own inner depths.... Christian civilization has proved hollow to a terrifying degree. It is all veneer, but the inner man has remained untouched. Everything is to be found outside in image and Word, church and Bible, but never within his soul—out of key with his external beliefs."

Scientific studies *prove* belief in magik, or the supernatural, powerfully impacts personal performance. Children's creativity assessments have shown exponentially higher scores after exposure to magik before testing. It's not nonsense; it's just been kept secret, hidden so long we forgot it was always ours.

The phenomenon of Harry Potter, the highest-grossing book and movie series of *all time,* is not coincidental. We all long to discover that we too possess magikal powers. Fairy tales remain the last bastion of the possibility that there is, in fact, more to life. The Fairy Godmother wears a tiny, pointed hat and waves a magik wand to manifest hearts' desires. She's a *witch*! Albeit with a sweeter, more inviting label, so everyone loves her!

Nothing could replace being raised in a culture untouched by conquistadors and crusaders, but most of us weren't. So fairy tales, fantasy, and sci-fi become essential gateways to magikal, Witchual living.

Beyond practicing yoga or meditation, we're deepening our sense of magik and wonder, seeing sacredness everywhere, finding the mystical in the mundane, from applying face cream to performing involved moon ceremonies with every color, number, and symbol aligned for your entire coven. What's required is intention, effort, reverence, discipline, and honoring the Goddess and God archetypal frequencies we all possess, shaping our own school of thought.

Witchual never requires following a set path, just forging your own, reigniting collective communication with the Divine through Nature and each other, celebrating your individuality and spiritual freedom, redefining and rediscovering magik and power on your terms.

Putting the world's current state into perspective is imperative. Feel Mother Earth's heartbeat. Listen to Her song and language. She's clearly signaling Her pain. Abandoning and disconnecting from Her, from our true, wild nature, is why suicide rates, especially in young people, are alarmingly high. School shootings, obesity, overmedication, and stress cause illness every day. *Antibiotic* literally means "against life," yet we're pumped full of them.

The world is crying out for rebirth—new systems, strategies, and spirituality to return us to equilibrium and our wild instinct, eliminating dissonance and imbalance. Something has to change, and the only place we can guarantee that is within.

Imagine a global governance who cares deeply, like our ancestors did, for not only our human species but all sentient life on Earth, seeking counsel from trees, rivers, and animals.

Imagine breathing immaculately clean air. An unpolluted mental realm of loving thoughts rather than toxic beliefs. Crystal-clear waters caringly kept pristine, free from oil, sewage or plastic waste— our tears, blood, emotions, sexuality, and creativity regarded as purely soulful expressions. We'd shine bright like the sun, fueled by inner power so radiant we'd never burn out or hide our light. Resplendent and recharged, we'd be motivated to serve.

We'd have vibrant soil feeding healthy bodies, relationships and abundance nourished and revered. With their needs met, people could work together to harmonize their mental, emotional, physical, and spiritual health. *Having* this discussion plants seeds of hope. I have faith we can and will usher in a new era where ancient ways safely serve the modern day for a world co-created with directed and devoted attention and intention. A new way awaits in Witchual.

Uniting ourselves with Universal energy and consciousness reweaves our life force with Nature. Sacred inspiration guides habituated actions, slows our steps and breath—putting away our phones with friends, opting for presence, we speak more kindly to ourselves or about others; we move mindfully. Escape the current bandwagon, let's hitch up our own!

The Goddess is a living, sentient deity upon whose skin we walk. The fastest way to actualize your greatest visions is not one-and-done ayahuasca ceremonies. It's your lifestyle, belief system, and interplay with existence, your Witchual way. Listen to your body; follow your IntuWitchin, your inner wisdom and guidance system; acknowledge Mother Earth's blessings. Reward yourself with the true treasures of life—joy, love, peace, magik, inspiration—wield Her powers to make your dreams come true.

INTO THE BODY

Take a deep breath. Fill your lungs completely. Hold for 10 seconds. Experience that fullness, stretch into your own expanded *inspir*ation.

Release slowly. . . . Feel yourself as the source of wind.

Air: our very sustenance, gifted from and inhaled by the trees, plants, and algae, in sacred exchange. Breath is gusting cosmic exhales, governing the realm of mind, communication, intellect, and inspiration—the life we're breathing into one another right now.

Experience your body weight. Feel the bones like mountain stones, muscles like mud and clay. Your Earthly body is the body of our Holy Mother.

Twirl saliva with your tongue. Feel the tears behind your clear vision. Rivers, creeks, and streams of blood pump through the canyons of your veins—the waters within.

Now, feel your beating heart. Can you hear it? Your electrical system is fire—hence properly functioning neurons are aptly deemed "firing." The rhythmic drumming of our mother's pulse, the permeating primordial sound we heard before we emerged into the world. The light in every cell.

Experience this moment between you and me through words *and* the deeper desire for connection with ourselves, each other, and reality's magikal hologram. The fifth sacred element, Spirit, animates all life, unites us as one, and emanates through every fiber of existence.

Take another big deep breath. Release a sigh. Make a sound. "Ahhhh . . ." Better. (Sighing signals safety; silent or held breath implies danger.)

Easy, right? You have just engaged in the fastest OG Witchual of all. The awareness that you are not only inherently connected *to* Nature but a reflection *of* it. Made of the same elements as our majestic planet and holy Universe. It's that easy. Attention and intention. All that's required to live a truly magikal life is listening to and connecting with those foundational pillars within and all around you. Then every action becomes ritualistic.

We call it *spelling* because our words chart the course of our destiny—the original meaning of the word *word*. Your words and ways make the difference. No matter how juicy my vernacular may sound, it won't mean as much as your own. If you experience angels where I have dragons, calling on those who guide *you* will be far more impactful than those who guide *me*.

Are you preaching peace, tranquility, acceptance, and safety? Or greed, hatred, fear, and doubt? I don't teach spells; I teach spell-*crafting*. I'm not going to catch you a fish and feed you for a night. I'll teach you to fish and feed you for life! Because what's most valuable long term is showing you how to heal what's in your way. *Being* your spells is the absolute most powerful manifestation tool to bring your visions to fruition. Please always find your most resonant prose and powers.

Yep, this is a different book, because I am a different witch. I don't identify as Wiccan or pagan; I got into spirituality through quantum physics, fairy tales, and "conspiracy" theories. Through my scholarly esotericism I have worked deeply with the Seven Hermetic Principles and 12 (originally 13) Universal Laws that govern reality. Which grant the outstanding opportunity to explore ritual as a lifestyle more than an obligation.

Devotion isn't about what or how anyone tells you to be, including me. Don't strive to emulate anyone else; commit to carving your own path. Every step offered in this book is a suggestion, an opportunity, or a foundation to build upon to cultivate spiritual, ancestral, and transformational healing. But *you* have to take the steps.

Maybe wearing blue makes you feel more powerful than red—great! Make it your own. Practice, hone, develop, and enhance your skills and gifts.

Envision feeling completely and utterly safe to be all of who you truly are. To say what you think, express how you feel, dress, play, pray, fuck, live how you *really* want.

How different would the world look?
Who would you be?
What would you do differently?

Genuine freedom is possible. Some of us dance and shake our asses to experience God. Others sit silently. Quiet your mental chatter long enough to listen to Nature's guidance and consciously communicate with the cosmos, aka Witchual. The most powerful of which you receive and immediately know you just *have* to do.

Walking beside a stream, you're *compelled* to jump in.

or

You have an idea for special quality time with your partner to try something new.

or

You feel the urge to stand beneath the moonlight and howl.
Now you're on the path that lights *you* up.

I wrote *IntuWitchin* specifically because those inclinations are *the most important practice*. When you listen to yourself, you are divinely guided. *Witchual* carries the torch forward into inspired action so you can wield infinite forces of creation in your favor.

In *IntuWitchin*, I explored the Universal Law of Correspondence, ("As above, so below. As within, so without."), which I'll dive deeper into in Chapter 9, "The Imperial Secrets of Adornment." Chapter 2, "Mother and Father Nature," illustrates harnessing the Law of Gender's spectrum through its expression in our environment. I'll present the Law of Cause and Effect in Chapter 3, "Singing for My Seven-Year-Old Self," depicting how challenges of our youth show up in adulthood's habitual actions and responses. Chapter 6, "'Sleighing' the Dragon," discusses shadow work, parts integration, and how facing off with your internal demons can lead to life's greatest riches, aligned with the Law of Compensation. Chapter 7, "Circle of Life," works with the Law of Rhythm, going with the flow energetically and physically. You could work with these invitations your whole life and always keep learning, so I'm going to share my most potent discoveries with you.

Because even the most magikal world is enhanced by having others to share it with, I wish for everyone to feel safe in their power, exploring and discovering what it means for them individually.

Your path might go one way, then turn 180 degrees. There's no right or wrong. Everything contributes to your evolution. Both paradises and erupting volcanoes have carved my route. Let *your* most healing, transformational, and impactful practices be your guiding light, and you'll never go astray.

My wish is for your reawakening to all the beauty and ancient wisdom offered by our sacred planet. To know the miracle of existence with an integrated certainty, which is no small feat. Rather than adding new things to your to-do list, it's more about what you stop doing (like overconsuming, mindless eating, scrolling, or dating) and *how* you do everything.

Ask yourself:

What feels most nourishing, joyful, and pleasurable? (not escapist or numbing—real pleasure)
What ignites my Divine spark?
How do I connect to or express my *Divinity?* (if you have been taught God is external)
What did my inner five-year-old love? What were they interested in?

What may sound insignificant to one person ("How could that be so life changing?") could have made all the difference to another. No one will ever be able to fully understand what you've been through. Never let anyone tell you what you do or don't know, did or didn't feel. Mystical experiences can't be translated. Our visions, releases, epiphanies, *and* suffering are our own. Honor your process and become unfuckwithable—this is radical evolution. Thank you for joining me on this journey.

COME ONE, COME ALL

Having worked with a diverse array of people, I am certain these Witchuals will work for anyone. Whether you're seeking love, joy, freedom, or fulfillment, take a chance. Experience living a magikal life.

As discussed in *IntuWitchin*, following breadcrumbs is key. So if the same book keeps coming up, read it. If you feel drawn to a location, that land's *genius loci*, "spirit of place," has medicine for you; go visit and explore. Travel is a magikally transformative experience—the only investment you can buy besides personal development, that makes you richer.

If the same modality, training, or class is recommended multiple times, try it! See if it resonates. I've tried many lineages that weren't for me. I've completed certifications that contributed to my personal growth and healing that I never used with clients. Specific goals in each training propelled me further into my power—that was enough. Even if you glean only what *not* to do, that too serves you long term. You're not wasting time; you're learning.

What have you always wanted to study, learn, or feel in your body?
What are you called to explore?
Where have you always wanted to go?
What knowledge have you always wanted to acquire, or what sensation have you always wanted to feel?

There's a reason you're drawn to that call; answer it! Let magikal morsels guide you. Following this guidance, creating rituals as tribute to or in consideration of your goals, brings your aspirations into reality. *Anyone* can do this, they don't have to be complex.

The only rule: Avoid manipulating another person or their will. Witchual is for *you*. Keep your workings focused on yourself or the highest good of all unless explicitly requested to use your magik on someone's behalf.

Remember, the micro truly affects the macro. No act is too small; everything holds significance. Witchual doesn't have to be an act of doing; it's about being exactly who you are, right where you are. There is a realm beyond your wildest dreams awaiting you, which I hope blesses your life every day, in every way, as it has mine. Time is our most valuable resource, so I appreciate your presence and can't wait to see how Witchual changes you as it has changed me. There is always a middle way, and yet the act of committing to this life really is all or nothing, go big or go home. Quite frankly, what else are we doing here?!

Let's GO!

✶ ✶ REFLECTION ✶ ✶

What is your lineage of magik, genetically or energetically?

Where did you first recognize, remember, or believe in it?

What names do you have for Divinity?

Where do you feel it in your body?

What activities make you aware of it more than others?

What rituals do you already have?

How could you bring more intention to what you're already doing in your daily life?

What affirmations could you add to these processes to help you believe in yourself and become more magnetic to your dream life?

What could you enhance with greater intention?

What would that look like?

How could you add at least one simple intentional practice to your routine today or this week?

CHAPTER 1

A New World of Witchual

If I had a time machine, my first stop would be seeing what *really* happened from BCE to CE to dethrone feminine Divinity. I wish I could prevent witch burnings and genocides of peaceful, harmonious tribes with plentiful resources by greedy, viciously warring colonizers asserting religious righteousness. Alas, despite endless hypothesizing, the great mystery destined this. Perhaps so we could now rise like phoenixes from their ashes.

Imagine if, instead of violent conflict, arguing over which "chosen people" have the right to be here, we recognized we've *all* been chosen, incarnated to share this paradisiacal planet. If we gathered as a global community *to choose* peace.

How much more productively and peacefully could society function if we accepted that we're all talking about the same things but using different words and languages?

Envision the effect across humanity if we united with a collective vision, using ritual for connection rather than a tool for projecting oxymoronic supremacy.

Leonard Shlain, in his groundbreaking book *The Alphabet Versus the Goddess*, offers a theory to explain our psychological regression. He suggests there was a literal shift of function in our brain's processing as we transitioned from symbolic or pictographic language to abstract written words.

The feminine, creative right hemisphere governs symbol interpretation, imagination, spatial ability, and the artistry that fosters sustainable and symbiotic life. A picture of a bird means "bird" but can also signify flight, freedom, higher perspective, or wind's wisdom, for example. Non-pictorial written language, on the other hand, migrates to the masculine, logical, critical-thinking left hemisphere for interpretation. These symbols put in this order means one thing, but shift them around and it means nothing. Used for necessary strategic bursts in hunting or building tasks, the left hemisphere had never previously been required for communication.

Unprecedented behavior ensued: plundering of planet and people, inciting mindless violence, and imposing patriarchal, religious dogma on others. A massive shift of myth from one ruling civilization to the next eventually resulted in the impetus of birth from anyone's *mind* or *rib* rather than straight out of the *womb*. Artistic depiction changed too. Where ancient illustrations show only reverence to vulvas, breasts, and the Great Mother, for the first time, weapons appeared against people rather than just animals.

For 2,000-plus years, major religions have warred against one another, annihilating the sacred, far more ancient wisdom and spirituality of indigenous civilizations worldwide. It's time to lay down crusading swords and daggered tongues. No one's God or relationship to Spirit is superior; they are simply different.

Ritual was a primarily communal and altogether consistent activity. It can be knit into any interaction with another—uniting our collective energies significantly synergizes the impact of our power. Though now carrying a religious connotation, in truth Ritual emerges from elements that Nature, humanity, and Creator all share. Calling all faiths home, remembering we are inherently one, brothers and sisters united by our Mother. Integrating intention into everyday actions mends our modern separation from ritual, unshackling it from relegation to private, personal practice or secret spirituality.

Scaling jagged peaks, reaching a sky-high summit to look out over an endless expanse of beauty requires perseverance, dedication, and desire. Reaching great heights in our own lives asks the same. You have to want it, *and* you have to go get it.

Whether proverbially or physically, mountains have always anecdotally represented the ascent of our spiritual path, reminding us, *everyone* reaches the top differently. Whenever someone says, "This way is the only/fastest/purest/best way," that's generally a red-flag warning—it's *not* the way for me. Everyone's healing, programming, and gifts are unique.

Eagles soar; goats scale cliff faces; snakes slither through underbrush; humans take trails; fish stay in lakes and creek beds. Some people have no interest in seeing the view, so *they never start the trek*. There is no *right* way to climb the mountain; we're all going to the same place. Don't get distracted from your path because of someone else's. There's no comparison. *Your* way *is* the only way.

When we set out for a summit, straight up is generally inaccessible, even impossible. One best practice is to wind around, rising in a spiral. Though it can feel cyclical, even appearing as if you've returned to the same spot, in actuality, you've gained altitude, a higher perspective, literally and figuratively. Yes, the landscape looks the same, and our ego tries to react with, "Oh no, not this again?! How did I get *back* here?!" as if we've somehow digressed. But though the view is similar, you have not gone back. You've gathered more information and tools to face your patterns or challenges. You know and have experienced more; lessons have been learned.

As you integrate this newfound knowledge, it becomes the wisdom that guides how you live your life from this moment forward. In the new world of Witchual, magik is in your every breath. How you embrace it is up to you.

ONCE UPON A TIME

Rites of passage were once necessary symbolic initiations from one significant season to the next. Completing vision quests (or other tests of character) officially welcomed you into your tribe. Failure could mean exile, rejection, or imminent death. From infancy to elderhood, ceremonial milestones rooted us in personal and communal growth. Now, these important celebrations have been minimized or lost completely.

For many, "adulthood" is marked only by high school graduation's solitary, systemic rite that hardly encompasses the personal evolutionary growth out of dependent teenagerhood into self-reliance. The transition from communal attachment in a family unit to independence surrounded by strangers (though many quickly become family) marks a powerful transition no one talks about.

This potent shift lacks deserved formal recognition and the adequate preparation you need to function on your own where others have previously upheld your responsibilities. Studies show that mental illnesses gone previously undiagnosed, or even unnoticed, flare up during this time. Children who never managed their own survival are suddenly thrust into leading their households without any training, and long-suppressed issues can flare up unexpectedly.

Technology places practically everything at our fingertips. Yet many kids grow up without basic self-care; they can't cook or do laundry and struggle with what's required on their own. Absence of structured community involvement and recognized rites of passage, especially concerning sexuality and creativity, leaves a confusing void that can lead to isolating mental health concerns.

We're all well-versed in pop culture, brand names, and celebrities but lack primal skills like building fires or darning socks. Contributing to further environmental pollution, we discard more plastic masquerading as fabric that's replaced textile and tapestry weaving.

Instead of cultivating food in backyards and kitchen windows, we poison it with DNA-altering RoundUp, stockpile it in Styrofoam and plastic-wrapped supermarket aisles, devoid of nutritional value. Systemically subsidizing monocrop agriculture over local farmers forces humans to ingest chemicals that harm every cell in our bodies just as they damage Mother Earth's body and soil.

Eating seasonally available produce reduces stress, autoimmune conditions, and mental health challenges. Shopping at local farmers markets makes a huge difference for you *and* farmers. Even the social interaction of doing so rather than using InstaCart makes a difference! Raising or hunting meat and cooking it from scratch rather than packages fortifies our microbiome and immune defenses. Modern industrialized "civilization" isn't cutting it for our well-being long term.

Beyond diet, consider other interactions with your local ecosystem. U.S. lawns alone cover an area larger than 65 percent of the nations on Earth, wasting massive amounts of water, eliminating biodiversity, and requiring many toxic chemicals. Dandelions, one of *the most* medicinal plants—used for skin issues, inflammation, digestion, detoxification and more—are classified as "weeds" and are attacked into oblivion despite their persevering strength and resilience. Pesticides harm wildlife from pollinators to predators. Replacing lawns with indigenous plants, gardens, and meadows reinvigorates ecology, encouragingly increases biodiversity, grows natural medicine, and strengthens flora and fauna, many of which propagate that which we rely on to maintain the equilibrium required to survive. Watch how land changes and thrives in response.

You can save electricity (which means reducing fossil fuel extraction) *and* money by turning all outdoor lights off at night, decreasing light pollution to help our nocturnal animal neighbors. These easy actions serve Earth, bolster environmental health, and foster deepening bonds with Nature.

Community, human and beyond, was not a backdrop but the very bedrock and constant participant in passing its members from one stage to another. The vital nutrient crafting values, honor, integrity, and behavior. Offering nurturing encouragement, guidance, and presence through transitions. We watch "how it's done" and emulate what we've seen. We are starved for tribal living. The full spectrum of rites of passage incorporate ritual into significant transitions, enriching our connection to our essential role in life's revolution. The best way to find loving, uplifting people is by becoming one.

TIMELESS LEGACY

People around the world use ceremony as pivotal cultural initiations to demarcate transitions from youth to maturity. Readiness for adulthood is shown by demonstrating certain skills or undergoing a rite of passage. In some cultures, because women give birth, they are not expected to "prove themselves," and this transition is marked with pampering and celebration. Navajo, or Diné, celebrate the significant milestone of young women's menstruation by treating them like a queen for a week.

Our first bleed is a mysterious moment in womanhood—a divine initiation. In Red Tent circles, women once gathered during new moons when we all bled together; seasoned sisters shared knowledge, welcoming young women with rituals that honored her journey into childbearing. Moon blood was the original Blood of Christ, created without violence or harm every month from women. Drinking wine to represent it is *far older* than the church. Menstrual blood is full of stem cells which are now being proven to help heal Alzheimer's. It is literally the liquid of creation. Supportive validation for its magik demystifies and destigmatizes menstruation's seasons of growth, harvest, decay, and renewal. Its mighty feminine reflections revered in Nature, mirror the waxing and waning moon.

Every woman has seen a friend who's bleeding, and within a day or so, they are too. That's a *biological* impulse. We're designed to sync up *to gather in Witchual*. This was our oracular time to divine wisdom for guiding our entire tribe and family. We sat together without the men, cackling conspiratorially, the way women always do when left to our own devices. That's why connecting when we're bleeding feels so yummy. We've been doing it since the beginning of time. We're remembering our body's wisdom and how we're meant to relate to it. The heightened sensitivity while Mooning, also called Dragon Time in some ancient cultures, is my favorite. It's about nourishing sensual practices; hearty, replenishing foods; juicy lovemaking; and giving absolutely zero fucks about anyone else's needs or wants.

Communal education about the true sanctity of menstruation would alter humanity's perceptions and connect women with themselves and Nature. Celebration alleviates the shameful societal burden projected on us; rewrites the story as a collective pause to take a break together; and enriches our support, strength, and shared enjoyment along the feminine magikal path.

I dream of giving my daughter a celebration like those that are commonplace and expected in indigenous civilizations. Telling my dad was embarrassing; my mom, who was three years into menopause when it happened, offered little solace. I simultaneously mourn for my inner 13-year-old and jump for joy that she and I will both know bleeding is sacred again. The whole community honoring transitions from childhood into young womanhood.

Ceremonial hunts, for buffalo in North America or lions in Africa, were integral to masculine growth. In the Mount Kilimanjaro basin, one of the most breath*giving* places I've ever seen, these initiations are more than relics of the past, they are living, breathing aspects of our present. Across vast regions of Kenya and Tanzania, Maasai men defeated lions to become warriors. A loss deemed him incapable of protecting his people. Beyond traditional victory, these were crucial elements of identity and social standing. Due to conservation efforts for lions and their disappearing habitat, this act has become rare. Rather than a hunt, many now participate in a ceremonial "Maasai Olympics" to demonstrate traditional warrior skills.

How different might the world be without us deeming certain societies primitive, conquering and plundering their lands, killing their animals as trophies with exorbitant price tags? What if we'd been inspired by their ancient wisdom instead? Sitting around a crackling fire you built, creating that magnetic gathering place, is a primal skill that will serve you all your life. Knowing which plants will hurt you, heal you, and sustain you is a whole other realm of power.

Intertwined with cosmic cycles, Nature, and the afterlife, ritual traces back to the dawn of human civilization, shaping our spiritual journey, weaving a tapestry of mystical knowledge and conscious connection with creation.

Although confronting, the truth can be almost too unbearable, we cannot remain idle any longer. Pretending we are disparate from a legacy as ancient as cave paintings and hieroglyphic storytelling decimates our spiritual wellness.

What if tribes and shamans still led communities?

What if we never poisoned land with plastic?

What if we were never prescribed false piety, pharmaceuticals, and petrochemicals?

What if we freely had sovereign relationships to God as long as we harmed no one?

Imagine if we truly safeguarded this planet and her people with *every* action—how different would our world look?

How might you plant a seed of greater tending today?

Each time I ask myself these questions, I adapt my behavior to align with my answer. Try it. Commitment to this vision can set us on a new trajectory.

OH HOLY DAY!

Once upon a time, wild, ecstatic rites accompanied spiritual observance of Nature within and all around us. Reenacting the nativity or resurrection is ancient ritual theater offering guidance through mythological wisdom. Greek philosopher Celsus, in his treatise *On the True Doctrine*, described early Christians who "excite their initiates to the point of frenzy with flute music like that heard among the devotees of the Goddess Cybele." Now, religion has altered most Holy Days (holidays) from solar and lunar observances to rituals of restriction imposed and inflicted upon us. Christmas was originally the birth of the *sun* (not the *son*) on Winter Solstice. Hanukkah's eight nights ended the same day. Easter and Passover once honored Earth resurrecting verdant flora and vibrant fauna at Spring Equinox.

Scholars like Graham Hancock suggest ancient Egyptians' rites date back over 20,000 years, like Mayan, Hupa, Apache, and Siberian shamanism's rich histories. The oldest shamanic site ever discovered was pre-Ice Age, over *40,000 years old*. Menstrual blood and swan wings were the tools used for rituals back then. Gobekli Tepe, a 12,000-year-old temple in Turkey, was buried by hand to safeguard its secrets. These uniquely bountiful traditions are connected by a common reverence for the natural world and the unseen forces animating it.

Circa 5,000 BCE, Witchual flourished on Crete. Priestesses held noble status highly regarded as being integral to spirituality and society. Art is one of the main ways we understand cultural function in history, and Cretan paintings don't have a single depiction of violence, war, weaponry, or bloodshed. Just peaceful nature, beauty, and feminine reverence. Unfortunately, if you tried to use the word "Cretan" today to reference this sacred place, the modern ear would most likely hear "cretin," meaning a stupid, vulgar, or insensitive person. In the Roman Empire, bathhouses served as sanctuaries of communal and existential connection, returning us to the Great Mother's womb for cleansing and purification.

Priestesses were more than highly esteemed; they were nobility, revered Divine conduits, counsel to kings and emperors with pivotal, influential roles. Incarnations of the Goddess herself, they shared status with royalty, inspired awe, and commanded respect. Within one generation, their standing changed. Sharply contrasting broader societal views suddenly saw women as lesser, with confined roles and restricted freedom.

Roman civilization, known for mighty conquering heroes born from Venus herself or favored by Nike, had similar dichotomies. Certain women held significant influence. But as the culture transitioned from polytheistic into monotheistic, the broader patriarchal framework of strength and dominance in one realm distracted from underlying restriction and limitation in others.

Jesus's story marks a transition where the Gods no longer returned to the earth to become soil and nourishment for the future, but ascended into heaven. His body disappeared. It's no longer of this realm, fully eviscerating him from the earth.

In the grand tapestry of history, Golden Age societies like Egypt and Greece rose to magnificent heights of conquest and sophistication yet eventually declined. Though we say the Roman Empire fell, it didn't. It converted to Christianity and became the Roman Catholic Church. Having stripped the metaphors from the myths and rewritten them as a literal, "historical" narrative, the Vatican became one of the richest "countries" on Earth. Its global stronghold is a protective, safe haven for known pedophilic child abusers without repercussions, restitution, or rehabilitation.

This is what we're supposed to regard as our pathway to Godliness?

We've been systematically removed from the most ancient form of worship on Earth, *of* Earth, left to idolize allegories rather than the Nature we're made of and the transcendent kingdom of heaven within, right here on this hallowed ground. Divinity is now limited to something or someone outside of us, demonizing the Great Mother

Nature we're an extension and reflection of. Yet the prostrations that organized religions have prescribed, enforced, and performed for centuries haven't helped much. Because they aren't *our* rituals.

Clearly, we have more to learn from the mistakes of our past. The rise-and-fall cycle prompts reflection on paradoxical antiquity, especially in the evolution of feminine regard. Society grapples with contradiction on an evolving path. Understanding our ancestral complexities underscores integral lessons of continuity and change. Inevitably, this empire will either crumble *or* rise into a new magikal sacredness. I believe the latter is its destiny, dependent upon its citizens.

Reconnection with ancient magik makes these stories, fraught with contrast and paradox, groundwork for our endeavor to harmonize and heal the pain in our world. From my tiny human perspective, as difficult as it may seem, how could all of this be unless it serves some higher purpose? Would we be so motivated otherwise?

While I have no definitive proof, I can only do my best to ensure those who lived cooperatively and magikally did not suffer in vain. They drive me to eliminate existential agony and bring magik home to us all. Because there has never been a more crucial time to reestablish our innate, inherent connection to creation and Great Spirit. *Resurrection* originally meant "awakening," and the best way to support a societal rebirth is devoting to awakening ourselves.

MONOTHEISM: PARADIGMATIC SHIFT

Monotheism marked a significant shift in the practice and perception of Witchual. Long before Christianity adopted the practice, baptism absolved one's *mind* before debate and discussion. Cleopatra epitomized the fusion of political power and spiritual mystique. Druids and Celts on the British Isles celebrated festivals such as Beltane, lighting blazing bonfires to welcome summer, for more than 6,000 years. Everywhere you look, ancient history highlights the connection to land and Nature's cycles.

With the spread of Judaism and Christianity, our spiritual landscape changed. In the 300s CE, Emperor Constantine, a polytheistic sympathizer to Christians emerging in Rome, was corrupted. Who really knows how it happened, but by the end of his rule, he'd abandoned his faith, ordered erasure of magik and pagan practices, and coerced many rulers to suppress Roman polytheistic spirituality. His reign saw the impetus of confiscating and demolishing ancient temples and sites of worship to become churches.

Spirituality once celebrated and revered pleasure, beauty, and sexuality, but the influx of Christianity cloaked rituals in fear. Intentional ceremonial life shifted from seeking blessings and celebration to begging for forgiveness, attempting to avoid punishment. The once-vibrant tapestry of diverse spiritual practices frayed under the weight of monotheistic dominance.

Amid this turmoil, the Great Mother Goddess remained a beacon of hope and empowerment. In contrast to the increasingly patriarchal image of God promoted by the church, the Goddess's unconditional love and desire for the best for her children endured as long as it could.

This deity wanted to help, serve, support, love, empower, enliven, excite, and inspire: a nurturing, forgiving Divine, a kind, loving presence that comforted in times of sorrow and healed in moments of pain. She who brought us all into the world was stamped out by those with violence in their hearts.

THE CRUSADE

As the church's influence expanded, it systematically extinguished natural and feminine Divinity, labeling them sinful and impure. Outlawing anyone's autonomous connection beyond their rules, regulations, and restrictions allowed for corporal and financial punishment. Ships set sail on a global purge to exterminate Central and South American tribes, forcing punitive and disembodied doctrine to replace sovereign and autonomous spiritual beliefs.

Vibrant and multifaceted declarations of Divinity were branded heresy. Those who upheld their practices were persecuted. Refusing conversion meant dire consequences. This dark era saw the forced erasure of our ancient spiritual knowledge's prolific tapestry.

The only option against such violent oppression was adaptation. Those devoted enough to persevere worked magik in secret. Elders and grandparents too afraid to share died with their wisdom, never offering it to children raised in a scary new world. Publicly, rituals were reinterpreted, aligned subtly (and not so) with religion's imposed framework to conceal the connection to traditional beliefs.

The church abandoned the many-faced Gods—that did not fit its definition. Formerly balanced, empowering pillars of loving safety as Divine counterparts and families who stewarded the elements and watched over life were forgotten. The original Holy Father—beyond a figure of authority—was kind, loving, and encouraging; he guided and directed his children in times of pain, protecting rather than penalizing them. But the singular, punitive male deity he became ultimately overshadowed his benevolence.

Witchual has always been about connection—to self, others, and our holy natural world. Monotheism severed this connection, pushing true communion into darkness. Despite this, the flame of ancient practices, with its abiding connection to the magik of life, was never fully extinguished. Even in the face of persecution, Witchual endured, adapted, and evolved, waiting for the perfect time to reemerge. That time has come.

Exploring this complex, multifaceted history reveals a narrative of resilient transformation. From sacred Celtic oak groves to the Nile's mystical banks, Crete's ancient temples, Guatemala's pyramids, and the Himalayas' or Andes' soaring heights, a spiritual revolution unfolds today in the hearts of people like you and me.

Magik isn't distant or unattainable. It has and always will remain in your every breath, woven into the fabric of your Universal being. The way you experience it is up to you.

Ritual's constant, fundamental thread across culture and time has defined humanity's character, touching every civilization, person, and part of the planet.

Living as extended family, we went on vision quests, danced for healing and blessing, petitioned for successful hunts and abundant harvests. Humanity once mirrored the animal kingdom, not in its lack of "civilization," but in harmony with Earth. We took only what we needed; "waste" was biodegradable and fertilized, never poisoned, our planet. Now, despite living beside one another in endless apartments, we go years without knowing our neighbors. What we refer to as "leadership" takes from us more than it cares for, providing its constituents (us) with the basics of a good life. The loneliness epidemic generates so much suffering. Commuting alone for hours every day to sit beside people we barely talk to, at jobs we resent but depend on, isn't *living*.

I look forward to growing food and babies on vast land with my best friends. Cool, clear water to drink and swim in nourishes a lush riparian backyard and permaculture garden. We know *things* can never fill that void. Only that which is *intangible* truly fulfills us. Instead of falling for the media's tireless efforts to convince us that emptiness can only be filled by external means—the next car, clothes, or accumulation of material wealth and possessions—we source our fulfillment from within.

Money doesn't make us happy, but when it is earned through a devotional, purposeful mission, it comforts us to know we're doing what we came to Earth for. Love, purpose, joy, pleasure, connection—cultivated within and grown together—can never be bought. Nature and travel, again, are exceptions, expenses that make you richer. We have strayed far, to the detriment of all species, especially ourselves, but I have the utmost faith we can return to it.

FROM FATHER TO DEVIL

Though feminism focuses on atrocities committed against women, how often are men educated to ask each other for spiritual counsel? Imagine if it wasn't deemed weak or laughable to seek support and guidance from others, but in fact strong to bring our wisdom together. How many men truly understand the ground beneath them or take the time to familiarize themselves with it? Many religious tales are of men who stayed in one place, often beneath a tree, to gain higher wisdom. Even the Bible carries remnants of a time when men listened to Earth.

Abrahamic religions diminished the Maternal Nature of God by confining worship inside churches, mosques, and synagogues rather than forests, moonlight, and thunderstorms, the latter having always been associated with the Divine because storms can devastate or propagate depending on the situation. Carvings and motifs emulate Nature's beauty but remove us from Her bosom.

The Mother's unconditional loving care for *all* Her children has been erased. In Her place, Lilith, demonized and exiled for refusing obedience, is an intolerable, rebellious outcast. Still, Eve's "immoral" desire for *knowledge*, questing for something greater, and connection to sacred kundalini energy (the serpent) condemns her. Yet our symbol for medicine, the rod of Asclepius, features a snake entwined around a staff to represent that most vital knowledge of all, healing.

The only acceptable feminine archetype remains overly pious and subservient. Mary isn't even permitted to make love to *conceive* her child. Despite all the modern scientific evidence proving female genitalia is quite literally designed for pleasure, the sheer idea was blasphemy.

No matter our gender, we *all* have feminine sides, emotions, and sensuality to be celebrated, not feared or shamed. Understandably, if I didn't have this ultimate, cosmic, creative power, I'd want it too! Women are inherently and perfectly suited for spiritual leadership. But we have been prevented from holding such positions by those who refuse to acknowledge feminine gifts within themselves, and the fact that they wouldn't be here without us.

Abolishing the Goddess in religious creeds bred endless internal battles. Against feeling and emotions, sexuality, and creativity, and the sustainability of internal and external environments. Destroying the empowered father's integration of those aspects to protect and provide for Her. To return to wholeness, we must reunite holiness through Mother God and Father Nature—more on that soon.

Modern feminism can be extreme, fighting the same way as those who inflicted the wound against us. We must uphold the Golden Rule here and treat others the way we desire to be treated. Reclaiming a relationship with the Goddess *never* denies the masculine. Witchcraft and pagan/Earth-based spirituality have *always* honored both. She welcomes hurting hearts of wounded boys who lash out aggressively into Her warm embrace so the healed and awakened man can once again rise to stand by Her side.

Jesus was a rabbi, and rabbis have always been encouraged to marry. Though there is no mention of Jesus having a wife, it never says he *didn't*. Which would have caused an uproar, as unwed rabbis were considered unfit to lead congregations. The Gospels of John, Philip, and Luke say that Mary Magdalene was his most beloved apostle, kissed him on the mouth, sat in his lap for the Last Supper, and washed his feet with her hair.

Jewish women of the time were allowed to show their hair only to their husbands. Mary using her hair in this way strongly implies that she was his wife, so why did many Biblical scholars deny this evidence while boldly calling her a prostitute, even with no support for *that* claim? Magdalene scholars argue that her story and role were intentionally changed, mistranslated, and misrepresented to degrade women. She had a Gospel like the rest of the apostles that was removed from the Bible. Its remnants describe Divine Union, unconditional love, and personal empowerment. Like all feminine power then, she was abdicated from her rightful place as Jesus's wife and spiritual counterpart.

The Great Mother, our oldest, original deity, had an accompanying Father counterpart as well. She was the fecund Earth; He, the ever-present sun, the stag to nurturing doe. Eliminating Her required changing the Divine counterpart: the unconditionally loving Mother was replaced with a villainous Father. And a collaborator became a combative nemesis, the Devil, whose hellish persona took on the appearance of a male horn-bearing animal. Female ungulates (cows, goats, sheep), producers of milk, our greatest food source without bloodshed, were sacred for millennia. Our reliance upon these creatures was cast aside for their enslavement and portrayal as part of the problem.

This singular, malevolent figure that replaced them was an amalgamation of demonized pagan deities and mythological symbols of Nature and fertility. Archetypal Satan poignantly illustrates the distortion of the Great Father's presence. Diabolizing pre-Christian traditions solidified Satan as a nefarious enemy, a narrative necessity for a warring male God to defeat him.

Prior to the church's creation of the Devil, which was part of a Herculean effort to divide and conquer with fear, there was no "evil." The afterlife was an expected, accepted transition. Lucifer, the father of pride *and rebellion,* for refusing humble submission, stood up for himself, rejecting unreasonable orders. The Bible says what made him "evil" was *desiring glory* for the *gifts God bestowed upon him.*

The original definition of *glory* was "the manifestation of God's presence" or "radiance." We feel the most radiant people's divine connection when they're fully expressed, serving Creation through art, purpose, or personal fulfillment. They love life and living it.

I wrote books to share wisdom with you. Is that not "glory?" Why would God give us gifts of knowledge and charm, courage and tenderness, to be locked away? Are we evil unless we try to suppress what was divinely designed for us? Bowing down in obedience to what? Whom? A lie we've been sold to force us to humble ourselves rather than naturally be lifted high?

How could the American Dream sold to all of us in the Western world, the glory of God's favor, be so disdainful?

Glory be to *all of us. Especially* those brave enough to let God manifest through the gifts we've blessedly received.

We are not meant to feel small or insignificant, *bowing down* to a facade of force, prostrating ourselves as worthless, desperately beseeching forgiveness. We are meant to know we are *necessary parts* of God, that everything we learn from mistakes makes us better, more powerful. It seems so blatantly obvious in hindsight. But these words would have gotten me killed back then, and many times since.

Humility comes from the Latin word *humus,* describing how the leaves perpetually rotting on the ground beneath trees create nutrient-rich, "black gold" soil—what *falls* in the *forest.* Humility is the willingness to let go of what has served us, what we've learned and grown through, which is ready to be laid to rest. Plants alchemize and reabsorb decomposing nutrients through their roots. We, too, are fortified by adversity, loss, and transition. Efficiently utilizing what falls away supports our growth. Composting old habits, patterns, and behaviors is the greatest alchemy for becoming who we dream to be. What dies teaches us, fuels our future. Humility is not sacrifice of self; it's *surrender to* it.

Even our language has been turned against us. There's no denying the denizen of deceit was duplicitously disseminated. We're finally pulling the wool from our eyes, realizing the real Devils are those who created him. In 2021, 43.9 percent of Americans identified as Christian; 50 years ago, that number was 90 percent. Church leaders are some of the greatest sinners of all, committing attrition as congregations have dwindled due to resentment and "church hurt." The word *God* has been bastardized by those hiding outrageous offenses to children and adults alike under the guise of "faith."

Catholic priests take three vows: obedience, poverty, and *chastity*. In 1531, German theologian Martin Luther, who criticized the Catholic Church for charging people to absolve their sins, exposed the papacy's attempt to maintain full approval for child abuse. He revealed their efforts to veto a decree that would restrict the number of boys cardinals were allowed to "keep for pleasure." Flabbergasted at how openly and shamelessly the Pope and Roman cardinals practiced statutory sodomy when they were supposed to be abstinent, he and many others in the Protestant Reformation referred to the Pope as the AntiChrist.

That children could have been "kept" as property to fulfill carnal desires of those under vows of *celibacy* breaks my heart—the Catholic purveyance of purity is a "Do as I say, not as I do" kind of creed.

Low estimates state that over 330,000 children were abused by Catholic priests or church employees just in recent decades. Those convicted were reassigned and continuously unsupervised with youth in mass coverups. The Los Angeles Archdiocese *alone* paid $1.5 billion of the *$5 billion* U.S. victim settlements awarded from the 1980s through 2025. The Vatican's coffers cover outrageous sums.

How can we be "delivered from evil" by its very incarnation?

Were fathers good before an unholy, punitive, harmful, disciplinary God was portrayed as our most prevalent "father" figure? Insecurity or fear overcomes the wounded masculine or "failed father's" sense of responsibility and dependability. Burdened by shame, he *takes* from society and community rather than giving.

Empowered and enlightened leaders desperately yearn for our purity to be exemplified in our relationships, treatment of Nature, and personal and objective truth. This is the exact intention of evolutionary ritual: maintaining foundations right here on the ground we spend our lives walking upon. Imagine if we genuinely and exclusively followed the truth in God's unique communication to us. We would feel certain of our worthiness here.

One of the great disappointments for my parents' generation is seeing how disillusioned mine has become with politics. We see through the facade; the veil has lifted. Unless you're one of the wealthy few profiting from the suffering of humans and animals, your say is minimal. Those in control are consumed by the illusion of power. Though greed accumulates wealth, it stems from scarcity. Modern society systematically siphons our power and resources. Artificial intelligence consumes more water to cool its servers than entire countries, yet even "conscious" people use it constantly and carelessly.

The planet gives perpetually in every moment, providing the air we breathe, water we drink, food we eat, and materials for shelter. Reclaiming that power and ancient magik to serve Her, thank Her, and help heal the wounds we've inflicted upon Her, is a duty and obligation. Nourishing ourselves spiritually and energetically ensures that, no matter what, we remain grounded in our sovereignty and inherent interconnectedness with life.

Thank Goddess there's now a growing righteous remembrance resurging—reclaiming the identity and practice of Witchual. It is truly my honor to be part of this movement of Divine Feminine leadership as, according to the *L.A. Times*, "a cross between Tony Robbins and a Victoria's Secret model." My chubby, ugly-duckling inner child loved that one!

I'm here to Trojan Horse this Muggle world as we rekindle relationships with mythical beings like dragons, unicorns, and elemental spirits. More information about extraterrestrial interaction keeps emerging, expanding our minds and returning Earth to the Galactic Federation.

Turning the tides is up to us no matter how insignificant we may feel in the face of overwhelming adversity. We are each a cell, a thread in the whole. A courageous global community is standing to fight for what's right, rediscovering and redefining what it means to be spiritual. We're freeing our voices and visions from their proverbial cages, reconnecting to our ancestors' ancient wisdom and reliance on Mother Nature's resources. We're adapting ancient ways to suit modern lifestyles; more than reviving old traditions, we're birthing a new era, directly contacting the Divine, carrying forward its messages and karmic invitations that humanity has been feigning ignorance about.

Isn't it funny how people say spiritual teachers shouldn't make money, that doing so contradicts the essence of our message? Meanwhile, megachurch pastors fly around in private jets, and the richest people are the ones causing the most harm. The Pope doesn't technically make a salary, but we've already discussed the Vatican's virtually endless supply of riches, with billions of dollars of investments in stocks and real estate made from money stolen from indigenous people.

This is why I'm passionate about supporting spiritual people building wealth. *True* power is less concerned with materialism and doesn't crave access to the same resources false power does, yet it struggles to effect systemic change on a global scale.

I offer healing techniques and modalities that have transformed my life and the lives of thousands of others. I feel worthy and grateful for earning money as a reward for my tireless effort and resulting growth. I love knowing I'm stewarding my financial resources to effect positive change. When we monetize or capitalize upon our gifts by aligning with Spirit, the Universe bestows its care for us.

Unfortunately, the patriarchy demonized the services of the feminine, abolishing their value and usurping the roles of oracle and healer to divert that stream of resources back into their own pockets. So, though survival and success require money, it's not inherently bad or good; it's just neutral energy. We're told money is "the root of all evil" by those who instilled it systemically to separate us from working together. Only in the hands of evil people is it evil. You decide what path it takes. During the same Dark Ages of the Witch Trials, the advent of imperial capitalism and privatization of land turned money against common people.

The church confiscated many things we held valuable and started charging "tithes" for absolution of sin they doled out relentlessly. The word *sin* actually derives from an archery term that simply meant, "to miss the mark"—mistakes are made, there's room for improvement.

Our time and energy are our most valuable resources, but because we exchange them for money, it's valued above all else. We each have a choice how we utilize and steward finances. Whose pockets do you want to line? Greedy billionaires or regenerative farmers? I love investing in companies who are working toward positive change. Will you support big pharma or naturopaths, herbalists, and people making seaweed out of plastic?

Each time we spend money, we vote with our resources, sending a message to the Universe about what we believe in and hold dear. This can be one of our most important Witchuals. When our homes are filled with cheap plastic possessions, we are communicating a reflection of our own worth and replaceability. I love spending in support of my values, what I stand for, and what is most important.

At the beginning of my path to prosperity, I signed every check or bill with words of gratitude and appreciation, smiley faces, hearts, and exclamation points. Affirming the blessing it is to be able to receive that which I desire or require, whether for food, rent, a fun experience, or an adventure. We call what investments do when they grow "appreciation" because that energy enhances whatever we direct it to. People light up when you acknowledge them. The crystalline structure of water, which comprises 60 to 70 percent of the human body, changes dependent upon the energy sent into it. Your body functions differently when you appreciate it, just like everything else in life.

WITCHUAL WEALTH

Society programs us with an insatiable hunger for wealth. Beyond life's necessities, this is an industrially inflicted trauma response. We want safety, certainty, to be seen. It's not money that matters; it's the feelings we associate with having it. I made more money than ever before when my health started failing. Lab results revealed stress wreaking havoc on me. I longed for the days of being broke but carefree and vibrantly healthy in every way. Nothing is worth more than wellness of body, mind, spirit, and relationships. Focus on establishing an energetically stable foundation, then you're truly wealthy.

Of course we want to improve financial well-being; just refrain from *solely* focusing on material wealth. There are too many people doing so, causing the abject desecration of natural resources. Did you know wood is one of the *rarest* materials in the *entire Universe*? Diamonds on the other hand form frequently, as carbon is one of the main substances in existence. There are whole diamond planets, others where it *rains* diamonds. Ouch, but *whoa*.

Wood, on the other hand, has *been found only on Earth*. Forests are beyond precious; they are a galactic treasure. Trees are worth saving and savoring our connections with. Yet timber companies have wiped out over *97 percent* of old growth and virgin forests worldwide *in the last two centuries*. We've got to be the new role models, to live and breathe the abundance that nourishes all. Having a large bank account does not eliminate inner turmoil, trust me.

If you're concentrating on financial gain beyond meeting your needs, ask yourself, "*Why* do I desire money? Where do my stories of unworthiness or hardship stand in the way of receiving the kind of stability I desire?"

In my money manifestation course, Witchy Rich, we dive deep into the consciousness of debt and scarcity versus investment and abundance. You are accruing what I call "dangerous debt" if it comes from a shopping addiction in an attempt to feel "better/hotter/more desirable/like you fit in." This scarcity mindset can drag you down.

Alternatively there's intentional investment. Putting $10,000 on your credit card for a business mastermind to help you become a more confident purveyor of your services is magikal Internet money you can pay off at your own pace. You're illustrating to the Divine that you believe in yourself and are devoted to your personal and spiritual evolution. That abundance mindset will lift you up and is one of my greatest money manifestation hacks!

Focus on *true* expressions of prosperity like love, fulfillment, purpose, joy, connection. Imagination is an incredible tool. Let genuine *values* guide your actions and decision-making like a compass, rather than buying what you've been told has value. Creating change in our own lives creates change in the world. *Do it for the better.*

Great powers emerge from Witchual, with great responsibility. Perhaps more than you can conceptualize. Use it only for the benefit of all. When we really think about what we hope money will bring to our lives, it's generally a deeper sense of stability and certainty.

What would safety look and feel like for you?
How can you start building it internally and energetically right now?
Ponder and proceed into miracle-manifestation mode.

My entire business and brand are built upon staying true to myself. The vibrational frequency of authenticity—being fully, unabashedly, and unapologetically yourself—is 400, yes *four hundred* times more powerful than love. If the "most loving" action is without integrity or denies your inner child's needs, you're actually *lowering* your vibration.

Withholding my authenticity, worrying I'll rock the boat or hurt feelings, and forcing self-sacrifice or abandonment were a detriment that only ever brought pain. Mustering the courage to speak my truth always serves me. In my friend groups I've been known to be the voice of honesty in a sea of silence, often the only one brave enough to articulate what needs to be said.

Authenticity is paradoxical. Letting ourselves *be* ourselves, showing our inner children they are worthy of love exactly as they are, is the most healing, liberating experience. But healing is necessary to feel safe enough to do so.

We receive massive spiritual rewards from unburdening ourselves of stories that we should be anything different from who we are. We feel alive, whole, safe, and comfortable within our own skin, magnetizing empowered relationships and opportunities. I aspire to be surrounded by authenticity not just in my Californian conscious community bubble, but everywhere I go: at airports, in restaurants and Lyfts, in education and healthcare systems, and particularly in legislation and government.

Authenticity has been the key to my success in every way.

I dream of collaborating with fellow conscious entrepreneurial light workers to rebuild governance the way we've rebuilt business and community. A united mission to reignite humanity's magik feels like a movement we can all get behind. The more of us who commit to living and leading our own lives in this way, the more rapidly we move together in this direction.

That's why I'm so grateful to you, dear reader, for being here, trusting me, and diving into the exploration of your own practice through these pages. This is how we become a leaderless community full of leaders, reverently stewarding rather than controlling and hoarding the resources, draining our planet.

My first utterly life-changing ritual was Burning Man; many transformational experiences I'll share with you happened there. Every year, 80,000 people build a temporary city in Nevada's desolate desert, celebrating full expression, communal collaboration, and liberation from societal conventions. It's mind-blowing and has fundamentally altered my lifestyle. The experience is profoundly satiating, inspires awe and wonder, and has given me lifetime memories of peak heart-blasted openness and ineffable connection to Spirit. Some of my greatest natural highs happened there: astonishing synchronicities, tearjerking performances by passionate Hula dancers, sunrise philharmonic orchestras giving their all, dance parties with my besties, booty shaking all night. I live for those moments, and there's always *one* that takes the cake at Burning Man.

What followed in the wake of my first experience there has also changed me forever.

A new friend I'd camped with brought me to a breathwork sound bath. I expected soft music; instead, I got scared shitless when I lost the use of my hands.

Breathwork can induce tetany, over-oxygenation of the bloodstream that tightens or even temporarily immobilizes extremities. My right wrist curled in on itself, clenched in a tight fist. It was already the only fully functioning hand I had after the other was severely damaged in an accident. When it stopped working too, I almost had a panic attack. *Oh my God, what's happening? I can't lose this one too! I won't survive. . . . Move! Move! Unclench! Oh my God, help me!*

Terrified, I almost screamed out in horror. These were the early days of breathwork, and no one had warned me this could happen. I assumed I was stuck like that permanently.

Forced to surrender, I heard Her whisper, "Calm down. Trust me."

Exhaling, I told myself, *I managed the last one. I'll figure it out. It's going to be fine.*

As soon as I relaxed, the rigidity started to release. Within minutes, I was back to normal.

Overcoming that terror sent me on a new trajectory: a bond forged with the Goddess guiding and informing my choices. I went wherever I felt called, let go of relationships that didn't serve me (although some cords were harder to cut than others), and devoted myself to Her.

Of course, I still made plenty of mistakes, ignoring suggestions more often than I'd like to admit. But my fundamental experience of reality had shifted. Crippling fear that had held me back was no longer the loudest voice I heard.

Now, my life feels like Burning Man. I am devoted to its principles of radical self-expression, decommodification, and leaving no trace. I wear fantastical outfits to illustrate who I am; I lead courageous women through purposeful work; synchronicities occur every day; I have transcendent weekly bodywork. The song "Circle of Life" was the soundtrack to my Serengeti hot-air-balloon silent disco as I watched thundering stampedes across the grasslands. I stood at the foot of the palatial castle for my fairy-tale France retreat, crying tears of joy, acknowledging my inner child's dream come true yet again. I am my wildest dreams. I've expected and received miracles.

That's the power of a single ceremonial experience. One Witchual. With this power, anything is possible. My life is living proof.

CROSS-CULTURAL EMBODIMENT

I hail from storied, precolonial, matriarchal cultures. Goddess-worshipping cults and sisterly Roman oracular priestesshoods, notorious kitchen-witch traditions and Stregheria. My mother's long line of Celtic clairvoyants descended from isles where Druid shamans reigned, wielding the mists of Avalon with a pinch of Norse Viking adventurer. Yet, despite this magik coursing through my veins, I was never taught to connect with it. It's a shame being "white" has come to lack cultural awareness and tradition, when our own indigenous roots honored the same elements as those in the Americas.

The hippie elementary school that helped make me who I am, Equinox, made me an outcast and loser in junior high. Backpacking camping trips into redwood forests cultivated individual and collective relationships with Nature. We planted trees; ate healthy, homemade food; studied the multitude of unique ecosystems around us in resplendent Northern California; and were inspired to dream wildly. It was a multicultural sanctuary that encouraged imagination. Always an advanced reader, I immersed myself in the most accessible lineage of wisdom available—fairy tales and fantasy.

Changing to public school for sixth grade was a rude awakening. The value system I'd been taught ceased to exist. Magikal creative thinking, which had bolstered our unique processes for integrating information, was erased. Learning was for standardized testing without concern for stimulating curiosity. I was suddenly self-conscious of *everything*; my body, clothes, interests, beliefs, and hopes were all fodder for the daily torment of the other kids' ridicule. There hadn't been bullying, cliques, or competition with the same eight classmates I'd had since kindergarten. Hearing catty girls tearing each other down blew my mind. I had no resolve to handle it and was utterly defeated. We'll discuss the atrocities of competition among women later, but there's a reason our cycles sync up. We're meant to be *allies, not enemies.*

I found solace in stories, the only place where the world I wanted to live in existed. The characters in my books mirrored who, what, and how I wanted to be. More than *believing* in magik, they possessed it nonchalantly, like other normal traits.

Pre-Potter, Tamora Pierce's books about fiercely powerful, courageously embodied, and tenderly loving warrior women enchanted me. In *The Song of the Lioness* quartet, Alanna masqueraded as a boy to become a knight. Her magik, or "gift," was healing. A Great Mother Goddess watched over her, and she had full telepathic communication with her black cat, Faithful.

The second book, *In the Hand of the Goddess*—right in front of my face my *entire life*—became my reality. When I'm overwhelmed or under-resourced (even in an otherwise healing space), I regulate my nervous system with the mantra "I am in the hand of the Goddess." In *The Immortals* series, Daine, a half-Goddess with "Wild Magik," communicated and shared consciousness with animals, including her baby dragon familiar.

Faithful and Wild Magik honed my otherworldly psychic relationships with my cats—some of the greatest power I've ever experienced. *My* "gift" is healing magik. My first service was hands-on energy work, which grew into remote ecosystems helping thousands of people heal mentally, emotionally, physically, and spiritually.

Everything I longed to be true, I willed from childhood fantasy into adult reality. My favorite "fictional" characters were the kind of role models I craved but never found, so I became them. Still waiting for that dragon ride, though.

WRITING YOUR REALITY

It stands to reason that if we are creating our reality, that includes the books we read and movies/shows we watch. It may seem far-fetched, but our quantum, holographic Universe makes this increasingly apparent and enhances our own imaginative powers and gifts.

The aliveness of the elements in the movies *Frozen 2* and *Raya and the Last Dragon*, and the faerie mating bonds of epic romantasy sagas, all feel like my higher self is revealing other lifetimes and iterations of my magik to me, opening my mind to possibility. In the show *Game of Thrones*, Khaleesi loses her lover king in the first season. But his death births her unparalleled strength and, more importantly, her dragons. My relationship had to die for a more powerful level and layer of my own dragon treasure to come alive. After the greatest losses in my life, I was rewarded with my greatest wins. These mythic tales help me break free from Muggle mentality's limitations and remember who I came here to be.

My dad is an avid outdoorsman and my mom an anthropological, philosophical adventurer. They taught me to love and worship Nature—never with explicit guidance or teachings but just in what we did as a family. They were conscious entrepreneurs who invented roofracks so people could enjoy more time outside. Though we had our issues, I'm so grateful for the idyllic lifestyle they brought us up in. I feel my ancestors' pride in my casually infinite connection with spiritual and animal realms, in my dragons' guardian-angel spirit guidance, how I use healing to change lives, and am making my wildest dreams come true. The blessings I've received simply from their *potential* have generated everything I've shared with students and clients all over the world.

I can't feign contentment with what society deems normal. I want the iconic stories in my reality to be *mine*, not just confined to books and movies. I'm here for a legendary life, to be the main character in the epic adventure of my existence.

If we can make the story of *our* world magikal, fantastical, fun, exhilarating, audacious, fulfilling, awe-inspiring, and sexy, why would we choose anything else? What greater service to humanity could we possibly offer than being beacons of this potential? Lighthouses guiding home our brothers and sisters lost in the societally sanctioned storm? How better could we use our time?

Yet another simple Witchual can be integrated into your daily life. We've talked about and will continue to dive deeper into consumption in terms of what you eat and how you spend, but it's also about what you absorb mentally through your attention. I use these stories to inspire grander expressions of magik in my life, and you can too.

When you consume horror movies and thrillers, you spike stress hormones and adrenaline, putting your body into a fight-or-flight response that it can't differentiate from an actual threat. My mom's doctor had to prescribe a news detox when her blood pressure was skyrocketing from getting so worked up about all the chaos she had no power to control. We call television "programming" because that's exactly what it's doing. Crime shows *program* your body with trauma and violence. Stop doing that to yourself willingly! The world is scary enough already!

I am vigilant about what kind of content I watch, read, and listen to, and I am certain it has played a massive role in the way life unfolds before me. I make sure the lyrics of music are empowering if I'm going to be repeating them to myself. So many modern melodies are versed with female subjugation and objectification. No wonder we have such a hard time changing our self-image and esteem.

With fantasy as the cornerstone of my mental magikal practice, yoga carried me across the threshold, opening my mind to a deeper relationship with my heart, body, and soul. I dabbled during high school but devoted myself at 21 when a guy said, "You're the most beautiful girl I've ever dated. . . . You should just do yoga every day."

Ouch, but thank Goddess, he was right. That backhanded compliment transformed more than my soft body—yoga changed my entire life. *Yoga* is Sanskrit for "union," and yogic *asanas* (which translates to "seat") are physical postures designed to support settling into stillness and silent meditation.

Initially physical, the posture and balance improvement, toning, and increased flexibility I got from doing yoga brought centeredness to my chaotic New York City life. Indispensable and nonnegotiable physical endurance led to spiritual resilience.

Synchronistic quotes or poems recited during Savasana to close the practice often moved me to tears. Magik's first little winks lured me away from my Muggle life, leading to the life-changing discovery of everything I teach. My first *real* daily Witchual, yoga, is integral to the woman I am.

Almost a decade later, I completed teacher training with Ally Bogard, a master who studied with the 13 indigenous grandmothers. The perfect instructor to deepen my knowledge, intricately interweaving the elements into somatic structures; there was no one else I would have trained under. Her transmission altered the course of my life yet again by bringing Witchual home to my body more elementally than ever before.

My first mindful job was leading meditation, connection, and consciousness to CEOs and their teams in the corporate hustle. My repertoire of startups and executive clients was significant. Feedback was overwhelmingly positive: "I've never had such a powerful meditation," "Wow, it's so nice to have spirituality at work," and "This is the best part of my week!"

My company wellness programs were implemented by leaders whose awakening touched hundreds of employees, families, and communities. I loved supporting people where they needed it most and reaching masses. But when I added *witch* to my spiritual development platform, my professional landscape dramatically changed overnight. Corporate clients vanished, and Christian friends asked, "Why would you call yourself that? It's evil."

Initially, I didn't resonate with "witch" either. Even Harry Potter's heyday was about *magik* for me. My elementary school teachers were witches every Halloween, and my mom (psychic lineage, remember?) was always the fortune teller at our school's carnival, and a very good one. Somehow, even before I knew the etymological origin of the word, I knew it was a misnomer for powers we'd been diverted away from. But when I donned the hat, mainstream acceptance evaporated while my audience skyrocketed. A world lost in the storm was looking to me as a lighthouse helping guide them home.

People had been longing for a witch who was friendly, intelligent, educational, and like that big sister next door. The wise woman within all of us was sick of only seeing decrepit or disfigured, wart-covered witches. Despite publicly defaming wisdom used against us as nonsensical silliness, many industrial figureheads believe in and utilize occult magik. J. P. Morgan regaled, "Millionaires don't use astrology; billionaires do." But only behind closed doors.

Working with an actor for bigger and bigger roles, it became clear my message was for the masses. I was his "secret weapon," too potent for the public palette, kept behind the scenes for one-on-one guidance.

I realized that without openly acknowledging it, Oprah is a witch. Working with miracles and healers, gratitude, abundance, and souls—witches' forces—to great degrees, she's built an incredible life. Manifestation is just the accepted mainstream euphemism for *magik*.

Thank Goddess the shift is occurring! Vanessa Hudgens, Madonna, Gisele Bündchen, Adele, and more high-profile celebs come out of the broom closet everyday! Ariana Grande's "God Is a Woman" video's powerfully evocative imagery of a chapel as a sacred pussy portal is about as witchy as it gets. When interviewed as *Wicked*'s Glinda the Good Witch in 2024, Ariana finally admitted to being "a real witch." Mainstream Muggle media freaked out—classic—but she and her co-star Cynthia Erivo brought a new level of comfort and support home to this title. Bless the bold, brave, high-profile babes who help heal, reclaim, and reframe the misconceptions about this ancient feminine archetype.

WITCHUAL FUTURE

The sickening, abhorrent genocide in Palestine is yet another result of separation from Nature and tribal living. Lacking global and communal unity, we've forgotten that we are not different peoples divided by borders or beliefs; we're a single species sharing a home. But with so few true *leaders*, people who care about one another and Earth have no one to count on.

My retreats are my vision for the future. I'm rendering the greatest service to the collective I can, impacting people's lives, and ultimately their families, friends, and communities. As violence escalates and religious warfare intensifies, all we can do is be fully immersed in transformational, intimate healing.

I wish for all people to be wildly liberated and free. We are capable of living synergistically, caring for each other, being transparent and vulnerable, acknowledging our one human family, and respecting each other as such. Our bodies' preciously designed nerve endings prove that we are worthy of deep pleasure and sensual satiation.

Imagine a world where everyone understands the nature of their magik so profoundly that they use it to live the life they desire. Envisioning each individual so capable and self-responsible—all beings happily, well-nourished, and cared for—is a bright future we can all work toward with Witchual. Rather than being forced upon us, it's intertwined with our breathing, knowing, and interactions. How we function every day lays or abolishes the foundation for this Golden Age of Heaven on Earth. My work is designed to anchor us all in complete inner safety to usher in this harmonious new world.

Sometimes thoughts are refreshing summer breezes; communication comes sweet and easy. Other times they get out of control or are unkind, leaving damage or destruction in the wake of twisted words. We can get lost in the fog of stories when thick emotions cling to our minds, preventing us from seeing clearly. When our powerful minds shame or judge challenging emotions like grief, sadness, or anxiety, they're like hurricanes tearing through us, flooding our foundations.

Viscerally recall your calm tranquility as the glassy surface of a lake. Your flowing rivers of blood pump through every part of your capillary's creeks across your inner terrain. It is up to us to remember that we are in constant co-creation with the Universe and can *always* choose how we respond to our circumstances. Always.

✸ ✶ REFLECTION ✶ ✸

These questions and practices can shift you onto your highest timeline. The more honest you are, the quicker you can get to work and start seeing results. You don't have to write them all down, but contemplate what you most find yourself wanting to avoid.

Get clear on what you want your life to look like:

What feels most challenging or important to face?

How is my life different from what I desire?

How do I feel on a daily basis?

How do I want to feel?

How do I spend most of my time?

What would I like to be doing instead?

What disempowers, frustrates, or hinders me?

What inspires and motivates me?

What gave me the most delight when I was young?

What delights me now?

What is my main character's energy in the legend of my life?

How have I been the villain or the victim?

What would it take to become my own hero?

When I look at my current circumstances, what phase of the hero's journey am I in?

Have I been mired in my own abysmal darkness?

Have I met my teacher?

Have I embarked upon the adventure or mission I've always dreamed of?

What is most dissonant from the tale I want to tell, the legacy I want to leave?

What shifts would need to occur for me to live as I envision?

(Do your absolute best not to outsource. This is not about being rescued; it's about YOU.)

Contemplate your responses, journal, and make commitments to new behaviors.

If you get stuck, connect to your inner child—the younger version of you who believed in infinite possibilities before they were punished for or discouraged from doing so. Inquiring about how they feel always helps you see where your wounding still informs your life, reminds you what truly matters, and lights you up.

If you've lost your joy, seek everything that reignites it. Finding peace or happiness in the midst of suffering can be the most harrowing task to face, but it's always there.

Engaging in these *activities*, literally Latin for "action in life," leads you home to yourself. Witchual will light the way.

MICROWITCHUALS

The beauty of Witchual is flexibility. Practice anytime, anywhere. Here are quick and easy MicroWitchuals—little doses of magik for everyday moments.

- ✳ Hold a crystal to charge with your intentions. Carry it with you or leave it in a special place you'll see frequently, reminding you of what you're calling in.

- ✳ I circle my car nine times before road trips, reciting, "I am safe and protected as I drive undetected." Works like a charm, because it is.

- ✳ Making coffee or tea? Send intentions or desires for the day into the water, affirming them as if they're already realized. Slurp in your blessings with every sip.

* Energetically reset using dried herbs like sage, rosemary, lavender, sweetgrass or pine to waft smoke through your home or around your body. Consider the spiritual or physical medicine of your chosen plant.

* Speak acknowledgments of beauty and vibrancy into your skincare routine. Send healthy vibrations of cavity prevention into your teeth while brushing.

* Add oils, herbs, crystals, candles, and maybe meditation to your bath for a cleansing, manifestation, or healing ritual.

* Waking up from a bad dream and having trouble falling back asleep? Try listing everything you're grateful for, expanding as much as possible. Express gratitude for someone, an experience you shared, their passion, kindness, or culinary skills. For example, here's some of mine:

  - *I'm so grateful for my team. For our beautiful sisterly connection, that we love each other so much!*

  - *I'm so grateful Ashlee woke up early to be with me filming today.*

  - *I'm so grateful Alexis is living her dharma taking such amazing videos!*

  - *I'm so grateful Rebecca flew out to help me with this project.*

CHAPTER 2

Mother and Father Nature

Gushing waterfalls, succulent riparian zones, intricate roots twirl through mycelial networks. Phallic trunks climb sky high; bees', birds', and butterflies' long, languid tongues pollinate, propagate, voraciously slurp sweet nectars. Life's masculine penetration makes love to feminine fecundity.

Mother and Father Nature's poetic, dancing union proliferates all species. Creation and destruction, decay and resurrection rising and falling symbiotically throughout billions of years. Ritual originated to please and petition this primordial pair. The Hebrew word for *knowledge* actually meant "sexual union."

We know we are one, but life constantly displays contrary evidence. "Good" battles "evil"; black is distinguished from white; gender is binary. Defying "norms," we breed discomfort in our own being—of eternal goodness beyond fathom. Harm to any is harm to all.

Denying or vilifying the "other" is an illusion of separation. We need both. The evil things that happen to us often become our greatest motivation away from suffering. They drive us toward change and our ultimate good. This is echoed in Alanis Morissette's song "You Learn," when she wisely recommended that we get our hearts trampled on, that we live and love and cry and bleed.

Big boys actually *do* cry. Watching men's tears fall is such a turn-on! Fully expressed women are *not* crazy; they keep us sane! *Sensitivity is strength*; it's all a spectrum. Vulnerability and weakness are signs of worthiness. Creativity isn't silly, without it we'd have no movies, music, museums, cars, planes, or trains! Stereotypes and judgments bring shame and criticism to us *all*.

Ecology is the study of how organisms relate to and interact with their environments. Journeying to the heart of *spiritual* ecology as highly conscious organisms, we can devote ourselves to stabilizing the sustainable stewardship of and reverence for Earth.

Every "offering"—sage, tobacco, seashells, flowers, cedar—comes from and is being returned to Her. Her trees and algae gift the oxygen in our breath. Speaking our praise to them, we're exhaling the carbon dioxide they inhale reciprocally. Using precious breath that fuels plants and trees, voices, prayer, and song for expressing thanks, acknowledging Her beauty, and appreciating life and all that nourishes us is our only genuine offering. If *all we have to give* is thanks, that's enough.

Our parents help us survive to physical maturity, caring for and educating us. Invoking *Her* unconditional love and cherishing it with *His* stable, grounding strength guides us into the fullness of our spiritual maturity as Earth's children. Such has been my love affair with my own Mother and Father Nature.

THE MOTHER WE SHARE

The permeating creative life force makes us all brothers and sisters. The feminine muse who inspires our mating dance, sensuality, and emotion, our very sustenance and nourishment, is fiercely ferocious if you cross her or her cubs, yet is ultimately forgiving. She gives of herself because she is compelled. The goodness of Her heart never greedily considers, "What's in it for me?"

She is freshly ripened fruit to be enamored of and enjoyed, along with the plants they're plucked from, and the sweetness that drips through your fingers and across your lips. Have you ever gotten the sense that She's demanding, "Don't eat the fruit"? Wants you to feel *bad,* be *damned* for receiving the blessed bounty she created for *precisely* this purpose? No, because she made it for you and me.

The truth is, She holds the wisdom we seek. Banished from dogmatic doctrine, the Mother remains the cosmic womb that creates us all—growth and abundance incarnate.

Ask yourself:

What does Goddess or feminine energy represent to me?

How do I experience the manifestation, feeling, sounds, or voice of feminine or Goddess's presence?

What beliefs do I have about femininity?

How do I perceive this frequency within and around me?

What would it look like to embrace this energy internally or express it externally?

How can Goddess energy—the conscious, Universal vibration of creation and abundance—support me with my gifts?

OUR FATHER, WHO ART ON EARTH

Father Nature is the powerful protector and provider. Masculine guardianship and caretaking are not instinctual to all people and animals. The thread and threat of violence in the reptilian brain has been mastered by some better than others.

The Green Man, or Father Forest, symbolizes Nature's active masculine presence. The bull to cow, stallion to mare, alpha king to his queen. In many ancient tribes, he is an antlered figure made of leaves and bark. Seasonally, his colors change from verdant emerald with bursting blossoms to golden-russet harvest hues or a beard dusted in snowflakes.

Animals we've evolved closest to and from—cats, dogs, and primates—defend prides, clans, packs, or troops to the death, and are tenderly affectionate with offspring, exemplifying engaged fatherhood. Emperor penguins take the cake for daddy devotion, sacrificing themselves up to two months to incubate their chicks before hatching them.

It's too bad the shameful (un)"Holy Father" has perpetuated mistrust of dedication to familial well-being. In the Gospel of John, Jesus even told the Jews that their Father is not God, but the Devil. Jehovah's violence was the real evil. We removed the wand from the hand of the masculine and replaced it with a sword, designed to maim and mutilate.

Beheading, physically and metaphorically, removes the mind from the temporal, the terrestrial, disconnecting it from, rather than connecting it to, the body, forgetting the wisdom he could wield instead. *Vagina* literally means "sheath for a sword." We've made the male member into a weapon rather than a scepter of power that can take us to the highest of heights. We've extricated the masculine from the roots, as if the tall, phallic trunks of trees are not pillars of their strength.

Yet another tale Christianity "borrowed" from paganism was about Dionysus, God of the vine, women, and festivities. He metaphorizes the magik and medicine of plants, their resilience, and how they pop up everywhere, like mushrooms, even in the hardest, harshest circumstances. He was known for appearing in many different cultures and traditions, and turning water into wine, which originally signified the blissful enchantment of spiritual transformation as told in the story of his marriage to Ariadne.

Women are uplifted, centered, and sacred in the cult of Dionysius. In ancient versions of his myths, women weren't raped, only made love to passionately, but that was changed to align with patriarchal dogma. In *Gender and Immortality,* Deborah Lyons says "female figures are prominent in his myths, and his cult is marked by a level of participation by women unknown for any other male divinity." Compare this to the way the role of women in Jesus's teachings has been downplayed and denied. Instead of acknowledging Mary Magdalene as a beloved, powerful person, biblical scholars would rather misrepresent her story to keep all women down. Only vicious insecurity and worthlessness could be the motivation for removing power from an entire gender in such a way.

Society says that "real men" take power over others, or just subjugate themselves to dreaded office jobs to keep food on the table. We've abandoned primal survival skills and have been taught to fear getting dirty; we eat meat but can't imagine killing it ourselves. The realm and duty of Father Nature, from persevering through its harshness to pursuing purposefulness, has been squandered.

Ask yourself:

What does masculine energy mean to me?
How do I feel or experience masculine presence?
How do I feel or experience the manifestation, sounds or voice of God/ masculine presence?
What beliefs do I have about masculinity?
What would it look like for me to embrace masculine energy within, or expressed externally, more?
Who is my inner warrior?
What steps can I take to create more solid reliability?

Epitomized in flora and fauna, Mother's creative force, nurturing, acceptance, and loving nourishment are held together by Father's logic, productive efficiency, strength, guidance, and purposeful direction. In forests, root systems are feminine, chaotic, wildly interwoven, like pussy portals that hold the phallic pillars reaching high. All life exhibits both energies, seeking and maintaining balance. The wild masculine deserves a safe, honorable space just like the fierce feminine. Playing protector *and* loving nurturer soothes much spiritual suffering and leads us to holistic success.

IT TAKES TWO

The greatest love story of all time is happening all around and through you, right now.

Mother and Father Nature are the ultimate romance. Have you ever truly observed their union, noticed how they celebrate life in love? This kind of fairy tale incites heartwarming sighs and gives you hope.

Before microscopes and paternity tests, we didn't know the masculine was required to create life. Women make love and don't show signs of pregnancy for three to four *months after* the seed has been planted. The contribution of semen isn't immediately obvious. Contrary to popular belief, it is in fact the egg who chooses which sperm she allows to fertilize her. She rests in her power, ready to receive without having to *do* anything to attract attention.

However, we've always celebrated the Divine Masculine as a protective warrior who hunts, builds teepees, or tends fire. Yes, we all come from the Goddess, and to Her, we shall return; but life, Her safety and survival, require the Father.

Artists need platforms or patrons to survive. Corporations need creative artistry to sell products and services. Masterpieces are born from contrasting darkness and light. It takes two to tango. We are born through pathways of structure and flow. We're not meant to do it alone. Father fertilizes Mother, spreading seeds and wild oats, fields and forests rising from their fertile loins.

In life and relationships, we often inhabit one role: nurturer or nurtured. But true harmony embraces the duality between the gardener *tending to* your growth and the fecund garden *to be tended* by others' love and care, providing for and protecting you. Restoring equilibrium in modern religion and society anchors our holistic awareness and embodiment of the maternal and paternal Divine.

Rivers aren't formed by their banks—water carves its own structural containment and support, beautifully illustrating this intricate balance. Small drops can, over time, wear away stone. Our capacity to both tend and be tended lets us travel like lush, flowing streams. Release the river within by accepting and allowing both archetypes to play their part.

As polar ends of the spectrum, drawing fortitude from Her endless cycles of replenishment and revitalization, your orgasms are unbridled, surging waterfalls; healthy relational devotion brings infinite blessed beauty. Engaging with, attuning to, and *surrendering* to the supportive Father, who safeguards and protects precious resources through sustainable living, connects us to conscious consumption, which integrally optimizes our existence.

A rose cannot be rushed to bloom—her petals unfurl only when she is ready, thorns protecting her every step of the way. Like seeds to become a forest, embodying Mother and Father Nature takes time and patience, then grants unimaginable mind, body, and soul pleasure.

THE WICKED STEPMOTHER

Our only culturally recognized mother wounding is the wicked stepmother. *Her*storically, it was honorable to care for another woman's children—signifying your trustworthiness, reliability, kindness, and compassion as a strong family leader, a good woman.

In tribal villages, mothers help each other, anytime. There's shared understanding among them: They all know the bone-aching exhaustion of motherhood and continually show up for each other, in public and in private.

Wicked stepmothers do the opposite. Beginning in fairy-tale lore and legend over 1,000 years ago, this archetype "coincidentally" coincides with patriarchy's dark villainization of witches. Shame of sexual impurity played a major role in bastardizing the opportunity to be a second, bonus mother rather than a "replacement."

Whether as a result of divorce or death (both traumatic for kids), a stepmother can become a blessing or a burden to her new charges. Jealousy of their mother, insecurity in being a secondary substitute, and concern for her inability to measure up manifests in neglect, manipulation, competition, or downright abuse. Which, like all our failures and shortcomings, result from trauma. Abusive women pass on the harm done *to* them—bad adult behavior stemming from pain in childhood. Anyone who abuses children, in *any* way, has *been* wounded, and will project what is too challenging to face. Feeling capable, lovable, and worthy of care, abundance, or pleasure, after being made to believe the opposite in your most formative years, can feel borderline impossible.

In classic heroine's journey fashion, my mom and I both had wicked stepmothers. Less than a year after my mom's mother died, my new "grandmother" forbade her and her siblings from speaking their mother's name and removed all the photos of her in their house, commanding, "I am your mother now." My mom was 22, not a toddler. It caused a rift between her and her father that was never repaired.

Mine, an insidious, manipulative alcoholic, spun different stories depending on her audience. My dad, blinded by "love" or too ashamed to admit what was happening, refuted her drinking and vehemently defended her, even when she stumbled in or out of the car, slurred her words at dinner, or humiliated herself (and our family).

I saw through her facade immediately. Attempting to protect him caused a rupture so large it became a chasm beyond recovery. He denied her addiction until she fell completely apart and stayed in bed (or rehab) for *years*. Then he divorced her to deflect from his own role and responsibility in the situation. I taught her meditation and inner child work for the traumatized little girl inside. But she's still choosing alcohol over awakening, slowly killing herself with increasingly intense injuries while intoxicated.

You know how people say, "Hate to say I told you so"? They don't. People love being right, myself included. But the validation for all those years I tried to warn him was bittersweet. She's all alone in a tough spot now because of shadows she never had the courage to face.

My friend Jess is the best example of an amazing stepmother. In the middle of her husband's and his grown daughters' ages, she could have been a disaster. But her courageously open heart never stopped loving them no matter how they felt or acted. They *adore* her. Like a favorite aunt or a cool big sister, she is the kindest, most loving presence. They share all their secrets because they count on her wisdom and guidance as a conscious woman. That's what we call a *bonus* mom.

Thank Goddess, blended families are returning to normalcy, with friendly relationships between parents and exes, harkening back to the days of tribal collaboration. Divine parents, biological and otherwise, are here to help, nourish, encourage, support, and guide you toward your healthiest, happiest, self. They make mistakes but will always rectify them and continue showing up for you without abandoning or leading you astray.

THE GREEN WAY'S DIVERGENT PATH

Walking the Green Way, we strive for harmony and sustainability rather than perpetuating war and violence; as leaders, we put the actual safety and well-being of people and planet ahead of profit. So practices like forest bathing, earthing, gardening, permaculture, somatic healing, and intentional eating—all Nature Witchual—guide us home to the Earth where we originate and belong.

Though the Witch Wound tries to convince you these practices are unsafe, what's *actually* unsafe is *not* doing them. They effortlessly regulate and regenerate your very cells. Negative ions, energetically charged particles present in natural environments, are proven to enhance productivity, overall well-being, and psychological health.

This systemic disregard for Father Nature (like Mother God) is the cause of most abuse: human, animal, and environmental. It breeds toxic masculinity: a violent, emotionally repressed, stoic entitlement. The mental plague of taking from rather than providing for has become a crisis of raping and pillaging women and Nature as commodities to be exploited for profit. Rape has been psychologically deemed far more often a crime of exerting dominance rather than carnal lust. Those who feel powerless themselves try to exude it over others they deem "weaker" in an attempt to bolster their internal standing in the world.

Too many have witnessed a father take advantage of or harm the Mother and her children, literally or figuratively. Our severed connection from Mother Nature makes us blind to Her reflection in the feminine, disrespecting and dishonoring women. Only those in deep existential agony could perpetuate violence in such disregard for the mothers, sisters, aunties, or daughters who are intrinsically linked to each man, inherently interconnected. We could never endure this behavior if we acknowledged our reliance upon Her.

That's why healing is my number one priority.

In response to the pain inflicted *upon* women, the feminist movement can overlook pain inflicted upon men. The true Holy Father of God as our loving protector has been hijacked by a small group perpetuating this harm. Men are not immune to being abused; sons and brothers get hurt too. "An eye for an eye" only makes the whole world blind.

Without acknowledging the Goddess, religion can't lead us home to genuine equality. Without acknowledging the suffering the patriarchy's toxic masculinity has inflicted on men too, we have no hope to course correct.

Healing requires more than mending this disconnect from Mother Nature—it means, first and foremost, bringing the Holy Father home to his rightful union with Her in our minds. We yearn for relationships where the masculine feels celebrated, honored, and appreciated, with loving reverence for the feminine so he in turn celebrates, honors, and appreciates Her. Taking it upon ourselves to uphold new standards and repair this dynamic is paramount. This means accepting yourself when you need to rest just as much as you celebrate yourself for taking action. Following your IntuWitchin as much as you let logic guide your choices, balancing work and play.

Stay steadfast and present with your pain. Face your fears and inner demons head on, with compassion and curiosity. Don't succumb to abandonment or rejection, running away like the failed father. Watch every excuse you make arise. Choose to stay. Confront convincing critics (in your mind or your life) by refusing to react to their taunting. Notice if any parts of their attack ring true and create change around them. Then the power they held over you melts away.

Achieving this highest alchemical integration of lead (limiting, painful beliefs) into Gold (Divine, shining power) is an ineffable experience and sensation I wish for us all. See who you are beyond the societally controlled narrative. Find your Divine Union within.

Think it sounds easy? Try it!

Ask yourself:

> *How different would our world look if gross domestic happiness, biodiversity, or mental health were the markers for a successful nation?*
> *How does the Witch Wound impact my true Nature?*
> *Do I feel ashamed of my sexuality?*
> *Afraid of my power or Nature's?*
> *Feel unworthy of speaking my truth?*
> *How am I showing up for the planet? For people? For all beings?*
> *What am I turning a blind eye to? Feigning ignorance of?*
> *How do I treat the elements within and around myself?*
> *How can I empower my connection to them?*

Heed the suggestions that arise.

DADDY ISSUES

The religious Father's love shames rather than uplifts. It unforgivingly belittles us, demanding rigid obedience, but not from those who preach about it.

The Father Wound painfully manifests in internalized abandonment of kind, caring direction meant to guide powerful warriors for projected punishment, judgment, and shameful fear of our power and pleasure.

Religion's spiteful, vindictive, and disciplinary leaders become the voices we use to criticize ourselves. Their propagandized Holy Father forbids *us* from sinning while using and *vehemently* abusing his name in vain so insidiously that we inherit and hear it through our mothers. Patriarchal trauma perpetuating what *she* was told to do, say, or look like in order to be "good." We're terrified of being violently disciplined, either physically or spiritually, as many young women in prepubescence were when hormones started changing or their sexuality awakened to be explored. How lost our sacred reverence has become.

Parental influence can instill agonizing deference to our desires, convincing us to settle for less. I have worked with so many people who are so terrified of what their family will think if they really commit to achieving their authentic goals. Left with unfulfilled potential, disappointed in themselves, they worry failure will befall you too, so you might as well just give up and find something stable. They're trying to keep you safe according to their frame of reference.

Time and time again, I have to ask, "When you look at your parents' life, is it what you want for yourself?" Ninety-nine percent of the time, the answer is no. If you don't admire or feel inspired by someone's way of being, achievements, or lust for life, *do not* take their advice! They couldn't possibly know how to adequately counsel your striving.

See who you are beyond society's or your family's controlled narrative. If your parents didn't fulfill their own dreams, and don't support you pursuing yours, it's time to become your own daddy (or mommy). Find your Divine Union within.

The Father's dharmic purpose is being the warrior lighthouse whose beacon shines in the most ominous tempests, illuminating the superior passage home. He's present at every game. His discipline guides who you were born, who he raised you, to be. He's a blessing. If no one ever defended or encouraged your dreams, you have to show up for your inner child, stepping up to evolve into your own internal father. Take a stand for your gifts, abilities, and hopes. Commit. Overcome obstacles. Defy odds. Maintain motivation no matter what obstructs your path.

Writing is an evolutionary gauntlet for me. Speaking is second nature, so filming is effortless, but sitting at the computer requires effort. To be productive while writing, I confront parts of myself who would rather procrastinate and spend time almost any other way.

In the snowy Rocky Mountain winter, my *IntuWitchin* "writing retreat" was isolated and lonely. I almost gave up the grueling process multiple times. I couldn't write *Witchual* like that, so of course, it came to life *as ritual*.

I met my editorial scribe stringing garlands of roses at a Mary Magdalene ceremony. Five days later, she joined my enchanted Scottish castle retreat. At the fairy-tale woodland estate, I lounged in my candlelit spring-water tub with seaweed while she typed and ran a transcript. Her questions and extensive notes kept my tangential thoughts and anecdotal monologues organized.

Goddess spoke through me delightfully, pleasurably, in this ideal book-birthing method. "Writing" became enjoyably easy. *Witchual* brought the magik to me.

On a 12-hour flight from Zurich, I was craving a relaxing movie; nothing interested me. My assignment was clear. With my kitten hiding in my pod beneath a blanket, I spent the entire flight typing love letters to magik, and you. In the end, I found myself *back* in the

Rocky Mountain winter, this time in Big Sky, Montana, and it was the most nourishing season of my life.

Despite discomfort, when we know juice is worth the squeeze, we persevere and we're rewarded. I cultivated resilience, fortitude, and dedication that benefitted every other area of my life. Win-win!

That's how powerful devotion is. Life is devotional to you in return. Same ceremony—writing a book—different energy behind *how* it arrived.

I'm sitting here typing while I'm bleeding, the most energetically low phase of a woman's hormonal cycle, when I could just lounge about. Instead, I'm showing up for the work because *that's what Daddy does.*

Implement Father Nature's power by alchemizing ancestral wounds from your dad and the inner masculine behaviors they inform. That can be as simple as not forcing yourself to push when you're tired, overcoming the urge to procrastinate when you know your mission is calling, or working with a therapist to understand how you are being loyal to his trauma with how you operate in life. For me, it's primarily in how I speak to myself. I hear my dad's harsh criticism when speaking to myself most of the time. The more conscious of it I become, the more I can choose soothing kindness and nurturing when overwhelmed rather than blamey disparaging.

Become a beacon for the Fortunate Father's clear direction, determining the course you want to set for yourself—in this case, a gentler inner dialogue. For you it might be drinking less, being more emotionally available or attuned. Whatever pattern you're confronting, start taking baby steps toward the end goal every moment you notice yourself doing the opposite. When you reach for the booze, say no as often as you can. When you feel yourself shutting down, try sharing with a friend or partner. That you even noticed the instinctual reaction is a great first step!

This frees you to let in the feminine, listening to IntuWitchin, creative expression, and sensational senses. When my energy wanes while I'm in my daddy mode, I curl up for a 45-minute nap with my kitty and wake up ready to dive back into business bossery. It's all about balance, baby.

These questions will help you work out how you may unconsciously be perpetuating negative patterns that won't help you in the long run. Don't skip over this; take the time to journal your responses.

- *What was your dad like?*
- *Did he encourage your dreams or shut them down?*
- *Do you know what he wanted to be growing up? Did he achieve or give up on his dreams?*
- *Was he programmed to fear yours?*
- *What do you know about his childhood trauma?*
- *Can you sense your father's wounding and how his father impacted him?*
- *What does your inner critic say?*
- *How does it judge or criticize you most?*
- *Can you see patterns in your relationship with your father (or parents) that feel similar?*
- *When yearning for love and care, did you receive retribution instead?*

What three to five primary fears feel most daunting or real when you think about your dreams and goals? (Generally, they boil down to the fear of being fully seen, which could lead to rejection or abandonment, ranging from physical or existential pain to mortal danger.)

Examine your beliefs about fearful outcomes: "If I do X, then Y will happen."

* Where did this story or belief come from? Where did you first hear it?

* Was it previously proven to you? What in your past solidified "certainty" of this outcome?

* When you think about taking bold action or following your heart's desires, what do you hear or see? Where did this imagery come from?

* What would be the opposite narrative you could use as your North Star? What kind of encouragement could you repeat to yourself to reprogram outdated beliefs?

Write a list of small preparatory steps you could take in the direction of this goal and prove your capability to yourself.

We know we've all got Daddy Issues, but just as often, we suffer from challenges with our mothers. For women, fathers are different from us—we don't expect to emulate them, but for men to. As women, mothers mirror, inform, and offer our notions about our femininity—we get our sense of self from, then become extensions of them, especially in relationships. Our mothers' behavior influences our interactions with men *and* women, as well as how we feel about ourselves. With rampant sexual abuse, mothers can panic when they see us beginning to explore our bodies and shame or discourage our sexuality (abusing us in a different way) in an unconscious effort to protect us.

Perhaps your mother body shamed you—weight restriction or constant dieting was the only way to maintain her acceptance. Or did money and status seem more valuable to her than you? Narcissistic, overly vain female caretakers can generate self-loathing, low esteem, body dysmorphia, hypercriticism, and much more. Emotionally oppressed mothers never felt safe to feel their feelings, so they have no idea how to help you with yours. Or worse, they punish you for being anything other than complacently content and compliant.

My mother was humiliated by staying with my father for so long. Then I exhibited the same pattern, unconsciously adhering to what had been modeled for me.

Most of us have negative programming from both parents, with one generally more acute. Either the passive or aggressive one offers a lens of what not to do; the other, we imitate in response. The Middle Way in Buddhism is an avoidance of extremes. Masculine directive energy makes space for the feminine to be expressed.

I'M MY OWN SUGAR DADDY: BALANCED BUSINESS ENERGY

I grew up thinking success leads to rejection and abandonment, that it was "lonely at the top."

But after many years of watching friends rise professionally, I got sick of worrying I'd be left behind. Powerhouses in my community created niche offerings, and I wanted to serve too. Solely focused on maintaining freedom and following my highest excitement, the only limitation to a wholehearted "yes" was financial. The Universe often handled even those issues for me, *fortifying* my faith in Her abundance, but still restricting my choices.

Luckily, my parents implored me never to depend on a man for money, that I needed to learn how to make and value it myself. "You're cut off after college; figure it out." Staunch unwillingness to sell my soul for a high-paying, meaningless job or date a rich guy to fund my life left me broke. Even if I wanted to, I would have been too embarrassed to let anyone take care of me. There was only one person to rely on: me.

I didn't realize I had built a cage of scarcity that was trapping me inside its flimsy walls. The poor little princess's tired tale of needing something to rescue her had far outrun its course. Women are ready for a new story of heroism. A hero is called a HER-o, not a HIS-o, after all.

When I finally couldn't stomach the damsel-in-distress phase another second, I committed to building a business. To rise out of the immersive, feminine-flowing, spontaneous, and creative energy, beyond flip-flopping between feast or famine, I had to be my *own* sugar daddy. Yes, I wanted to make money, but more than just provide for myself, I wanted to thrive in devotional service! Thus, diligent dedication to actualizing abundance *within* commenced. I wanted to viscerally feel a richness of energy, aliveness, joy, and pleasure. So I started changing the way I spent my most valuable resource, time.

Turns out, it *wasn't* lonely at the top! All the best people, the dreamers and doers, are up there! And the climb is where the magik happens. My Goddess-Based Business team is a daily blessing of professional fulfillment beyond our wildest imaginings. We prove that entrepreneurship and capitalism don't have to be extractive or manipulative. Conscientious awareness of impact on planet and people run the show.

Masculine structures are filled with feminine operation principles of inspiration, collaboration, connection, and service. We attempt to plan our entire year around when I'm bleeding for relaxing rejuvenation rather than pushing forcefully from my lowest output. What truly matters most is people's transformation, which extends our focus beyond sales. The source of our creative inspiration and basis for company procedures is sharing the magik that allows us to lead extraordinary lives.

We hold my retreats *together*. Managers and operations officers adjust their roles and don different hats. Boss babes in the business become my most trusted handmaidens in castles and cabins. They don't mind getting tea and helping me pack in a week of wonder. They delve deep into this work alongside me, recognizing its power as a fundamental part of leaving a lastingly liberated legacy on Earth. They know how appreciated they are, and how I cherish our profoundly familial, intimate, sisterly connection.

We are seen and loved as our authentic selves beyond typical "employment" boundaries. Our missions unite far beneath the surface. It's a new way of collaborative leadership pioneered by priestess peers we'd never seen role modeled. I could not do what I'm doing without their support. I still pinch myself that I am so entirely uplifted by these sacred sister queens. I wouldn't have it any other way.

This is how women in power functioned for eons. In ancient times, a Healer or High Priestess like me would have been fully supported by her tribe, a respected, noble leader. Her devotional service to the community would have been fairly and graciously exchanged for comfort and nourishment. Spiritual leaders have always been cared for.

Queens' handmaidens or ladies-in-waiting were their best friends, closest confidantes, ardent ambassadors, and fierce protectors. In turn, they took care of them and joyfully provided them room and board. Reciprocal safety and protection offered familial intimacy. You better believe those handmaidens would lay down their lives to save the queen with concealed weapons in every corner, gown, and bedchamber. It's an age-old way of working together.

While building business and calling in partnership, I repeatedly ask myself a question we all must consider to really be the change we wish to see in the world: "How can I harmonize the God and Goddess within?" How can we nourish the driving force that motivates us while tending to the parts that feel afraid or exhausted?

Though Earth School curriculum is individual, entrepreneurship provides a plethora of significant learning. Successfully being who I get to be is my purest, essential joy. But entrepreneurship requires things that aren't my highest excitement every moment, like any business. I don't always (or ever, really) want to sit down and write an e-mail or work on my computer when it's sunny.

I (mostly) live in Southern California—it's *always* sunny. When I'm in a new place with different Nature to explore, which is quite often as an avid traveler, I'm even less likely to get anything done.

At first, having the discipline to do anything I didn't want to do was extremely taxing. I'd *been* doing exactly what I desired at any moment in my flighty fairy life. . . . "What do you mean I have to do something I don't want to?!"

Suddenly, more was demanded from me. My disempowered masculine side was running away, like the absent father archetype who picks up and leaves. I'd abandoned my mission to accomplish, my message to share. I was absent and neglectful of the gifts I'd cultivated through devotional Goddess energy.

This required my *inner* Daddy to step up. Dedicated time and energy in my *spiritual* devotion was familiar; implementing disciplined structure to uphold my personal destiny in my *professional* practice was new. Shifting to embodying a badass boss babe had business booming quickly and altered the trajectory of my life.

Despite being very petite, I have a massive energetic presence. I did lots of visioning and got acquainted with this Warrior within. I wanted to know who he truly was. Seeing the strength it takes for me to show up was both rewarding and such a turn-on. I revered him and got all worked up, like we do watching someone we love doing what *they love*. Staying in to be productive, and not escaping responsibility, sent chills up my spine. I pictured myself in a tailored black suit and corner office, all business, and felt *attracted*, instantaneously magnetizing my feminine muse.

As the Father, I gently compelled myself with, "Okay, sweetheart, it's time to get up and go." I took breaks lying on the earth, practicing yoga or singing, drumming, and meditating. The sexy new lovership *inside* was a wild ride. We owe ourselves the same treatment we lavish upon others.

Owning my balanced, powerful polarity, I felt whole and complete. Once I could trust, rely, and depend on myself to take care of everything, it brought peace, fulfillment, and faith to every day of my life. In a feminine body naturally oriented to Goddess energy, acknowledging my medicinal masculine spirit was a pivotal shift.

On the other side of the spectrum, extreme rigidity is a different kind of imbalance. Conditioned by toxic-action orientation and hypermasculine productivity, our original way of life has become the hardest practice. We feel lazy taking breaks or solo time, or like being is never enough. We forget simplicity's profound power, solitude's strength, stillness and quiet contemplation's clarity, and appreciation's sacredness.

"You don't deserve a nap in the middle of a busy day."

"Don't waste time dancing when you feel melancholy."

"Avoiding hard conversations is more convenient." Or forcing your body into a brute workout when you're exhausted.

Worrying that breaks in routine will lead to chaos, sticking to your calendar like it's law, or feeling guilty for resting means you need to get into your feminine side. Ask for Goddess's guidance. Build Her a pussy-powered altar with flowers and thank Her each morning.

Empowered masculinity is driven by persevering love. Burning the candle at both ends is driven by terror that taking a break means inevitable failure. What's actually failing is missing out on the beauty of being alive. Even if you have to schedule it on your calendar, true *rest* means *in*activity. Recharge your batteries. Sometimes the most important action is doing *nothing*, breathing in stillness.

Nature's raucous symphonies of birds who sing during the day rest at night, crickets and frogs come alive at sunset. Earth takes deep and regenerative rest in winter.

In the *De Natura Deorum*, Cicero said, "If anyone cannot feel the power of God when he looks upon the stars, I doubt whether he is capable of feeling at all. From the enduring wonder of the heavens flows all grace and power. If anyone thinks it is mindless, then he himself must be out of his mind." Yet rest evades many because we sit inside inundated with light and noise pollution, disconnected from the dark, quiet, regenerative celestial blanket of night. We have lost our minds. Dictated "shoulds" and "supposed to's" driven by scarcity (rather than abundance) drive the machine separating us from true power.

Rest	**Recharge**
spending time in Nature, ditching your device, praying, napping, meditating, taking a bath, getting a massage, sitting beneath a tree, reading a book	swimming, walking, hiking, making art, playing board games, playing with your pets, surfing, making love, spending quality time with friends, dancing, intuitive movement

Take movement breaks. Invite a friend to try a new hobby or workout class. Let spontaneous inspiration guide you at least a few times per week. Remember, *scrolling isn't resting.*

Inspired action fuels the fires of juicy, feminine gestation/manifestation powers. It proves loyalty to our dreams, communicates trust in the Universe, and exhibits worthiness of their fruition. Showing up consciously and courageously with the kind of support we always dreamed of receiving helps us rewrite patriarchal narratives.

Engaging in one or a few of these practices for five minutes instantly rejuvenates you. The most important step: familiarizing yourself with feminine receiving.

Place your hands on your body and feel into the Nature that is you.

Ask what it needs from you. Don't shut down or cut yourself off from your own love and attention. Prioritizing your body's requests and acknowledging its state can prevent major future health challenges and anchors inspiration (feminine) to follow the direction of (masculine). Inquiring what's most nourishing in a given moment evokes the fatherly energy to make it happen, especially when that means doing nothing at all.

Out of control, emotional flooding may wreak havoc on our proverbial homes and landscapes. Without context, emphatic weeping, even if it's empathic rather than our own, can be confronting or intimidating for people whose emotions have been shut down or suppressed. How can we hold ourselves, and let ourselves be held, while simultaneously holding others' needs with compassion? Let them pass through without drowning you or fogging the mirror in your mind with stories. We can't shame our feelings, nor *feel* shamed by other's projection of "wrongness," being deemed "inappropriate" or "too much."

When emotions feel more powerful than our capacity to witness and work with them, we are in trauma response. Bring in your wise inner parent to soothe the hurting child, asking your little self what they need and doing your best to provide it. Your Divine pair(ents) will guide you to your synergistic pinnacle without retraumatizing or discouraging you. They actually *do* know what's best.

If you get stuck or are prone to laziness, sloth, lack of motivation, or depression, getting up and moving that energy out of stagnation is the *best* medicine. The opposite of depression is not happiness; it's expression! Showing yourself and the world you feel safe to express who you are in ritual is one of the most powerful stands you can make for yourself. Then depression and anxiety become uncomfortable rather than familiar. Witchual moors Nature's frequency of peaceful calm as our center point to walk forward from.

My yoga teacher always said, "The hardest part is getting on the mat." You have to actually get up off the couch. If you are more comfortable avoiding invitations from Spirit, this is not a permission slip to keep doing less than you're capable of. Nine times out of ten, as Robert Frost so poetically reminds us, the road less traveled makes all the difference.

THE INNER DANCE

Those of you who have read *IntuWitchin* are familiar with the Law of Correspondence: "As Above, So Below; As Within, So Without." Implying that everything outside of you, whether you like it or not, also exists inside of you, so if you want something external, create it internally.

If we want abundance, let us be generous. Want safety? Heal your inner child's fear and instability.

If I want everyone to embrace the harmony and beauty of Mother Earth, I embrace my masculine urge to conquer and build, without shame or resentment. Recognizing the necessity of things we don't want to do means overcoming resistance to effort and discipline with compassionate patience.

We are both Earth and sky. Accomplishment requires grounded, steady progress *and* expansive visionary imagination. Innovating logistics with delegation led me to achieve my goals. Discipline doesn't limit my freedom; it *expands* it. I say yes to more opportunities, travel more often and more comfortably, impact more people, make financial contributions, learn, evolve, and heal—amplifying my freedom of choice. Win-win.

I constantly work on trusting each aspect of my inner dynamic duo. Some days I'm up bright and handling business. Others, like the first day back after a long trip, I don't accomplish much. Despite wanting to hit the ground running, I'll take naps and move slow. Surrendering to rest, I rise motivated and ready to tackle tasks.

My fervently pleasure-seeking femininity resists the disciplined direction of masculinity too often in favor of just about anything else. I have to be able to rely on her for the creativity that fuels my business and fun that fuels my life. But I also have to be diligent and follow through on the tasks that bring those creative visions to life and allow me to provide financially for myself in order to enjoy all the adventures and activations that keep my inspiration flowing.

There is always a balancing act. The side we resist, or are less comfortable listening to, whispers the advice we really need to hear. Do what it takes to listen. Build the foundational temple sanctuary to worship at the altar of your life.

✶ ✶ REFLECTION ✶ ✶
Use the Elements for Your Warrior or Wise Woman Within

Examine both sides of your coin: introspection and action. Attune yourself with the archetypal energy you need most.

What does wholeness ask of you?

Earth: Feminine

Is your feminine yearning for more structure, guidance, and purposefulness?

Or is your masculine asking for connection, healing, and creativity?

Do you need a little earthquake to shake things up?

Have things fallen apart and it's time to rebuild?

If you've been overly stubborn, rigid, and unmoving like a mountain, use the medicine of movement and connecting with the body.

Ask yourself:

How do I nourish and care for myself?

What did I come into this lifetime to accomplish?

When am I most connected to my body? How can I connect more deeply?

Water: Feminine

Has the flow of your emotions been dammed or your sexual or creative current staunched?

Have you flooded your world and feel stuck in the mud, begging for a sunny day?

Let those tears fall, giving your body the love it deserves. Or dry your eyes and surf that wave.

Your brain cannot experience pain and pleasure at the same time. Do something that makes you feel good, happy, excited, or connected to your spiritual nature and the Divine.

Ask yourself:

What emotions have I prevented myself from feeling?
When do I feel genuine love and affection for myself (not just superficially)?
How do I express creatively? Or devotionally? How can I recommit to these pursuits?

Air: Masculine

How is your mental health? Are you asking for more clarity and trust in your authentic expression?

Are you really in your head and need to drop into your body? Maybe you have trouble sharing your truth, feel unworthy, or are overwhelmed by negative thoughts.

It's time to clear the air. Get a fresh perspective. Use your senses to ground you into the present. Try breath work or mirror work to speak what you need to hear to yourself.

Ask yourself:

What stories do I tell myself about who or how I am?
How free do I feel to unleash my full expression?
How do I communicate who I am to the world?
When I talk about my experience of life, am I coming from villain, victim, or victor consciousness?
What inspires me most?

Fire: Masculine

If you've been burning the candle at both ends, it's time to momentarily extinguish action.

If you need to stoke the flames and generate some fiery, passionate heat, take action on whatever you've been avoiding that's been burning a hole in the back of your mind.

What motivated you as a child? What drives you today? Get the show on the road!

Ask yourself:

> *What is my relationship with rest?*
> *Where do I need clearer direction?*
> *What motivates me?*
> *What do I need to do more of? Less of?*

Reintegrating, revivifying, and fulfilling femininity can be as simple as savoring your food. That "I'll have what she's having" energy, sensually enjoying the pleasure of different fabrics, natural environments, or letting your creativity run wild with imagination. Coupled with the masculine energy of accomplishment, stillness, and momentum, we become unstoppable and profoundly fulfilled in every area of our lives.

Whether building structures or embracing fluidity, embodying both Mother and Father Nature is an enchanting exploration and discovery. Understanding and integrating both archetypes requires honoring your needs, embracing power, and being guided by what truly resonates with your soul.

Like us, Earth is a living, breathing consciousness. Holistic living requires returning to Her symbiotic qualities—strength and gentleness, ferocity and fertility, abundance in complexity and simplicity, depth and vastness. As we nurture this relationship, we attune to Her spiritual essence and our true selves. She is infinitely more intelligent, advanced, and billions of years older than we are.

See Nature's Divine reflecting your own. Remember, your bones are the stones in the mountains. Your blood, sweat, and tears are the rivers, creeks, and streams. The wind is your breath, and the same shining sunlight is the fire that keeps your heart beating. We are both flower and bee, roots and tree, sky and sea.

MICROWITCHUALS

* Go outside without your phone to a wild, natural environment. If your local park is all you've got, that's okay, but try something less manicured. Record in your journal or contemplate Nature's femininity and masculinity. Notice flowers and pollinators, leaves, stalks, and branches, where there is strong direction and more gentle flow.

* Expand by lying down, enveloped in Nature's embrace. Feel loving arms wrapping around you, letting unconditional love soothe aches in your soul. Ask Her for guidance or words of wisdom. Stay as long as you can.

* Dance to embody your inner warrior (or masculine), then inner Priestess (or feminine). How does your body move distinctly in each? Which sensations make you more comfortable?

* Take a life inventory through the questions already posed and the sensations from your dance practice.

* Invoke your inner masculine in a more empowered, action-oriented way while ensuring your body's trust in the Mother's nurturing nourishment you may be more familiar with.

* Schedule at least three nonnegotiable two-hour work windows this week. Sit with your to-do list and notifications OFF. Bang out as many tasks as possible.

* Or schedule your time to rest and recharge. Take yourself to the spa, or do whatever you need to feel replenished.

* Set a timer and clean your room for 30 minutes; organize a closet that's been bothering you; get rid of outdated wardrobe or household items.

✳ Get an intense workout in, meal prep for the week, or start *and commit to* the supplement regime that's been lurking in your kitchen cabinet for months.

✳ **Practice Inner Union:** Every day for seven days, celebrate the balance of these energies. If you're slammed with work, take 10 or 15 minutes between calls to stretch, get sunshine, read, sing, or dance. Carve out a creativity night; engage in a pleasure ritual, like a massage; plan that trip you've been putting off; or just a dinner party! If you love cooking but never make time for it, be the chef (or tag-team it). Enjoy your time, decreasing stress in whatever ways feel devotionally creative and abundant to you.

CHAPTER 3

Singing for My Seven-Year-Old Self

I am everything I am because my inner seven-year-old's deepest desires drove me to achieve my dreams.

Back then, I wanted to be a singer. Belting '90s hits, '70s disco, show tunes, and my own "channeled" works, I *knew* it's what I was *meant* to do. One summer, while my parents and I drove home to Northern California from a Montana river trip in our minivan, Joni Mitchell, Nirvana, the Eagles, and Sinead O'Connor circulated through the speakers. On a quiet audiobook stretch, Alanis Morissette's album *Jagged Little Pill* blared from my Discman for the millionth time. (That's a portable CD player for you youngsters.)

As I sang along, I heard my dad, my biggest fan, tell my mom, "I can't take that screeching anymore."

My jaw dropped, agape. *Screeching? Me?* Earth-shattering cognitive dissonance fundamentally transformed my identity instantaneously. I was *beyond* devastated. I'd never questioned myself, my destiny, his word, or masculine trustworthiness before.

One sentence altered the course of my life. I stopped singing. My annihilated trust impelled my Daddy Issues.

Two decades later, home in the redwoods for Christmas, I got some context from him. "Your mom wanted to leave that morning and not come back."

They hadn't spoken in hours, and he had made a bid for connection, attempting to break tension with a smile, and those words just came out. He'd seen my reaction in the rearview mirror. "I knew I'd made one of those irreparable parenting mistakes. I begged your forgiveness for months, apologizing every day, trying to convey I didn't mean it, get you back to singing lessons. You refused."

To this day, I only remember the incident itself. Blacked-out memories are common physical or emotional trauma responses. After all, *internal* scars are far worse than scrapes, bumps, and bruises. Toxic mental and emotional behaviors we witness in childhood are just as likely to be residually replicated as rebelled against. Evolutionary human curriculum magnetizes situations that mirror past experiences to transcend and complete patterns.

The day after hearing my dad's explanation, I was at a dance class. Summer, a fiery redhead with an infectious giggle, announced a song circle, and I was instantly compelled to be there. My inner child's greatest crusade was unknowingly charioting me to my fate. It wasn't about being good; it was about enjoying ourselves. I did. I had fun singing for the first time since I could remember. That Scottish Faerie became a treasured friend. She knew endless Goddess and Earth worship songs. I couldn't get enough.

Coaxed into spending unanticipated weeks in my hometown, after many years of suppression, I found that using my voice was an antidote to the anxiety and depression caused by hiding who I am. Singing became a testament to my joy, worthiness of my dreams, and authenticity. Despite hearing, "You're screeching!" in the back of my mind every moment, I focused on how good it *felt* to free my voice. Even years into working with it, and my virtually limitless comfort as a speaker, I still struggle to just let my voice *sing* freely. The moment it starts to feel good, unencumbered by those old, painful beliefs, it starts to strain, or I instantly start crying. It's wild how something so seemingly small and insignificant can impact you unconsciously.

I have revisited that minivan moment countless times in inner child healing sessions. I grasp those tiny hands, gazing at that little version of me as the Goddess I am today and tell her the truth: "You're not screeching. You sound beautiful. This voice is going to ring out across the world. Thousands will be healed by it. Keep going, my girl; you're meant to be heard."

She swallows the lump in her throat and goes right back to Alanis, belting out how ironic it is to have rain on your wedding day.

A voice for Earth, the feminine, all the children who just want safe spaces to express.

I'm so grateful the path led me to my destiny. This wild spiritual journey made the medicine of my message. My *teaching* is my soul's song, no matter how it emerges. It's *so fun*, such a *celebration* to be who I am, do what I do. I still have fear around singing, and that might remain forever. But now I'm proud of my voice, the way I'm spiritually expressed in all mediums.

This is the essence of subconscious inner child healing outwardly manifesting. You came to Earth believing in the infinite possibilities of your dreams and can again, leading you to your most magikal life.

THE WIND BENEATH OUR WINGS

Our Inner Child's *dreams* beckon to our divinely designed destiny—following them leads to purposefully fulfilling and magnificent lives. And our Inner Child's *wounds* are beacons illuminating milestones on our healing road map to get there.

Inner child work is the most foundational aspect of personal growth and healing if we want a peaceful, happy, purposeful, and accomplished life with a regulated nervous system. Our original wounding hinders *and* motivates our success and evolution.

Though the initial impetus can feel isolating, perseverance magnetizes people with shared values, celebrating our breakthroughs and comforting our breakdowns. Loneliness is an epidemic because we're not meant to live separated by borders, boundaries, and apartment walls. "It takes a village" to raise children because we need community support and help to uplift us when our babies cry or we're overwhelmed. Villages function symbiotically—we can't do it alone, and we were never supposed to.

Reparenting means responding as the kind of parent our inner child needed then and still seeks now. We hear about money before we're old enough to spend it, for instance, and we see masculinity through male presence, or lack thereof, before hearing the word. We're told the likelihood of our dreams coming true before we have autonomy to pursue them. Our beliefs in magik, men, mission, and what we're worthy of, all originate in childhood. Using tools from meditation to ayahuasca, we're adequately nurturing the version of us who existed before the negative programming we work so hard to abolish as adults.

Inner child work is the bedrock for Witchual, authentic living, and creating invaluably sustainable, regenerative personal and professional success. Money buys facilitation and support, but it can't ensure soothing and nurturing responses to unsafety. Integrating joy and pain into how you're inclined to show up is priceless, crucial work.

As children, we believed freely and fully in whatever we chose, from the Tooth Fairy to the limitless potential futures. Identifying and alchemizing which imparted beliefs disempower, keep us stuck, or hinder progress returns us to original innocence. If we learned men can't be trusted from our fathers (or mothers), we attract partners who prove us right—until we change the narrative. All the ways I couldn't count on or rely on my former partners became the jumping-off point for the work I did to manifest my true king, proving that my masculine discipline and direction could be trusted.

According to trauma experts, often, childhoods perceived as "fine" or "good" lead to epiphanies that a lack of nourishing care has similar impacts to outright abuse. Some children witness alcoholism or drug addiction and learn what *not* to do. Others follow family footsteps, continuing generational patterns. In households with emotionally unavailable or abusive parents, some children become people pleasers, suppressing their emotions to keep the peace. Others act out, trying desperately to create connection. Some play small because no one ever supported them. If you were constantly seeking approval, questioning your worthiness without it, what would you need to feel accepted and celebrated within yourself?

Overbearing parents have been shown to breed children who become excellent liars because they're always fabricating stories. As adults they can't trust themselves, so they don't know how to trust others. A sibling who knew what was really going on may project dishonesty onto their partners later, exhibiting jealousy, possessiveness, and intrusive interrogation, attempting to maintain control. Others withdraw as a protective response, because if they stay small and out of the spotlight, they cannot be criticized or controlled.

Children's gifts need to be acknowledged and supported. The failure to recognize and nurture these gifts is another sickness in our society. It is crucial to embrace and support the unique abilities of children to foster a healthier and more accepting environment. And there are many herbs, such as passionflower, that can calm a nervous mind, promoting tranquility and easing restlessness without the methamphetamines in Ritalin.

One of my students who was sexually abused in childhood by her father (which is all too common) was terrified to tell anyone in her family. She'd kept it all to herself until she joined my retreat at 31. Her adamant secrecy stemmed from her aunt's accusing her grandfather of the same molestation. Their family locked her in a psych ward and ultimately had her *lobotomized*! Proof that if the patriarchy can go that far in a single family, there's no telling what they do to keep secrets from the world at large.

Kids are malleable, too easily harmed verbally, spiritually, or otherwise. The damage done by physical mistreatment, emotional neglect, or absence of safety all impart different defense strategies and survival tactics. Our inner children feel forbidden from their emotions after being told to be quiet or by interrupting them. Punishing children for innocent expression (touching, jumping, running, sounding) makes their natural impulses feel unsafe to follow, skewing who or how they must become to survive.

Sometimes simply letting your inner child do what they want is all you need to heal it.

My father was volatile; our emotional environment was unsafe at times. If my mom or I met his emotions with our own, he erupted. She, on the other hand, was emotionally suppressed and conflict avoidant. I bounced between overt emotional displays and internalizing to avoid my pain being seen. As an adult, I re-created that same insecurity in romantic partnerships, sacrificing my needs to maintain toxic familiarity disguised as "love."

Breakups are such a gift. I could never have done a full spiritual remodel without demolition. Only once I was removed from daily dynamics could I see all I had sacrificed by staying, abandoning myself for perceived safety where it never actually existed.

My desire to be cherished and of service drew me to people unwilling to appreciate me, who took advantage instead, so I could learn to celebrate myself. Though agonizing, this served me deeply. I became my own biggest fan, claiming and cultivating my own worthiness of acknowledgment, which is what little Mia needed all along and eventually magnetized a true king who matched that frequency.

One of the greatest challenges we experience as a species is combatting shame. I see this in myself and every student and client I've ever had. In order to glean the important insight from such situations, we have to be able to distinguish between guilt and shame.

Guilt: "I did something bad."

Shame: "I *am* bad; there's something *wrong with me.*"

Without eradicating shame, partnerships form as "woundmates," mirroring shadowy parts we resist or reject and don't want to look at—deep-seated injuries from our familial relationships.

How do you operate in response to your upbringing? Seeking approval from people you don't actually respect or admire, like your dad?

What does your inner child need to self-source approval and acceptance?

CHILDLIKE WONDER

Remember when cardboard boxes became spaceships? Bounding across living room furniture because the floor was lava? The doll or stuffie you shared an intimate and engaging relationship with? The gift of childhood is endless possibilities—kids climb trees and enter entirely different worlds. But have any dreams, desires, or fantasies you once only hoped for come to life?

We paradoxically obsess over movie and rock stars but ridicule "band geeks" and "theater nerds." Societal pressure has perpetuated generations of adults whose childhood dreams were tragically dismissed—dissuading yet naturally admiring mission-drivenness.

Diminishing imaginative powers reinforces what we *don't* want:

"I'm not an artist."

"I'm not smart enough."

"No one will like me,"

"I could never make it."

Crushed beneath negative self-perceptions, criticized creative impulses, and fearing rejection, failure, or abandonment, we slowly conform to more "realistic" expectations.

Our imagination is our *most powerful tool*. Just as caterpillars are transformed into butterflies by *imaginal* cells, we can *imagine* ourselves into someone totally different if we're *willing* to change and rise reborn as who we *choose*. Beyond daydreaming, caterpillars take necessary (sometimes scary) steps to metamorphosize into new dimensions.

Following our inner child's aspirations leads to personal and/or societally recognized success. Unmet childhood needs can influence adulthood's striving. Either for the courageously authentic ambitions someone else's fear convinced us to abandon, or the destiny we've always known was ours. Hoping for rectification through external achievement, people who pursue fame often felt unseen, or were told they'd never amount to anything. "I told you," "We'll show them," or "See?! I didn't need you," motivates the desire for proving others wrong.

During my tenure in Los Angeles, I watched people fight for respect they'd never cultivated within by striving to "be a billionaire," desperately attempting to show neglectful, absentee, or broke parents that they'd "made it." I opted to follow my inner child's joyful inclination, and my star rose higher and higher.

Wound-driven goals don't produce genuine satisfaction. Goals fueled by joy and wonder lead to inspiration, fulfillment, powerfully healing redemption, and ecstasy from the children within us who dared to dream and never gave up.

For the last 2,000-plus years, those who empowered the masses faced severe repercussions. Jesus preached personal *and* communal emancipation. His successors lost sight of his teachings, exemplifying the polar opposite of his philosophical pillars. I respect Jesus's teachings as a Divine avatar but challenge the authority and motives of those who speak on his behalf to exclude and judge.

Joan of Arc, an awakened mystic guided by angelic visions, was a formidable warrior at just 18 and put to death for her brazen valor. Modern figures like Martin Luther King Jr. were fully aware of the consequences, yet they stood firm in their beliefs to help humanity awaken, and spoke against oppressive governance.

Grammy winner Sinead O'Connor's revolt against the Catholic church rendered her blacklisted and virtually invisible after soaring to superstardom. Watching her documentary, *Nothing Compares*, I realized I had played small by not fully opposing patriarchal structures. Inspired by her resolve, I unleashed all I'd held back for fear of upsetting the status quo.

We speak Joan's name hundreds of years postmortem, a living legend. Sinead's courage sparked a movement and mass awakening in Ireland. I want everyone to feel welcome in this space, *and* I am devotionally dedicated to eradicating mental, spiritual, and physical enslavement by dogmatic chains. It's up to us to carry these torches.

Wield your powerful imagination by believing in (even the possibility of) magik. Books like Dean Radin's *Real Magic* and Daniel Lieberman's *Spellbound* divulge scientific *proof* that trust in magik significantly alters reality, improves cognitive function, and enhances memory or retention of information.

My favorite children's creativity assessment, which I also shared in *IntuWitchin*, proved that *momentary exposure* to magik *momentously* increases aptitude. Watching scenes from the Harry Potter film series with magik's presence as a nonchalant expectation of life boost brain function by *50 percent!* Simply *pretending* you *might* have unseen powers works wonders in *making your dreams come true.*

If you *knew* you had infinite wellsprings of magik, requiring only focused cultivation and practice, miraculous events would unfold, drawing exponentially more magik to you. You'd think more creatively and innovatively, cope with challenges better, and maintain hope when it seems lost.

Ask yourself:

What have I forgotten or rejected because of people's opinions/projections?
What dreams excited me?
Why did I give up?
How could I reintegrate them now?

Did you want to be a pro athlete? Join weekly pickup games. A zookeeper? Volunteer at animal shelters. Go to art, cooking, or archery classes; invite friends for creativity gatherings; hit the planetarium. Endless possibilities, remember?

Kids' movies, fairy tales, and fantasy help enhance belief and offer endless codes that inspire new Witchual practices because magik is real and anyone can have it. *Fern Gully*'s Fairy Godmother, Magi, oozes existential wisdom. *Frozen 2* is one of the few films adequately depicting colonizers' betrayal of magikal indigenous societies and that damming sacred rivers hinders their powerful ways of life. *Peter Pan* teaches that happy thoughts make you fly and magik *does* come from your heart. These aren't silly statements; they're true! Maybe only metaphorically sometimes, but still better than major religion's shameful disempowering allegories. Legend and mythology far predate the Bible, Torah, and Qur'an.

Your heart's electromagnetic field is *5,000* times greater than your brain's. Courage (from the heart, remember?) grants you the confidence to actualize and makes you magnetic to your greatest visions.

Magik's vastly underutilized resource is not just for getting *things* we want. It brings us together with others, reminds us we can heal ourselves, empowers us as leaders, and connects us to Nature and our original medicine—plants!

Now, casually unshakeable, fervent belief in magik tends to be a little more challenging when overcoming religious programming. But Jesus was a witch, akin to a Fairy Godmother himself. His magikal gifts and abilities brought beauty and healed aching souls. Why shouldn't you do the same? Some of my most popular content encourages talking to your Christian family about Witchual. I've never met a believer who didn't scratch their heads when describing Jesus's actions as exactly what witches were punished for. Real followers of Christ understand questioning the innocence of those who lit the pyres.

VICTORY OVER THE INNER VILLAIN

Every good story's hero(ine) faces their foe, and even if they don't emerge unscathed, they're always wiser for it. In our life legends, great adversaries are more often voices in our minds than external enemies. We rarely remember to see ourselves in these stories as adults unless it's in films or our favorite romantasy novels. More often we repeat, "You're unworthy; you're undeserving; there's something wrong with you; you're destined to fail. There's no hope, so you might as well just give up; don't even try." Sound familiar?

Think about the bad guy, or antagonist, in your favorite tales. Anything he says to the hero (you), you've likely heard yourself. Our inner dialogues can be the most vicious villains. We blame others while holding on to believing we're unworthy of great love or achievement, sabotaging our potential for happiness and fulfillment. We fear the consequences of success *and* failure. Miserable isolation isn't due to external opposition, but how we respond to and abandon the parts of ourselves we love most.

The inner villain exacerbates the elusiveness of whatever you've been trying to manifest or accomplish that keeps evading you, exclaiming that its lack proves their critical opinions right. Instead of just succumbing to their subterfuge, explore your inner child's beliefs and needs, tracing similar experiences (and the meaning you make of them) to your youth.

External villains or naysayers project, "Your dreams are unrealistic; you should settle for more 'security' (aka boring and unfulfilling)." The inner villain holds on to childhood pain as evidence that you're better off without that job/love/money/home, shaming your hope, steering you away from pursuing joy in favor of what "makes sense." Convincing you violent or unsafe situations, abusive relationships, and toxic behavior patterns are all you'll ever deserve rather than encouraging you to seek more. Then, advertisers, some of the most insidious and hypnotic propagandists, sell you their products through societal ridicule, and our poor minds think the solution can be bought.

Physical or existential pain and suffering is the perfect chance to show up as your own hero, bringing soothing solace, safety, and blessings. Though they can be harsh and unkind, underneath the villain's condemnation is a positive intention. Their certainty of failure is a misguided effort to keep you sensibly small in order to be "safe," offering you an alchemical opportunity should you choose to accept it.

The world hasn't looked kindly on those who are joyful or truly powerful. Because they scoff at small-mindedness and are always willing to face their fears.

I have waged war with my inner villain in full-fledged battles. It took over a decade after my accident to see my scars as dragon skin rather than deformity. When I looked at my reflection in the mirror, disfigurement and ugliness greeted me, never beauty. Even though it was only my forearm that had been damaged, the inner injuries were all consuming.

Questing to quell your inner villain requires courage and perseverance, which are gained through our trials and tribulations. Reclaiming our heroism shifts life from happening *to* us to *for* us. I wouldn't have learned to heal myself if I hadn't been hurt so badly. I wouldn't have known how to heal others without first doing so for myself. This is the classic legend of Chiron, the wounded healer.

Suffering provides us with the tools to help others through their own trials.

Heroes come in a myriad of forms just like power does. I have a fierce power, but so many of my dearest and most cherished sisters have a kind of soft power that inspires and encourages me. At one of their birthday parties this very culty guy attempted to take over the ceremony to honor her, and it took me standing up for the unconsensual facilitation to bring us back to the original intention of the evening. All true power has merit, albeit with different context in different situations.

Maintain mindfulness not to aggravate current circumstances. You don't want to cross your own boundaries and retraumatize yourself. Your goal is to allow your original essence, the you before you fell victim to the villains, to emerge, returning to the innocence with which you first arrived in the world. The resulting trust and faith from repairing wounds makes us magnetic, vibrantly alive, and the kinds of hero(ine)s we always longed would come for us.

☾

I once found myself trapped in a cycle of learning through pain. Emotions would surge, and instead of allowing them to surface, I'd swallow my tears and keep moving. Within a few hours, I always had some kind of physical accident—I'd hit my head, bang a knee, or close my finger in a car door. Everything I'd bottled up was inadvertently forced out like a champagne cork.

After multiple occurrences, I had to reflect on when I first learned, "Growth doesn't come from soft gentleness and ease; it comes from pain."

I'd been in a horrific, near-fatal accident at 16, and another one 18 months later. I had ignored the Universal guidance that I was saved for a reason, my big mission to help and heal, which awakened the first time: "It's selfish to hide who you are, abandoning yourself and all those you could inspire and serve, by pretending to be so much less than magikal."

It took me a decade to finally step into that truth and chose to learn lessons differently, less painfully. Mustering the courage to stop hiding was the first step toward changing my response to inner turmoil. Now, when emotion arises, I let it come up and out, moving through quickly when I don't stifle its power. My neural pathways finally diverged to more tender transformation. But you better believe, when I ignore any inner truth, there is always a consequence, like my higher self is saying, "I told you so. I thought we covered this already. Do you want the easy way or the hard way?"

One summer, while way behind on this book's deadline, I decided to skip Burning Man—which, by this time, you know how much I love—with *all* my friends. My inner villain had a field day. I knew there was a reason, but I regretted it immensely. Until I realized quantum leaping onto my most optimal future timeline had kept me grounded.

So I dove in: *What have I been avoiding feeling or missing out on by distracting myself, chasing so many activities? What's bigger, better, and even more glorious that I get to channel or harness because I'm choosing me and the mission I was assigned with this life? What am I trying to get by going? What* more *might I get by* not *going?*

Choosing to *self-source* divine connection was the latest, albeit unfamiliar, transformative experience. When we are so accustomed to distracting ourselves from what we actually need to do or don't want to feel, silence, stillness, and solitude can be incredibly confronting. But the inner villain's antidote lies within. Avoiding responsibility or the emptiness of feeling alone and cut off from connection is succumbing to societal kryptonite, keeping us stuck as Clark Kent.

I rejected this invasive illusion's poison. Triumphantly, I tended to the parts of myself that felt like anything external could somehow give me more than I could give myself, which I'd have been running from in Burning Man's novelty, escaping the responsibilities that are greater than me, in service to the mission I'm here to accomplish. I *chose* not to go. But my inner villain chose regret and suffering.

Reacting like I did will not support you in living your best devotional, purposeful life, or being your own Super(Wo)Man.

Insidious dialogue can be earth-shattering and steal your life force. Think back to behaviors you brushed off that actually didn't feel good. What have you let slide, put off until later, or refused to accept? Are you hiding from a larger purpose, a deeper devotion that would grant you long-lasting fulfillment and self-realization? Uncover the negative beliefs that are equivalent to ignoring gut feelings.

What seemed like FOMO was greater forces orchestrating my evolution. We are always in charge of our capacity to enjoy the present. It's called that because it's a *present*! By staying home, my princess's villainous fear of missing out and victim's self-doubting unworthiness that leads to procrastination were gifted a priestess's victorious personal metamorphosis, a queen's mission accomplishment, and redemptive recognition.

The villain says, "You made a mistake." The purpose-driven, spiritual CEO whose mission is saving and changing the world (by writing this book instead of being at Burning Man) *knows* nothing trumps accomplishing Goddess-given gifts and goals. The victor says, "I'm always exactly where I'm meant to be. I am whole. This new choice leads to a new timeline serving who I've worked hard to become." I have integrated the love and lessons from Burning Man. What is this new choice offering me that I haven't yet mastered?

MOUNT OLYMPUS

This is one of my simplest and most enjoyable Witchuals. When digressing into a spin about whatever nonsense is bothering me that day, I (in classic Gemini fashion) chariot my mind from the gloomy underworld of abysmal self-sabotage onto the glorious empowerment of Mount Olympus.

I plop the negative or self-deprecating thought into a golden carriage or atop Pegasus. Whisked away through luminous pearly gates, my sorrow and self-pity trail behind as they open onto a glowing, golden mental mountaintop palace of joy, gratitude, and wonder. My mind and body experience what it would be like to arrive there.

Instant, visceral, all-consuming blissful delight, calm tranquility, heavenly vibrations, and celestial celebration arise like clouds parting on gloomy days to brilliant skin-warming sun. Sighing in relief, I revel in Mount Olympus Magik. Your mind doesn't know the difference between what's real and imaginary, so give it the gusto.

Finding myself single in my 30s had my inner child worried I might not find anyone else who would ever love me. My novelty-chasing, naive relational novice constantly fell victim to old narratives echoing throughout mental caverns, begging to be put to rest. "Does the kind of love I dream of and desire actually exist?" Completing the cycle of these misbeliefs requires satisfying my inner child's needs for safety and strong, reliable care.

Unfortunately, my romantic partners have been more intimidated by than intimate with me, shamed more than celebrated me, and wanted me to play small to counteract my fervent success. I wouldn't want that kind of love for anyone, least of all myself and the little girl who's manifested her most magikal life. So I scooped her up, provided the movement, support, pleasure, fun, or excavation she needed and cooed, "We're living our fairy tale. No chance we're settling for anything less than legendary love and a mating bond to match. It was right to leave. Let's go flying."

After shifting identity and outdated beliefs irrelevant to my badass boss babe, I rallied my mythic magik. I show up with men differently now. I call them forward even in surface-level interactions and reject the status quo of what's acceptable to impress women. Men have been floored and thanked me for being different than anyone they'd ever met, even in momentary acquaintances.

When it's just a broken record, and not the actual trauma response, my wise adult says, "No. I'm not going down that dark hole again! I'm on Mount Olympus!" Then I put a huge grin on my face and close my eyes to imagine it is so. *Smiling* (then letting the warmth of your visions cascade over you like honey) literally changes your brain chemistry. Use mantras, affirmations, orgasms, Nature, singing, or empowering music to activate imaginal cells and envision your future, anything to evade villain territory.

You might think something like this is easier said than done—it's not. Your mind is a *tool* and *servant*. *You* are its master.

Ancient seminaries that initiated adept students into mystical teachings of wielding universal powers for personal development and advancement, known as mystery schools, proffer, "By will alone, I set my mind in motion." When you're reeling, your body responds with stress, sadness, frustration, disappointment, or anxiety, viciously cycling. Rejoicing generates happy hormone responses! Flip the switch. Reclaim the reins. *Choose.* Your *will* is the *only* thing you're in absolute control of.

You're ready for Mount Olympus only after you've done the work to defuse triggering charges behind the spin—to handle reverberating residual, antiquated stories. You can't bypass the necessary wisdom that arises from feeling and facing the root cause of your struggles that lead to villainous voices like:

You can't . . .
You don't deserve . . .
You'll never . . .

They must be dealt with first. So the hero your inner child needs protects them no matter how large or small the battle, standing for who they hoped to grow into. Invoke your victorious, archetypal champion capable of slaying any foe. Use superheroes, childhood idols, or Natural elements to envision the sacred warrior devoted to your personal crusade. See them galloping forth onto Mount Olympus atop Pegasus whenever you feel like you're losing to limitation, and choose the reality you desire.

KEEP IT REAL

Modern treatment of children glaringly reflects deep-seated societal maladies. Child abuse is unfathomable to most, yet perpetrated by those who have clearly not received the kind of help a tribal community could have offered. Studies show many perpetrators were victims themselves—only someone so hurt, so disconnected from empathy and kindness could harm helpless, innocent beings. If you suffered at the hands of another, I am truly sorry, but you are not broken. Healing is possible for us all.

A safe environment for inner-child flourishing is essential to vanquish inner villains. Comfort and soothing replace shameful punishment when mistakes are made. Faith conquers doubt when we're uncertain. Compassion greets embarrassment. Sending signals of "You're safe with me" dissuades wounding from running rampant and ruining your life. Something as simple as deep breaths with audible sighs and singing signify in the brain that there is no present danger. Because if there was an imminent threat, we would breathe and be as silent as possible to avoid notice.

Every child needs to feel supported, uplifted, held, acknowledged, and celebrated. To halt the cycle of abuse perpetuated throughout the world, we must begin by nurturing our inner children with the reinforcement and recognition we needed as little ones.

It's *never* too late.

Whether you've locked them away, hidden in pain, denied their desires, rejected them, or avoided them, your inner child remains your entire life. Fear not: Despite a lifetime of terror, unlocking their cage and embracing them forges a new relationship with the most important aspect of yourself.

Nervous-system regulation radiates safety to others' inner children. When we let ourselves play like kids—be silly, embodied, vocally expressed, tender, authentic, and friendly—we're shining beacons of the acceptance everyone craves.

Childhood is fleeting. It's too easy to be caught in current struggles and create schedules forgetting playful carefreeness. Western culture troublingly promotes escapism through alcohol and other substances, attempting to recapture what we've lost. But *life* is meant to be fun!

Despite our justification of substance use for unwinding and relaxing, using them long term has the opposite effect. When we're subconsciously reaching for the unburdened exuberance adulthood obscures, under the influence we're unrestrained, uninhibited, even reckless, like children. Numbing past pain by severing connection from the present is *not* genuine freedom.

Modern neuroscience's intersection with spirituality is proving we *are* creating reality. Belief about our lovability, worthiness, and inherent value stem from our families of origin. Which draws similar situations to us again and again. If we didn't feel seen, accepted, or celebrated by original attachment figures, we'll expect lack of acknowledgment and rarely demand more of ourselves. If love was unpredictable in our household, we'll settle for unpredictable romantic relationships. Belief that we're unsafe magnetizes more evidence to prove this true.

We magnetize similar circumstances until we finally utilize the curriculum as an opportunity to learn and transcend habituated responses. Secure, stable partnership is possible once we unwind that instability's internal impact and informed behaviors.

See repeating red flags with "your type"?

Ask yourself:

What must I stop accepting?
What am I ignoring or excusing that keeps rearing its ugly head to get my attention?
What do I believe about myself that I'd like to change?

"I'M NOT A KID PERSON"

"You're so enthusiastic!" The word *enthusiasm*'s root means "the divine within." *Ism*, from Greek, means "a system, practice, or theory." Enthusiasm is the practice of letting God into you! My childlike exuberance and genuine excitement are contagious. I love playing dress-up, being theatrical, eating, skipping, playing games, splashing in waters, snuggling puppies, feeling sand, seaweed, grass, or warm stone between my toes, on and on. I can't imagine being any other way; I'm obsessed with the zest.

What else are we doing here other than enjoying this human experience?

On playgrounds, when shy, solitary children get invited to play by audacious ones, kindness replaces lonely isolation with connection, kindred spiritedness, and fun. Inner children feeling safe transforms sad solitude into pleasure, playfulness, and connection with community.

People who get triggered by kids have often been shut down by life's harshest realities. When their uninhibited childlike wonder and joy were repressed, they weren't safe to be themselves or grew up too soon, so children's playful, unbridled audacity can be overwhelming. Such people build barriers against environmental or emotional unsafety and are buttoned-up and withdrawn, repelling pure, sometimes chaotic energy.

The reminder to have fun, play, be curious, feel, and appreciate the aliveness in our bodies, explore, express without a filter, speak our minds, and maintain awe and elation (the high magik behind Mount Olympus), draws most people *to* children. Childlike enthusiasm, especially when compared to misinformed projections to "grow up and get serious" in an attempt to keep us safe, infectiously encourages others' innocent rejoicing, whether they're 9 or 90. What a gift!

Anchoring safety for your inner child begins with understanding where it's been lacking.

Ask yourself:

How were my emotions, body, passions, or dreams related?
Who was I told to be?
Was my environment nurturing?

There's an exploratory practice at the end of this chapter—for now, how could you provide yourself physical, emotional, or professional safety today?

VISIONARY ECHOES

Prior to attaining wild success, people call entrepreneurs and artists "crazy" for compulsively following visions only they can see. It's not madness; it's inner child risk taking.

Dreams and aspirations are not arbitrary, whimsical desires, but life's guiding force. We're born to play our unique part that has been dreamed and passed down through lineages, often as the first descendants who can! Women weren't even allowed to have personal bank accounts without a man's permission until 1974; what we are able to achieve and attain today is astounding! If dreams were supportively nurtured, we'd never give them up. Their brave pursuit reclaims and fulfills wonder we've always imagined, breeding constant growth.

Contributing unjaded hope and gleefully fueled action is *monumental*. Accepting your mission reinforces belief in your heroine's path rather than the villain and victim's domain. Possessing the potential to win is a big responsibility. Trusting yourself with childlike confidence, you rise victorious over the insecurities instilled in you by illusions. Beyond personal aspirations, dreams are essential threads in the fabric of humanity.

When I connected with a top female podcaster, five weeks after she'd given birth, she yelled for tissues right as we were about to start. Within moments, her big, beautiful breasts were leaking golden milk. I'd been hungry, so my assistant had used the studio kitchen to make me some food, and our teams bustled in to satisfy each of our needs. We laughed over the milk, shared a few bites of nourishment, and got down to business. Our independent safety and comfort initiated an authentic environment. My kind of friendship is real, raw, authentic, open, and *natural*. We don't have to stand on ceremony or be anything other than who or what we are.

At "Write Night" in sixth grade, the class shared stories from our favorite assignments. Reading "Your Future," was a big mistake, apparently. That evening—the last time I felt genuinely high on myself until I was an adult—stamped out my excitement for what lay ahead.

In a gorgeous silk tiger shirt, I animatedly regaled my fate. The tension swelled. Destined to become a big star, speaking *(and singing)* on massive stages, I'd save tigers, and the world. Despite having outwardly abandoned my musical dream, I'd never envisioned any alternative. Still alive enough to write a day-in-my-life scenario, I remained thrillingly certain this magnificent existence was not only within my reach but my ensured future fortune.

The aftermath wasn't just hurtful comments; it was downright war. Suddenly, the other kids were so intent on tearing me down, making me doubt myself and abandon my aspirations. Their mockery, ridicule, and torment were incessant for *years* after. I swiftly decided such dreams were outrageous, so stupid.

I got rid of that shirt, which I wish I still had, and detested myself for *considering* escaping my small town and smaller-minded people. I quit theater, altered my interests, changed my wardrobe, and desperately sought approval from vapid mean girls. Known for academic achievement over creativity, smart but in obedient ways, athletes destined for conventional careers and messy marriages, they were a safe haven in mediocrity. I betrayed my authentic visions by adopting their values, attire, and attitudes. Within a year I was unrecognizable.

No one stepped too far outside the box of acceptability, had interesting quirks, or unique abilities, except Emily McCoy. She stood up for and always saw me. She's a psychedelic therapist now and still the sweetest person I've ever met.

Rather than forging the path I'd incarnated for, pursuing dreams became synonymous with rejection and abandonment. Thinking big, having high hopes, embracing talent, and believing in magik were dangerous. "Fitting in," conforming, and pretending to be someone else was the only viable survival path.

Misinterpreting this opportunity was a harsh lesson I paid a steep price for. I lost over a decade of time I could have devoted to my purpose. When rock-bottom depression, existential angst, and anxiety made spiritual growth my top priority, I realigned with bigger-picture people who played in more powerful realms. Luckily, my parents' caveats to traditional success—philanthropy, artfulness, contentment, and adventure—made me stand out. Afraid of big lifetime dreams coming true, I focused on fulfillment instead.

I wanted to be happy, peaceful, charitable, and to uproot negative patterns. Which unknowingly builds genuine, sustainable success rooted in healing and faith.

Finally, with some semblance of inner stability and equilibrium, I was able to target misbeliefs and perceptions that had informed my adulthood. Write Night's subsequent misery frequently resurfaced during healing sessions. Transported back to the playground after that pivotal performance, I'd revisit the subconsciously implanted beliefs without alternative input.

My higher self, the Goddess, or a protective archetype would descend upon the scene. "Sweetheart, they're afraid of the big things they want to do too but have been told aren't possible. You've always had something special. That can be scary for people. We all come to accomplish different missions. Yours requires being exactly who you've always known you'd be."

Drying her tears, I revealed a future that is even more magnificently magikal than the one she'd written about.

"It's *not* actually lonely at the top! It's so fun and has the best people! The wizarding world became *my* world?!"

I've also revisited the hospital where I almost became an amputee at 16. Though I was beyond "childhood" when I had the experience, the major physical and emotional trauma altered my entire life.

In fantastic regalia, I sat where my mom read Harry Potter aloud beside my battered, bruised body with tubes in more places than I care to remember. Instead of *The Prisoner of Azkaban* for the millionth time, I showed my younger self how real magik is, all she's become, the places she's seen, the goals she's accomplished, the love she's found—congratulating and celebrating her.

"Despite decades of playing painfully small, you clawed tooth and nail, escaping that darkness, conquering your inner Voldemort, and learning to ride your dragons."

She wept in awe and disbelief, sweetening my accomplishments. Both the pain and the fantasies birthed a more powerfully enlivened woman than she'd ever met. I stood before her beyond her dream girl—the fairy-tale queen.

Returning compassionately to pivotal past moments encouragingly gifts our inner child faith, hope, and resilient perseverance that leave lasting imprints. Fully feeling previously painful emotions, going deeper for the 3rd, 4th, or 100th time, becomes nourishment, soothingly revitalizing our energy through acceptance.

Avoiding, resisting, shoving down, suppressing, or hiding from them *won't work*. Letting them feel safe, which is what all beings want, and welcoming them with acceptance as they are, grants those emotions something they've rarely, if ever, experienced.

Imagine operating from profound worthiness of the kind of love, touch, friendships, purpose, and finances you've always wanted. What would life look like if you felt fully worthy? Spiritual work is the hardest and most worthwhile choice you'll ever make. Some painful wounds stay forever—veins of grief, sadness, and anger—but they don't have to control you. I have so many scars on my skin, each with a story, but our deepest scars are usually invisible. They're our stories of lost love, abuse, and failure. The scar on my arm actually paled in comparison to those I carry on my heart.

Freeing yourself from those wounds is worth feeling anything. So become the protector your inner child never had. The courageous warrior willing to stand and fight for you, to rescue your own inner princess (or prince). Then you become the queen (or king).

I pray this chapter illuminates your joy and reignites your delight, inspiring you to play, pursue your dreams, follow wonder, and have fun! I hope you make life sweet. Magik awakens bodies, minds, hearts, and relationships. Become a toroidal field of generative service to yourself, humanity, Earth, and the entire Universe for the sake of our future. Surrender to your highest state of play and pleasure. *That is* Godliness—your birthright, destiny, and true Nature. Let your inner child light the way.

MICROWITCHUALS

Forgiveness

Write a letter apologizing and asking for forgiveness using specific examples of harming, abandoning, or neglecting your inner child.

Respond using your *nondominant hand*, writing *from* them, granting your forgiveness. It's okay if it's illegible; this allows you to tap into your subconscious and respond from what's been unresolved.

Read aloud in the mirror or repeat, "I forgive you; I forgive myself; I love you."

Baby Steps

Identify where you need reparenting. Ask yourself:

* *Which aspects of my life are not the way I'd like?*
* *What thought patterns are most harmful?*
* *What stories hinder my expression?*
* *What did my parents believe about my dreams?*
* *How was love modeled in response (or not)?*

Map out how wounding informs energy-draining actions that serve others rather than you. Determine the most important healing to focus on and take aligned opposing actions. For example:

* *I can't disobey my father.*
* *I have to work hard to survive.*
* *I have to fit in.*
* *Love isn't easy.*
* *I can't be culturally taboo.*

Practice:

Begin by creating a safe, sacred space. Gather nostalgic or sentimental items as talismans to anchor you: photographs, cherished teddy bears or blankets, and your journal. (Doing healing outside, Mother and Father Nature, the world's most accomplished alchemists, hold and offer you their ultimate support.) Light candles, cleanse and clear with water or smudging herbs—whatever supports focused presence for you.

Breathe slowly for a few minutes, entering a meditative state.

Visualize the challenging moment or memory where you first experienced this belief.

See yourself in the scene, observing your surroundings.

As your current or higher self, approach your inner child. Stand or kneel before them as a figure of strength, safety, and compassion, gazing into their eyes. Take their hands—embrace, hold, or comfort them (either physically using a pillow or teddy bear, or symbolically in your mind). Feel the emotions you experienced then.

Ask, "What do you need?" "How can I help you heal?" "How specifically can I support you?"

Listen attentively each time. This crucial dialogue guides your healing and will change your life.

The most important step is *following through.*

Imagine yourself actualizing their request or desire. Maybe they want to fly dragons over the mountains, dance, sing, speak words they've never shared, or trust you again. Envision yourself giving them whatever it takes to do so.

If possible, once your process is complete, follow through in *real life*. If they want play, a hard conversation, or a new hobby, *this step is the most vital ingredient.*

Bridging the gap between understanding your inner child's needs and *actively meeting them* builds trust, and rewires and rewrites the neural pathways that subconsciously inform your responses and behavior. Your tender mentality has been waiting *all your life* for this acknowledgment and care. Listen.

What were you discouraged from or not celebrated for doing?
What makes you most playful?
What brings you joy and delight?

- ✳ Identify where you take deep, satisfying breaths or burst into laughter, and actively incorporate these into your life. Release endorphins, natural mood-elevating chemicals that enhance your well-being. Embrace beauty, awe-inspiring Nature, art, song, improvisation, and epic dance parties. Feel the wind in your hair and let joy flood your senses! The pursuit of joy is more than fun; it heals.

- ✳ Dress up and create characters or archetypes you always wanted to be. Allow your inner child to experiment with different identities in a safe and encouraging environment. My personal style is my character, my vibe. What's yours? Tim Burton characters, fairies, Lord of the Rings, or Vikings? Freely play with different styles, switch them up, explore who your inner child is aesthetically but also who they are *essentially*.

- ✳ Use that powerful imagination! Daydream about what you want for your life. Then take tangible steps to get there!

- ✳ Try somatic, movement, art, or equine therapy.

- ✳ Bodywork and reflexology are so healing. Every single part of your body is linked to the foot. Unlocking physical spaciousness and stored trauma makes room for your inner child to grow.

* Observing wildlife is such an easy, instant way to activate inner child excitement. Avoid zoos and aquariums that torture poor creatures, though! Safaris or rehabilitation sanctuaries are amazing alternatives. If that's not accessible, visit a neighborhood horse (they love watermelon), play with pets, volunteer at a shelter, or pretend to be an animal for a song. Dolphins inspire community playfulness, eagles commune with Spirit, chameleons are shapeshifters. What pattern interrupt will reignite your freedom?

Try Psychedelics

Psychedelics are widely proven through studies at NYU Langone Health Center, the National Institutes of Health, and Johns Hopkins University to heal cancer by boosting immune function and to heal trauma by rewiring deeply ingrained neural pathways. They are incredibly supportive for inner child healing. Work with a psychedelic therapist from the Psychedelic Coalition for Mental Health, or directly navigate your own journey. Blend it with bodywork, and you've got yourself an *experience.*

Enlist Professional Support

Inner child healing is entirely possible, albeit more challenging on your own. Having a therapist doesn't mean there's something wrong with you—it means you're brave and sane.

When signs point down, go down. . . . Work with your inner child to cultivate resilience, expanding love to really enjoy the precious impermanence of life.

CHAPTER 4

Becoming Her Body

We've all met one. A person with powerful presence. You can feel their pulsing radiance emanating the moment they walk through the door. You are magnetized, drawn to them like a moth to a flame. You want to converse, know their secrets, get close enough to let that spark of brightness burning inside them illuminate the flickering ember inside you.

Embodied aliveness is felt in every room you enter, experienced in all you do, and seen no matter what you look like. Even by those who can't quite put their finger on what that "special something" is. It's the artistry that colors life incarnate, transcends mundane, black-and-white existence, elevates you into a multidimensional masterpiece. Like wombs every month and trees every Winter, what's ready to be let go of is shed and released. It's Goddess's creative genius alive and thriving, regardless of your gender.

The word *persona*—*persona*lity and *person*-ness—means "mask." Specifically, those used in pagan ritual theater spinning explanatory tales of myth. We have all been taught to cover up who we truly are, layering on more and more masks based on what we think we need to do or be to receive love.

Babies aren't born riddled with anxiety or fear; instead, they are blissful and inquisitive, curious and receptive. Gabor Maté's extensive writing on trauma asks us to consider, "How much of who I am is derived from childhood defensive strategies or coping mechanisms?"

A *lot*. We don't *randomly* become insecure, reactive, or unkind. We are either deprived of basic, required nutrients or get punished for needing them. We believe we just "are the way we are," but how we are treated *makes* us so. Caring for yourself is hard if you weren't cared for as you learned in the last chapter. Many of my clients grapple with consistent morning routines because reliance upon routine in childhood equaled disappointment or punishment for having expectations.

Overt sexuality or vehement oppression, people pleasing, rebelliousness, domination, or doormatting are all learned survival reactions. Habits that have hurt or harmed you or others are trauma responses. Even physical symptoms, like autoimmune or weight issues, can be manifestations of deeper disease calling for Her spiritual medicine.

As discussed in the previous chapter, everyone has a feminine side, the Mother of all's full-spectrum creation and destruction expressed through us. Even my former partner, a 6'5", 230-pound warrior always said, "I'm a Goddess on the inside." We are all both. Yet our world functions on toxic (and over-) masculinization, so we're all pretty clear how that's going—not very well. Father Nature illuminates how important it is to actualize the *empowered* masculine within ourselves—to be able to provide for and protect our inner children, to inspire their creative, emotional, or sexual expressions. However, what fewer of us are familiar with is how to heal that feminine wound, which has plagued each of us and our planet, to bring us home to harmony.

SIGNS YOU'RE DISCONNECTED FROM YOUR DIVINE FEMININE:

* Lack of fulfillment
* People pleasing
* Avoiding "getting dirty" or fear of Nature

* Lack of boundaries
* Unworthiness
* Sexual shame or shutdown
* Feeling unlovable
* Creative constipation
* Feeling stagnant in life
* Disease or imbalance in your body
* Distrusting yourself and your gut feelings or heart
* Believing you don't deserve good things
* Struggling with scarcity
* Hiding your true self, feelings, desires
* Avoiding vulnerability
* Toxic relationship patterns
* Overmasculinization, overworking, burnout
* Lack of purpose or motivation

Becoming Her body, Her vessel means removing the masks and allowing Divine Femininity to course through you like a crystalline river of creative reverence. Let the shame of your body, sexuality, magik, and majesty fall away like autumn leaves, allowing your full, unabashed self to be seen. We have so many terms that come from our body, such as "heartwarming," "breathtaking," "swelling with pride," "a knot in our gut," "weak in the knees," "heart skipping a beat," and "butterflies in our stomach." When you reconnect with your inherent body wisdom, you wield the same powers that created our Universe.

Make *your* life the mythical tale of lore and legend without holding back, fearing what others think or are too afraid to do themselves. It means bringing compassionate care and nourishment to how you feel, live, talk about, and treat yourself to determine the beauty of your landscapes. Becoming the prodigal painter.

☾

Massive success can still be deemed meaningless in our eyes if we never feel fulfilled or worthy of it. We can cast all the spells, but if our body doesn't believe we deserve our desires, they'll never come true. If they do, they're empty of the emotions we associated with having them.

No matter where you're from, if you've struggled with health, financial security, relationships, inspiration, mental or emotional well-being, dynamics with your mother or other women, fear of Nature or feminine energy, the land beneath you can heal you.

Even bossbabes and baddasses have scars and suffering, boo. We all do; no one gets out of here alive. If it doesn't kill us, it builds resolve and resilience, gives us an opportunity to fortify our spirits, and helps us have greater compassion for others. Feeling ashamed about what has made you stronger prevents it from doing so. So if any of these symptoms stir something in you, don't fret. That's great! You're one step closer to being able to change them.

Crossing the threshold to loving yourself, even as you take part in this societal charade, takes Herculean effort. But just as regenerative agriculture heals soil, we can somatically repair our trust in ourselves as emanations of the true Source. Invoking Her infinite strength will serve you no matter what you dream of accomplishing. Remembering you're a walking expression of Earth chariots you home to your spiritual magik through the illusion of separation from Her. Her effortlessly abundant energy will support all your achievements and help you remember why She brought you here in the first place.

A motto I live by is: Easy choices, hard life; hard choices, easy life. To truly embody the infinite abundance and regenerative power of Earth, we must abolish familiar patterns of scarcity, emotional or sexual suppression, and violent self-criticism. Which is casually just about the most difficult endeavor we can embark upon. It's not easy, but it's *so* worth it. Making life easier and you exponentially more magnetic to what we all truly need most to thrive. Facing off with the parts of yourself that still succumb to outdated, limiting beliefs takes ardent self-love and is an absolute necessity.

What falls from winter's chill nourishes summer's succulently sweet, indulgent fruits. Letting go of past behaviors, emotions, and beliefs offers you life's ultimate nectar. You get to reclaim the reins of your life and alleviate the burdens of what you did or didn't receive in favor of living as who you *truly* are. Existing mindfully *in* your body, listening to its requests, honoring its needs, and appreciating its tireless effort innately translates to relishing the earthly body. Experiencing yourself as the Goddess's Divine channel, you operate as you were designed to. Breaking through binding concepts of acceptability, piety, or perceived perfection enforced upon you (or the woman who raised you) sends a ripple out into the frequency of femininity encouraging greater freedom for all beings.

You *are* the forces of Nature incarnate; everything prepares you for your purposeful dreams, easily magnetizing your manifestations. Proclaim with each footstep, "I am a cell upon, and direct emanation of, Her body, as She is a cell in the body of the Universe." Becoming Her body, wielding the full breadth of your awareness *as* the flow of water, strength of earth, ignition of fire, and belief of air, you become unstoppable.

How will you let the wildly, unapologetically beautiful aspects of you finally run free?

ALL ACTS OF LOVE

The word *courage* comes from the French *coeur*, for "heart." It takes much courage (a connection to and willingness to follow the wisdom of your heart), to bravely face hard conversations, to love yourself enough to walk away from relationships that are out of alignment.

Witchual lives in how you think, speak, act, and serve—how you spend time, energy, and money communicates what you value. Start right here and now. There's no chaste, monastic, restrictive devotion required, just nurturing Her blooming flower in you to bring the sweetest fruits. When you trust the Goddess, more choices feel exhilarating, fun, and aligned. Recognizing *life is the ritual*, we become Divine beings.

We can always find reasons not to make healthy meals or accomplish tasks we've been putting off, like (spring) cleaning! But removing chaos from our environment alleviates it from our minds and vice versa, making all the difference in the long term. Though unusual compared to conventional ideals of love or pleasure, that doesn't discount their importance.

Naturally, reestablishing our original blueprint of certainty and safety will present challenges. Love transforms; people die; what you've been through and what's still running your life are deeply interconnected. There's never been a time, even in my worst pain, that I wasn't soothed, even momentarily, by sitting in Nature. The comfort of Her loving arms can brighten even your darkest days. You develop a deep trust in yourself simply by hearing the call and listening, going out to greet Her, gaining certainty in your capacities and gifts. Witchual is a collective call to action invoking our embodied Goddess energy to foster empowered relationships and live symbiotically between masculine and feminine within and all around us.

Start small; set an intention for ease and inspiration every time you sit down with a project. Bless your food, sing your prayers, speak to your water, breathe mindfully, savor your walk to work, and then go big! Do ceremony; try transformational personal or spiritual development work; go to retreats; take crazy leaps of faith. *Anything* infused with intention is a Goddess ritual, including delving into darkness.

Old beliefs say it's scary to let Her in. You're reconnecting with the greatest, most powerful force in the Universe, which has been manipulated and falsely propagated as the greatest evil. Don't fall for it.

Like jumping off a cliff into a cold, clear river, that first step can feel impossible, and the time spent falling, terrifying. But you're always glad you took the leap. As you let Her consume you, consider: What would She change about your habits? How could you involve Her in your daily practices and decisions?

ARCHETYPES, AVATARS, ICONS

The Goddess has been referred to as "She of 10,000 names" because there are that many different words for Her ineffable creative force. The feminine archetype is not monolithic but as varied and multi-faceted as Earth Herself. From mountains and mosses, lakes and seas, Grandmother Spider, Kali Ma, and Vestal virgins—Roman custodians of the sacred flame for hearth and home—to pioneers and painters, scientists and CEOs. Every archetype carries codes, but they all lead back to Her. Listen to Oshun or Yemanja in pounding waves. Gaia's boundless generosity inspires an eco-sexual reverence. Like diverse craggy peaks, dry deserts, verdant rainforests, and lush meadows, we too embody Goddess in our personal perfection.

Virgin originally meant "sovereign," and referred to the powerfully autonomous priestesses or women who made their own way in devotion to Her. They chose who was blessed enough to enter *their* body temples. It was a high honor to be deemed worthy to make love with such a treasure, a vessel of the Divine. Then the church maligned this archetype as a symbol of purity and innocence *void* of sexuality, in an effort to forbid, tarnish, and conquer these angelic forces. Reclaiming sovereignty honors our bodies as temples of spiritual power and preeminence.

What you believe and how you practice is what brings your sex magik, sensual, and creative power into your body. Contemplate the qualities you admire or desire in others. Might a broader paragon open your heart for Her power?

How might you utilize associations with Her?

What manifestation of the Goddess would help you cellularly integrate and carry her transmission into your life?

Of every name describing Her, what resonates most?

When questing for clarity, courageously standing up for yourself, or fearlessly facing fierce emotions, invoke Pele's fiery spirit to ignite your inner flame. Pray to Persephone in your Dark Nights of the Soul or existential underworlds, Seek Isis's guidance to unlock sex magik mysteries and energetic transformation. Whether you're drawn to Mary Magdalene's devotion to sacred union or creating your own blueprint, allow their teachings to energize your life.

Prayer lies at the heart of any spiritual path. Whether to something external, or invoking our internal reflection of the eternal spark we are emanations of, dialoguing with the Divine, transcends words, casting spells across every dimension.

Trees and animals send messages through scent and sound, silent vibration, or songs and calls. If we followed Nature's guidance on growth, synergy, resilience, and regeneration, we would see massive change in just one generation. Shutting those vital nutrients down, suppressing our animism, is damming and poisoning our literal and metaphorical rivers. We are seeking validation and attention in the wrong places; satisfying emotional and sexual needs and primal urges in spaces that take from and give nothing in return prevents us from embracing Her.

Becoming her body is an act of service, to Earth, to our collective creative capacities, and for healing humanity. Sensuality, abundance, and our untamed Nature *are* Her communication and connection methods. So when we familiarize ourselves with them, we are in constant conversation with Her. What you do, who you are, and how you feel matters. You're contributing. If you can anchor safety, love, and healing in *your* world, *our* world will thank you.

APPLES FALLING FARTHER FROM THE TREE

In ancient civilizations, leadership and lineage were passed down from mothers to daughters rather than fathers to sons. (Remember, there was no way to prove paternity; it just made more sense.) Women kept Her stories alive, strung in secret, whispered into granddaughters' ears through generations. Remembrance of the Goddess is reawakening from our very blood and bones.

Feel Her in life-changing sacred sites or places people have gathered over time to bask in Her beauty. Her eternal frequency of aliveness exists everywhere. Amplifying the elemental voices in forgotten places less commonly acknowledged can reinvigorate and release you from the mind's trapping limitations set upon you by others. She's always beneath your feet, no matter how high in a skyscraper you are. Revive this cellular memory through your own ancestral or spiritual lineage of Goddess worship. Listening to and letting Her freely move through you heals you holistically. So don't worry about how you do it, just reconnect to your instinctual wildness whatever way is most exhilarating for you.

One summer I went on a river trip staffed by an *entirely* Mormon team. I later found out everyone had been either curious or downright concerned "a witch was coming," but no one let on when we met. When I realized the situation, the Witch Hunter was *loud*. I nervously worried I might have to completely hide who I was.

People always underestimate my outdoor skills and savvy, thinking I'm some high-maintenance diva instead of the ruggedly wild, tree-hugging, adventurous paladin I am. So, as usual, I show up in my expertise, and gain respect and admiration the old-fashioned way, by proving myself. My spirituality was no different.

All Nature lovers, they were curious about how my philosophy differed from their own. I illuminated how God isn't just *creator of* Nature but *is* Nature. This prompted riveting conversations about the Goddess and Mother Earth, as Mormonism is esoteric and ritualistic in its own way. One insightful young man asked, "I know what God wants for us. What do you think 'Goddess' wants from, or for, us?"

"We are Her children; like any good mother, she wants the best for us," I said. "To laugh and play; to be happy, healthy, and fulfilled; to fall in love with ourselves, life, and others. She wants us to enjoy everything She worked tirelessly to provide. To be essentially 'good,' of service, and find our way home into Her arms as often as possible so she can give us all the love she possesses. What saddens her most is how we treat Her and each other." They were pensive, yet agreed wholeheartedly.

When an elder gentleman graciously asked for the sacrament of a mushroom ceremony, I was flabbergasted. I caressed Her mossy cliffs, sobbing apologies to Her for all the pain our species continues to inflict and thanking Her for everything, as I always do. He was nearby, witnessing this. Later, beside a crackling fire he asked, "What were you apologizing for?"

"How much we've forgotten to love Her in return."

"It was one of the most beautiful things I've ever seen."

Simply by being Her body in *my* way, serving the best I can, I left one or two imprints that might just last a lifetime.

RESPLENDENT WRATH

War, despair, loneliness, and poverty are not our natural state; they are the result of *separation from Her*. But the Goddess never gives up on us. No matter how many mistakes we've made, how many times we've ignored Her, how young or old we are, she keeps offering opportunities to remember you and She are one. You never know when She's going to come through, or to, you. Whether blatantly or in disguise, it's never too late to let Her in.

Relishing in your pleasure and power *and* appreciating pain is the essence of existence, what she made us for. Imagine how good it must feel to let a volcano erupt from within you, to twirl like a tornado twisting tempestuously across terrain, or be lightning crackling through stormy skies as thunder roars in your wake. She doesn't suppress those urges; that would be *unnatural*.

Throughout mythology, Gods and Goddesses unleash wrath, decimating foes with formidable power. Yet, when a woman expresses anger, asserts her strength, or exposes her power, society villainizes her.

Unearthing long-buried emotions and instinctually moving through trauma *can* resemble what has been *misconstrued* as "demonic," or "exorcisms." Psychosomatic mending is mandatory for broken hearts and minds. It's been shamanically practiced for millennia. We get the word *cathartic* from ancient French mystics: Cathars, who used *catharsis* for personal growth and spiritual development.

After so many generations of being forced to undermine them, our bodies' *innate impulses* have become ingrained to trigger stress responses, rather than the remedy to them. Peter Levine's *In an Unspoken Voice: How the Body Releases Trauma and Restores Goodness* discusses how automatic responses of shaking, trembling, or other unconscious movement are directly related to our resilience against post-traumatic stress. Allowing our bodies to process instinctively alleviates the long-term impact. Unfortunately, restriction or suppression is what leads to an ingrained response to a single incident, for the rest of our lives.

Because fear is mostly momentary in the wild, our mammalian brains are not accustomed to its presence as a low-grade constant in our minds. Whether real or imaginary, fear leads to instantaneous, unconscious suppression and shutdown of many biological systems. In the animal kingdom, when a threat passes—the lion gives up— its potential prey gets to return to business as usual. We are not so lucky. Though most of us don't have to worry about lions, we are on constant high alert for perceived danger that our bodies rarely get respite from.

Sanity comes from Latin meaning "health." We're so worried about what other people think because historically, displaying anything that *deviated* from the norm equaled *deviance* and had dire consequences. We abandoned how we *felt* and what we *needed* for fear of appearing "crazy." But every animal shakes off a chase; it's the *most* natural response.

Societal projection of "demonic exorcisms" has censored and misconstrued the vital, necessary, and evolutionary releases or somatic activations that lead to healing. It might *look* unusual or unsettling, a little too weird or "crazy" to a conditioned mind, but you are actually *becoming* sane. Stifling these instinctual reactions is yet another modern mental-health malady.

I admit, when I let myself writhe and shake, screaming at the top of my lungs, even I still glance over my shoulder, making sure no one's watching.

Studies on trauma show cathartic, somatic release is actually one of the healthiest and most sustainable ways to unearth stuck tension, which can lead to disease. We need to accept these primal instincts and the wider range of expression as paramount parts of our primordial, essential nature. Feeling its tingle, vibrant sexual vivacity, and aliveness is tapping into the pulsing Shakti, the Goddess's energy coursing through you. Sensing your heartbeat, expansive breath, or *any sensation* is Divine Femininity.

Rage rituals—structured, safe spaces to express suppressed emotion, perhaps for the first time—are always a favorite at my retreats. They really should be called release rituals because you're not just raging. You're letting go of grief, disappointment, heartbreak, betrayal, frustration, sadness, anguish, and every other feeling we suppress or tend to shy away from when it emerges. In his book *When the Body Says No*, Gabor Maté quotes Dr. Candace Pert, who says, "Sometimes the biggest impetus to healing can come from jump-starting the immune system with a burst of long-suppressed anger." I have certainly experienced this for myself and with many students throughout the years.

Immobilization is another instinctual mammalian response because it often deems prey boring to a predator. This is why women frequently report feeling frozen while under attack. So during this process, we let our bodies experience the freedom of movement we were incapable of, speak to our abusers or anyone who has wronged us, what we were unable or too afraid to say in the moment. We're not *indulging* in rage but channeling it constructively, providing sanctuary for its powerful, healing release.

When my rage ritual went viral with nearly a billion views across social media accounts and platforms, the vast majority of men called it "Karen summer camp"—marking themselves the real "Karens." They misconstrued and made fun of the sacred freedom denied to women for *millennia*, implicating the denial of their own need to feel emotionally safe and expressed.

Critics—including false preachers of "love and light," notorious for spiritual bypassing—caution against emotional release, suggesting love and forgiveness as the only acceptable path. Anger can be a necessary spark, igniting movements or signaling boundaries. It can help us respond to injustice and suffering, but it's also a critical indicator of "Don't tread on me." Love and forgiveness are imperative! *And* those noble goals are nearly impossible without facing what stands in the way of reaching inner peace and acceptance.

Millions of women banded together with countless supportive, commiserative comments on my video:

"I cried the moment I heard their screams."

"I had an immediate, visceral reaction!"

"I need friends to do this with me."

Sometimes our deepest pain makes us mistrust Her. But healing it leads us home to Her. Recognizing and respecting anger is essential in asserting our rights and dignity as Goddess conduits.

My awe of the ocean deepened this understanding for me. She has no qualms about being massive, intimidating, or powerful. Waves of emotion rise and fall, ebb and flow, but with the ocean, we *know* our respect is deserved. I have almost drowned several times, held down thrashing beneath massive swells with no respite for breath. She could kill me in an instant. So I respect and revere her, yet I still surrender to her infinite embrace.

Many days swimming on her coasts are calm, even predictable. I observe her mighty vastness—unafraid and majestic.

"Do not fear me because I am formidable. This is simply who I am."

Inspired by her unabashed strength, I echo her message into the current. There is nothing inherently frightening about engaging and expressing our strength.

Our precious inner children suffered at the hands of others who stifled them and remain hidden in the face of a society that does everything to keep them caged. People have always been afraid of or intimidated by my ferocity. I dreamed of and always hoped I'd find a role model who exhibited every facet of femininity, fought unabashedly for what she believed in, and turned fantasies into reality. I never found her, so I worked tirelessly my whole life to become her. The kind of woman little Mia needed.

SEXUALITY IS BIOLOGICAL CREATIVITY

Our sacral chakra is the Holy Grail that should be revered, not shut down across humanity. Sex, our most natural and essential endeavor, is commercially exploited yet vilified endlessly. The very fount of life is made all the more fecund with love. We're passionately devoted to what we love. Just as plants treated hatefully wither and die, those nurtured with attentive care flourish and thrive—like kids and all of creation.

As our consciousness elevated, we realized the body is our sacred pathway to experiencing the Divine, a holy temple to consecrate and pray upon. Our tribal ancestors lived naked. Sex was another natural part of life without shameful taboos. Then, sexuality went on a societal rollercoaster ride.

Ancient arts of sex magik were taught and practiced worldwide—best known from traditions like Chinese Dao, Indian tantra, Celtic rites, and Egyptian sexual and energetic alchemy. Each lineage dates back to the origin of our higher gnosis and mysticism. The latter filled temples to Isis, training Jesus; his mother, Mary; and Mary Magdalene in transforming sexual energy into healing power for manifesting miracles. The reason Jesus's wife, mother, and grandmother were all called "Mary" is because *mar*, the root word for "mother" and "ocean," was actually a title of the high priestess initiates in ancient Egypt. Anglicizing the demarcation turned it into a name.

Beginning with anointment, priestesses used magikal properties of different herbs and flowers like frankincense for blessings, spikenard for devotional peace, and blue lotus for psychic vision. Beyond physical cleanliness, spiritual purification was preparation for dream activation or enhancing metaphysical gifts and mediumship.

Mary Magdalene, Jesus's wife and spiritual counterpart, is rarely acknowledged for Her imperative and synergistic role. Her magik combined kundalini activation through sacred sexuality, energetic amplification, and alchemical redemption. In historical rather than

Biblical allegory, Jesus attributed his miraculous abilities to their relational transmutation and cultivation of energy sent intentionally for healing. Magdalene's traditional foot-washing rites exemplify acts of humble acknowledgment and profound benediction.

Egyptian mythology revered Isis, goddess of fertility and magik's powerful healing and regeneration. Worshipping her involved ecstatic and luxurious adornment, archetypal activation, and transcendent sexuality.

Religious patriarchy made everything in the feminine, earthly realm, especially our bodies, sinful. Therefore sex was shamed as something evil, reserved for married people's procreation and not enjoyment, despite the undeniable design of our genitals for pleasure. This rejection of our own physicality led to blindly raping, pillaging, and plundering the masterpiece of divine providence—Earth. If we believe something is "bad," we have very little trouble treating it badly. Look at our prison systems' complete lack of rehabilitation and ensuing recidivism. We've villainized the true sources of life rather than those who destroy it and the planet. We're projecting the same hateful treatment onto women, who are the vessels created for us to experience life and who provide us with everything.

Now, sex has been commodified. "Thirst trap" social media photos have women objectifying themselves for attention, like their bodies are the only way to be valued. Selling monthly porn to creepy strangers on the Internet from their bathrooms for small or exorbitant fees has desanctified this precious act that can be our greatest pathway to God.

Too many people seek sex that isn't actually in service to our inner dimensions, perpetuating more pain. Shitty jobs and junk food aren't all that sucks the life out of you; sex can too, when it's for the wrong reasons. Disconnection makes us think it won't affect us, but *everything* does. Sex driven by wounding just pours salt into it. But in a safe container, it can be one of the greatest healing remedies.

You can keep it casual if that works for you, just know your "why." Intentional sexuality doesn't mean prudish piousness, just purposefulness.

Why are you engaging in sex?

Pleasure is a perfectly good reason, one of the best, but what kind? To distract or numb? Fleetingly placing a Band-Aid over deeper pain? Is it energetically draining or emotionally dissociated?

Devoted to integrating sexuality and spirituality, Witchual transcends the act of penetration itself, with those two simple ingredients: attention and intention. The most valuable assets you have (not in the way society wants you to think), pleasure and orgasm are powerful tools, whether they're for personal healing, strengthening relationships, deepening Divine connection, transformation, greater intimacy, or any other dream! In partnership with Earth, the Universe, God, or Goddess, sex can heal disempowered beliefs you have about it or yourself.

More intentional engagement transforms your relationships, health, and manifestation potential. This creative energy fuels personal growth and intimate connection.

Imagine if we all came home to our sexuality rather than being performative, attention seeking, or shut down and shamed. If sex was never a survival tactic for validation, conquest, or harm. Imagine if we understood sex's interweaving energetic fields, karmic imprints, and soul contracts. No matter how it occurs, every realm of our being is involved, uniting our physicality, mentality, emotionality, and spirituality.

MIRACLE MESSAGES

Undoubtedly, when you've been programmed to believe that your feminine essence is evil and dangerous, you're going to bump up against edges or resistance. Notice what feels uncomfortable about Her in you—what have you believed is "wrong" or "bad"?

Humanity's general shame of the femininity in creativity, emotions, and sexuality—denies our dependence upon and necessity of women. We're afraid to be artists exuding or, God forbid, *relying upon* creativity, when that's how the world came to be and exactly what we need more of. Life as artistry. Without creativity, we'd have no movies, music, museums, cars, planes, or technology. We encourage invention's gestation process, laud "self-made" men, and congratulate captains of industry. But women *created every* creator, inventor, and innovator on Earth.

Without emotions, we'd all be numb. Without sex, we *wouldn't be here*. There is nothing *more* reliable than the feminine. Nothing has made me feel more unconditionally loved and supported, and blessed by miracles, than my devotion to reunion with Her.

We're reawakening to the fact that what we do to Her, we do to ourselves and vice versa. When I quit processed food in favor of farmers market freshness, I felt Her life force in my sustenance. When I acknowledged money for all it affords me with the worthiness of having it, I became more abundant. When I replaced negative thought loops with Beautiful Chorus lyrics, like, "I am everything I want to be, I have everything I need," or "I feel peace near, I am safe here"; ho'oponopono; or other ancient mantras of forgiveness, my life became infinitely sweeter.

Thank Goddess, the Queen of Heaven, cures you when she enters your heart, always whispering the truth for the highest path to you. Listen.

Your body opens portals to Divine consciousness all the time, whether you are aware of it or not. Tap into your wild physical energy to access elevated emotional states, bring visions to fruition, and use any moment for transformative healing.

When you hear fear or shame come in while making love, art, or just feeling, can you give Her voice the microphone? "My body is a living temple of love; I am a sacred priestess; this is my power; I deserve pleasure and love . . ."

Whatever the Goddess would say to or through you, make that your focal point.

Spending money or investing in yourself can be scary. When it comes to frivolous purchases like clothes, or more stuff, examine your "why." Why are you telling yourself you need it? What will it get you? When it comes to real expenses that tangibly transform your life (including electricity bills, dream vacations, and fabulous retreats), consider who you hope to be on the other side. Would that person keep denying herself an opportunity to grow, discover new things, or feel safe and cared for? No! Use your future self's wisdom and Her voice to take important leaps forward into becoming that person.

When you need to grow physically, financially, relationally, or professionally, take inspiration from the Earth, which doesn't let anything stop Her from growing except appropriate timing. Trees perch at cliff edges. Dandelions sprout out of concrete. Water finds ways around obstacles, carving through the easiest course. Roads run beside creeks and rivers, because water found the way. When seeking a creative outlet, let those first little droplets fall from the wellspring of your inspiration. Over time, even the smallest trickle can change the stone beneath it. Let water guide your flow and feeling.

When the Witch Wound or Hunter's claws grip you, use your breath—long, slow, and deep, or directed a certain way, unwinding painful patterns in your mind. Sing songs that soothe your spirit. Connect with your inner child. Remind them they are safe, and you're here for them. Choose a different thought, act the opposite as you are habituated, and let the winds of change blow through your perspective.

PERMISSION GRANTED

The church has missionaries. I consider myself a *per*missionary. Spreading faith in *yourself*, providing the service of genuine healing rather than an illusion of salvation from immorality. Promoting the gospel of Earth as an example that it's more than okay to give yourself the permission to live outlandishly and outrageously magikal lives.

Invoking the Goddess transcends prescribed methods, and permission is the first step. You have to accept your mission in order to accomplish it.

So, what feels authentic for you? Meditation, song, dance, lovemaking, exercise, cooking, or simply lying upon the Earth—what does She ask of you?

Creativity is Divine Femininity's conduit to communicate through us, translating the ethereal into the tangible. Our soul's language illustrates the deepest visions of our hearts and minds.

Invocatory music, dance, art, culinary delights, literature, or entrepreneurship manifest our innermost dreams and desires. Beyond production, we're externalizing our individual essence, joyful exploration of existence, and harmony with intricate Universal rhythms, reflecting the billions of unique and shared perspectives, reminding us of the power we hold.

Creativity calls for embracing playfulness and curiosity through realms of profanity and profundity. Get inspired by your inner five-year-old's freedom to be silly, to play without aim, and to indulge in the joy of creation for its own sake.

Discovering its boundless potential begins with simple acts. Sketch aimlessly; dance to upbeat tunes; improvise a recipe in the kitchen; do stream-of-consciousness writing. Each act is a step toward deeper self-connection and more refined spiritual alignment.

How can you create spaces where these aspects can flourish and express safely? How can you facilitate your own empowered feminine energy?

All I ask is that you use your creativity to rise above the material pursuit of possessions. There is enough stuff on this Earth to last our entire species for generations. Return to the original intent: Mater = Mother. Value *Her* gifts instead. Be a gift to *Her* in return.

✶ ✶ REFLECTION ✶ ✶

I invite you, dear reader, to ask these questions not merely rhetorically. Let them call you to action, prompting the empowerment of your full aliveness, allowing whatever insight comes (literally and figuratively). Identify the nourishment your soul craves, and harness the greatest powers on and of Earth.

What would your sexuality express like if it was only for you, not performative or attention seeking? If you only allowed the most empowered interactions with others?

What are you seeking in the moments it is otherwise?

What do you need to feel accepted, loved, and safe?

What kind of sex would you have if your every dimension was aligned?

What does embodying the Divine or becoming Her body mean and look like to you?

What choices have made you feel like less than a Goddess (or God) in relationships, health, career, family, or physical environment?

How can you make choices She would make?

What habits or behaviors would change if you were aligned with Her?

What did She bring you here to create?

How can you bring Her into your physical activities: eating, kissing, dancing, bathing, exercising, working?

What are your feminine archetypes?

What Goddess energy turns you on, ignites your curiosity, or would support you most?

What has lain dormant inside you that wants to come out?

It all starts within the temple of you.

MICROWITCHUALS

✷ Choose a name for the Goddess that calls to you or an avatar whose qualities you want to experience more of. Find or create an image to place on your altar or somewhere you'll see and interact with daily. Or greet Her ethereally throughout the day.

Go further:

✷ Use an image that feels like *your* higher self. That's what she is, after all. What does she look like and wear? Who is she? How could you adorn your body as an emanation of Her, to feel more like Her? Using either your image, silent meditation, or conscious listening, invoke Her guidance to support your decisions and guide your path.

* Ask, "What do you want to wear, eat, do, or see, or where do you want to go? If you're going to buy "new" clothes, please get them secondhand or support artisans using earth-friendly materials to maintain alignment with our Mother, *the* Goddess. Accept Her invitations!

* Begin each day by creating sacred space with Her. Use that image. Stand barefoot; feel the ground beneath your feet; call Her into your body and day. Move, sing, pray, self-pleasure, speak, dance (whatever comes through) for, or *as,* Her. Choose music with positive feminine messaging. Let Her energy move you freely without judgment. This isn't about form, grace, proper etiquette, or eloquence, just devotion. Be guided by Her; become a prayer and celebration.

* **Yoni Gazing:** (Men can do this too.) Set up a comfortable space in front of a full-length mirror. Remove your clothes and set a timer for at least five minutes to gaze into the pleasure portal between your legs, the place we all emerge into the world from. If this is enough, sit quietly, remaining present. Go further by speaking to Her with gratitude, admiration, and acknowledgment. She is the gateway for all souls to be born. Choose your own affirmations, but connect with Her reverently with awe and respect.

* Sex magik can start with eye gazing pre-foreplay. Straddle heart to heart (aka yab yum) to attune your energy before penetration. Direct your breath through erogenous zones,

synchronizing rhythmically with your partner. Move energy from the root chakra at the base of your spine up through into your crown during lovemaking. Have a shared vision for orgasm. Paint sigils, or symbols, on one another with moon blood for extra credit. Tone, chant, or speak intentions out loud, bringing in special sensual or ritual elements. The world is your oyster (also a great addition, depending on what you're into)!

✳ Most meditation techniques suggest inhaling love and exhaling fear. Ancient tantra indicates that the reverse genuinely liberates. Breathe in sadness, frustration, and painful emotions into your heart, swirl them through the vortex of infinite cosmic power, and exhale love to all existence. Opening its powerful portal to all the pain you never felt safe to feel, alchemizes it into love.

✳ If you find yourself seeking validation or attention from others, try mirror work, and give that to yourself. Give your body the reverence, sensual attention, and affection it craves. Cherish yourself. When we try to escape the power of our feelings, we end up feeling the loss of our power. Don't get distracted; get interactive.

CHAPTER 5

Anima Mundi

Witchual's first whispers were conversations with Divine Father Sky and Holy Mother Earth, with stars, plants, and animals. The ocean's salt falls in your tears. Fossilized marine life creates calcium for your bones. Earth and sun emit your heart and brain's electromagnetic energy; neural pathways mirror galaxies. Anima Mundi is inherent oneness with Earth's alive, vibratory consciousness through flora, fauna, fungi, crystal, and mineral kingdoms.

From Latin for "world soul" or "earthly spirit," *Anima Mundi*—mountains, winds, rivers, and light—beckon us to recognize Her alive, sacred sentience.

Before modern metropolises and social media, only symphonies of crickets, owls, and frogs, the melodic rain or crackling fire serenaded our sleep. Now we play recordings of Nature's nightly orchestra as we attempt to rest. Her spiritual Nature has been abandoned, locked away, and imprisoned by ignorance of our own. Tornadoes of doubt grip us; whirlwinds wreak havoc in relationships or work while we forget to celebrate the beauty of Her gifts.

Giant corporations are purchasing our pristine aquifers purified by carbonic sandstone, then packaging mineral-rich hydration in plastic, charging exorbitant price tags to disrupt *every* body system with resources stolen from the Earth, who receives nothing in return. Gifts, again, are sacred, yet now, everything Nature grows for us of Her own free will, we have to pay for. We've forsaken tending to sacred springs, neglecting their interconnectedness to our fluidity.

Like soil, waters are poisoned with industrial, nuclear, and human waste, directly reflecting our toxic relationship to emotions, creativity, and sexuality. Most cities operate on closed water systems, pumping what you flush down the toilet full of chlorine and chemicals, and sending it right back through your sink and shower. *Yuck*! Would you take an IV of sewage or pool-treatment chemicals? No! Yet skin is our largest and most absorbent organ, unknowingly ingesting poisons every day.

How often do you see yourself in Nature's mirror? Your veins of blood as waterways? Do you consider your shampoo chemicals? So removed from the cultivation of our sustenance, we wonder why obesity and disease epidemics are unprecedented. The government says processed food isn't the problem. *Science* says sugar is as addictive as heroin, and now it's hidden in every snack, sauce and supposedly healthy alternative. We pollute the air, then wonder why our mental health suffers more than ever.

Sustainability means "the ability to sustain long term." Plastic is *not* sustainable. We are desensitized from the atrocities committed against our only method of survival. Taught to carelessly assume it's just "the way things are." It isn't. Plastic didn't make it to many third world countries until the last century. We've survived for hundreds of thousands of years without it. This recent status quo is too unsustainable to accept.

But we can choose differently. We must opt for alternative solutions; vote with our time, money, and energy; be mindful of food consumption and waste from packaging, and our bodies where it once just went back into the soil. We flush toilets as if ruining drinking water is so nonchalant. We call it throwing "away"; there is no such place as "away." It all stays *right here* on Her.

It's *undoubtedly* easier to order new items online; trust me, I get it. Convenience has become the modern standard. But when you prioritize secondhand purchases, you end up with an exponentially more unique and meaningful environment that also takes better care of us all long term. Take the time for committed devotion to the kind of world you want to live in and person you want to be. When you shop, choose artisans or local businesses rather than chains and corporations. Deliberate choices significantly impact our relationship with Earth, always have a positive effect, and end up making you feel so much more fulfilled! Compost even if you're just tossing organic matter onto the ground instead of in the trash.

Jarod K. Anderson, in his poem "Naming the River," describes the water in your body as a visitor. In the past, this water was a thunderstorm, and it will soon be the ocean. He says the body is more like weather patterns than stone monuments and reminds us that our choices outweigh our substance.

Mountains weren't made in a day; they are the result of millions of years of chaos, destruction, evolution, and massive, shifting change. Climbing them, literally or existentially and proverbially, requires strength, resilience, and perseverance with the body.

Delicately balancing action and stillness, observation and operation, giving and receiving as important parts of the whole, moving at Her pace is the key for Earth ritual. Your heart rate calms, nervous system regulates, and stress hormones decrease. If you need to shine bright or be bold, bring the sun's fiery heat, or dance like lightning bolts.

Ask yourself:

> *Do I feel energized or exhausted?*
> *Do I need recharging or ramping up?*
> *Do I want to create or receive?*

Understand your needs. Follow inclinations to take inspired action. Each answer leads to entirely different rituals. Exhaustion, or needing to rev up requires changing your state, even if that's napping or guided meditation. When you're energized, what's the best use of that power?

Your fire can be gentle candlelight, erupting volcanoes, or infernos devouring internal landscapes. An acorn's cellular imperative to become an oak tree, blood and tides drawn by the moon, the rose's sweet scent. Divine power shows us who we are. We can shine like gleaming beacons of sunlight upon glistening peaks.

Stormy weather teaches us to weather the storm.

Let us be motivated by the destruction all around us to dismantle established dependence on conventional convenience over the Earthly Soul's consciousness inherently woven between us.

A DISCONNECTED GENERATION

Humanity's darkness denies Anima Mundi, commodifying and enslaving the majority of people, plants, animals, and resources to make the one percent richer, while impoverishing the planet. Adults sit scrolling or drinking beside kids, neglecting the young beings they created on a wide spectrum from covert to overt abuse.

Unconsciously, we all feel the gaping wounds inflicted upon Her. Refusal to excavate generations of old, outdated trauma patterns fuels voracious consumption and perpetuates violence. Terrified to face emptiness inside, we're abjectly disempowered from standing against those who greedily feast upon Her plethora of provisions, which has only been exacerbated with the advent of technology. Children hunch over their phones, incapable of stillness, obsessively checking Snapchat instead of exploring the magikal world all around them. We have to change.

Heartbreakingly, kids worry about creating content *of* life instead of actually *living* it. Lost is the instinct to climb trees, splash in puddles, use imagination, and be present. They are desperate for distraction, throwing tantrums if, Goddess forbid, they are required to simply observe their environments or internal state for more than three seconds.

Studies show that when electronic devices are removed, the outrage in resopnse is a withdrawal symptom akin to addictive drugs. Our species survived for *hundreds of thousands of years* before iPads. We *know* it's possible. Young people need to feel useful, engaged, purposeful, belonging, and contributive. Children in Japan are taught trust and responsibility by being granted the independence to go to school or run simple errands on their own from as young as three! Intentional urban design with low speed limits as well as commercial integration with residential areas makes this possible.

Unfortunately, the greatest risk in many countries is of kidnapping or endangerment, which, if we hadn't inflicted abuse upon so many generations, would not be a concern.

Families who forbid devices perfectly exemplify the innovative, ingenious, confident critical thinkers kids become when left to their *own* devices—they play! We all must spend time outside, learn skills, and have hobbies, as this is crucial for well-rounded humanness. Nature offers endless stimulation, so get kids to work outside! Identifying or foraging plants, or even simple tasks like picking "weeds," makes them feel like they matter, just make sure you're not doing away with medicine that might be making its way into your garden.

I love doing beach clean-ups and always pick up trash in Nature. Gamification motivates. My greatest hack is enrolling kids, telling them, "We're saving sea turtles, dolphins, or [insert your favorite ocean creature]. Whoever gets the most plastic wins!"

Science has *proven* that kids who believe in or are simply *exposed to* magik score highest on creativity assessments. The most present, self-reliant, loving, confident, happy children, with the most regulated nervous systems, grew up playing outside, getting dirty, and exploring life and their environment.

Learning to entertain themselves enhances problem-solving, self-sufficiency, and independence. Those thrust in front of screens for soothing suffer significantly more. We must reeducate ourselves about Earth's beauty and magik, or we're going to lose to the doldrums of devices.

THIS LAND IS OUR LAND

Perhaps we crave desolate desert expanses, crisp mountain air, alpine forests, or we find that craggy peaks' massive majesty inspires awe and wonder. Maybe we seek misty coastlines, deciduous rainforests, richly rippling riparian zones, or lush jungle mana's endless fruits. We are forest creatures, mermaids, snow bunnies, and everything in between. Some of us can't sacrifice serene lakeside summers or snowy summit winters. Our personal climate and soul frequencies resonate with specific places that impact our well-being with the ways of life they evoke from us.

Sacred sites are lasting relics of our once resplendent relationship with Divine Nature's holy ground. But they don't always look as grandiose as Angkor Wat or Machu Picchu. When I nestled into the foothills of the Daughter of the Sun Mountain on Salish and Kootenai land of the Flathead Reservation in Montana, I marveled at glory beyond any manmade edifice. Sitting beside a turquoise half-frozen alpine lake on volcanic boulders, struck with awe, I was one with God.

During my nomadic sabbatical after the L.A. fires in early 2025, I swam in crystalline waters at a local wilderness reservoir a few minutes outside of Boston. When a giant turtle floated by, whose medicine reminds us that home is wherever we go, and slow and steady wins the race, I felt the land's healing encouragement. Your backyard or neighborhood woodlands can become a sanctuary, the temple where you pray. Sacredness exists no matter where we are, we just have to open our eyes to see it or our minds to remember.

While excavating an underground garage on a wildly busy section of Los Angeles's Wilshire Blvd, for instance, where millions of cars traverse daily, workers discovered Earth's largest collection of Ice Age fossils in a quicksand swamp. The La Brea Tar Pits, one of the most ecologically significant discoveries at the time, suffocated animals for *eons*, offering so much information on our ancient past. They, quite literally, "paved paradise and put up a parking lot." Fossil fuels literally burn *fossils*—preserved, hydrocarbon-producing plants and animals, history from the ground. And we drive around feeding it to our cars or park on top of it. Whoa.

Similarly, in Prague, Czech Republic, scuba divers discovered an alchemical laboratory from the 1500s when flooding collapsed a town square. In the past, before demolition-removal equipment existed, people just built on top of such ruins—old European city-street levels have risen more than 20 feet since their founding.

The lab had been sealed behind a secret wall, with its chimney rerouted to a whole different rooftop many houses away. Even the homeowners hadn't known it was there! The alchemist's hideaway revealed a three-mile-long tunnel directly into King Rudolf II's chambers. Everyone who dug the tunnel had been killed to ensure secrecy for creating elixirs of life. While King of Bohemia, Rudolf made Prague, known for its Gothic occultism, the Holy Roman Empire's capital.

This treasure trove would have been lost, like many others, without those rains. It was *fascinating*. I could feel the sheer magik and brilliance when I was there. We need more spiritually open and progressively minded rulers so such places are venerated rather than desecrated.

After my 13 temple initiations pilgrimage in Egypt, I recharged in Greece, one of my spiritual homes whose sacred shores soothe my soul every time. A new island, Crete, complete with caves, caverns, and canyons, river gorges, waterfalls, and chestnut forests was true paradise. It's much lusher than other Mediterranean islands.

Some of you may remember from *IntuWitchin* that I stumbled upon a 9,000-year-old temple to Artemis that had been demolished only to be rebuilt as a church of the 99 Fathers. The rubble of this once-venerated place had become a place where she was not only unwelcomed, but unseen, despite epigraphs to Her holiness etched into the very stones.

A naked hike to the top of her pristine peak brought me to greater heights than I'd ever known alone. The first time I experienced the most life-changing Witchual of all, laying upon Her for endless hours, my body luxuriously melted into Her enchanted terrain. The longer I surrendered, resisting all urges to rise or depart, the more I merged with Her spirit, becoming the sacred site upon the verdant meadow among Her ancient temple ruins.

Earth's beating heart came alive in pulsing, primordial song, the voice of Goddess like clanging church bells ringing out through every corner of my consciousness. I prayed and prayed upon the altar of my own physical and eternal Divinity. That day she was more than the Greek Mother or Wilderness. She was beyond name—life itself. Melding with Minoan holy land, She who prays, and who I pray *to, united*. My most transformative moment of becoming Her body, shaken from the slumber of separation, by some of the most active Anima Mundi on Earth.

Hateful ignorance and spiritual warfare have destroyed sacred sites en masse. The church confiscated temples of antiquity and built from and upon their rubble. Cathedrals with motifs of fruits and flowers manipulatively removed people from Nature *into* their pews. The Roman Catholic empire conquered Europe, then Britain as the Church of England. Once upon a time, something far more exciting existed and delighted in life over violence. In such times of suffering, we learned to worship regeneratively.

Within a few hours of wherever you live, there is magik to behold. If flying across the world is out of the question, take a road trip in your own locale. If that just doesn't inspire or motivate you, ask why. You chose this place; learning about it might illuminate your reason for being there. Who were the indigenous people that inhabited it before "settlements"? What were their myths and Witchuals?

Every place has spirit. Engaging with the ways people communicated with them for generations offers a wonderful relationship to your homeland. Delve into the traditions of the original tribes and beliefs where you come from or live. Before a whale swimming journey to Tonga, I learned about Polynesian and Maori people, history, and culture, which generated such awe for their embodied wayfinding and navigation, and helped me connect exponentially more deeply with the locals. Thousands of European tribal cultures were wiped out like First Nations Americans between the 1400s and 1900s. Visit a cultural center; find informed tribal members who can guide your more intimately involved interaction with the legends beneath your feet.

☾

In Mexico one weekend, I had a beautiful experience with a tamarind tree. I had taken part in a medicine ceremony, and when everyone started chatting, I ventured off to explore solo—classic. I met some horses and was heading back when a golden pod crunched beneath my foot. Examining the sticky caramel fruit, a sweet, spicy smell greeted my nose. Though I'd never had it fresh before, I've tasted enough Mexican candies and recognized the scent. I wondered, "Is this tamarind?"

At risk of poisoning myself while alone in an altered state, I touched the tip of my tongue and was delighted my spidey senses were right! I thanked the tree for my pleasant surprises and perched to feast, gazing up at its feathery leaves. Sucking gooey flesh off the seeds, I unconsciously spit them out and *immediately* heard a booming voice shudder through me:

Respect the seeds the same as the tree. Where do you think I came from?

I'd had reverence for the being who stood before me, and its blessings bestowed upon me, but nonchalantly launched the creator onto the ground.

I picked up the smooth, shiny onyx pebbles and wondered at their magnificent intelligence. I sat, sang, and prayed into them for hours until I was guided to gather the delectable pods to share with my friends. Everyone devoured Earth's special treats with gusto. I never discounted the tiny origins of the fertile fruits and forests again.

The afternoon I wrote this story, returning home from the Mediterranean in Ibiza, I learned my front yard tree was carob. A hippie chocolate alternative in ebony pods with dusky hazel seeds—the inverse colors of my tasty tamarind friend. Nature is always interacting with us when we pay attention because embracing Anima Mundi is connecting to God(dess).

Medicinal plants abound all across the world! Indigenous elders from every tradition say they learned how to harvest, cultivate, and prepare tonics and tinctures from plant teachers themselves. They refer to them as "more than human people" and our "big brothers and sisters," who have evolved for millions of years longer than us. Yet we annihilate native species to plant invasive grass and landscaping that harms pollinators and requires copious amounts of maintenance. I grew up with a meadowed backyard "lawn" full of plantain and pennyroyal, clover, daisies, and dandelion, some of the most potent medicinal plants for wound healing, womb health, vitality, digestion, and even natural birth control! It's actually easier to let your yard return to its natural state, and better for you as well as the environment.

THE CLEANSING CANOPY

Religion's enlightened masters and avatars once had epiphanies or inspirational insights among the *trees*. Nature's healing wisdom could lead a new renaissance of regenerative innovation, magikally restoring our current timeline's trajectory. Honoring Nature's infinite abundance, ecstasy, or shameless expression again requires masculine action—taking time and creating space for the feminine receiving of Her transmission.

☾

Forest bathing abandons agendas for immersive woodland luxuriation. Engaging each sense, fully absorbing the atmosphere naturally (pun intended) melts worries, concerns, and regular thoughts away. Rather than purposefully crossing terrain from point A to B, forest bathing is about soaking it all in, basking in timeless canopies and carpeted roots.

Earthing or grounding is how we used to get around, connected to natural surfaces like grass, soil, or sand with bare feet and skin. Direct contact with negative ions and the generative electromagnetic field facilitates a transfer of electrons from Earth to us; kept our ancestors free from many modern maladies.

Hundreds of studies prove that forest bathing and earthing or grounding are the easiest, most effective ways to bring our bodies home to equilibrium and optimal functioning. Heart rates and blood pressure lower anxiety and stress hormones, and responses drastically decrease, and our immune system markedly boosts. Creative thinking, focus, and problem-solving functions get activated, inspiring new solutions to daily life's challenges.

I was unwittingly forest bathing for years before I learned the term. I can cover less than a mile in hours, meditating, journaling, identifying new species with Seek, my plant app, determining whether or not something is edible or medicinal, and touching (okay, let's be honest, hugging) every tree that calls to me. I'll often ask them to speak any messages they have for me in the moment through my pen to be recorded and followed. There are no wiser teachers on Earth than trees.

Intentional time in Nature has been proven to be the greatest benefit to your overall health. It's the best medicine you'll ever have. No matter what I am going through, I always feel better in Nature. Even with all the ceremonies and spiritual medicine I've done, merging with Gaia Herself over five to six hours remains the most wildly magikal.

Exposure to diverse microorganisms fortifies and reinforces our immune system's adeptness at fighting pathogens. Unpolluted environments were commonplace until the industrial revolution, linking autoimmune conditions and disconnection from Nature. We need antioxidants, negative ions, and Earth's electromagnetic energy to reduce inflammation, alleviate pain, and promote overall physical wellness.

Effective relaxation leads to better sleep, realigning your circadian and infradian rhythms to your location. Hence the best antidote for jet lag is a long walk on the earth or, better yet, a nap on the ground as soon as you arrive. I did that after traveling from Australia to Europe and was aligned with the time zone by the same evening. Hanging out in or near trees, especially barefoot, significantly reduces stress, illuminating the path toward reparation. Consistent grounding in serene surroundings, such as with barefoot walks in the woods, lowers cortisol, which reduces anxiety instantaneously and drastically improves mental health.

Forest bathing doesn't require extensive trips to remote wilderness, though that's highly recommended at least once a week. If all you've got is a local park or greenbelt, just find the quietest section and spend mindful time there. When I moved to the lake in Austin, Texas, just sitting beside the still water was so serene. I'd paddleboard past the lily pads to a nearby nature reserve and sit under massive trees with dripping moss to read, journal, or meditate.

Use every opportunity to walk barefoot on natural surfaces, even for just a few minutes a day. I revel in weeks where I never put on a single pair of shoes for retreats or adventures. Sharing this practice with a partner amplifies your shared magnetic field. Co-regulation generates greater health and happiness for your relationship and your individual well-being.

No matter what Earth ritual you choose, the key is presence. Go slow enough to hear Her. If you feel lost, unsure of how to move forward or what's most effective, lie with her and ask. After the L.A. fires at the beginning of 2025, I left my home in Topanga and didn't go back. The Goddess just kept repeating the mantra to me, "When you know, *then* you go." So I did. I waited to make any plans or take next steps until it was crystal clear where or what was meant for me.

Clarity from quiet contemplation in Nature is the best medicine. Take your time; relax; literally and physically mirror Nature. As within, so without. Lao Tzu said, "Nature never hurries, and yet everything is accomplished." She'll show you how to be with yourself with the same dignity you give Her. Follow through with Her requests and invitations. You don't have to *do* anything to feel Her. *Nothing* is actually required of you, though pausing long enough to accept that can be a defiant accomplishment.

Sitting beneath a tree, gazing at the canopy, clouds, riverbanks, or vast forest expanse phone-free for an hour does *wonders*. This immersive healing ritual can be effortless or confronting. Be patient. Start with 15 to 30 minutes. Work your way up to entire afternoons. Not a moment is wasted; it's all worthily well spent. The longer you stay, the faster it works and the better you'll feel.

Record visions, ideas, or messages you absolutely must capture without getting tempted by distraction.

A ritual lighthouse, offering safe passage through the storm, Nature may reveal other opportunities as you come home to yourself. Accepting your full spectrum means giving your emotions permission to be felt and held, your voice to be free and heard, and your body to be safe, loved, and cherished. This surrendered state reveres all beings and reminds you what an integral part of the whole you are.

CALL OF THE WILD

Configurations of flocking birds in flight, paths of ants, and bolts of lightning once held infinite information. How stalks and fields sway in the wind, waves crash upon shores, and the presence of totem creatures were signs from God to be interpreted. Augury was our original and oldest form of divination, calls from the wild.

Anima means "spirit." Animals were always our most compelling, sacred bridge between human consciousness and Nature. If you're like me, the most heart-wrenching stories are of wild creatures asking humans for help.

Minerva, my cat whom I lost tragically while writing this book, taught me about the magik of merging souls with animals (spirits). The *moment* I typed that sentence, a squirrel scurried up to me outside overlooking the canyons, affirming my acknowledgment. She and I had full psychic conversation—I called her in each night by sending a magnetic golden beacon down a bond I imagined between our hearts. Intentional interspecies interaction is a superpower we can all cultivate with any familiar: horses, serpents, cats, dogs, birds, exotics, and those in their natural habitat. People living with lions and panthers have wielded their energy to be able to do so. You can too.

Infinitely more intelligent than we give them credit for, my "pets," as well as animals in the wilderness, can psychically and physically communicate with me, some better than others.

During the funeral rite at a Samhain retreat in Ireland, we laid our past selves to rest. The moment I buried the stone representing old versions of me, horses surrounded me, nuzzling me with their velvety, pillowy noses, and I wept into their manes, feeling the therapeutic, restorative medicine they innately sensed I needed.

I used to babysit this dog Atlas, who was half Great Dane, half black Lab; he was a *hot* dog. You know what I mean! He was strikingly handsome; everywhere we went, people admired his gorgeous face. If he were a man, I would have been in love. We had a crazy karmic bond. His dad referred to him as a disobedient wild card. But I walked him leashless every day and telepathically sent him commands to stop at corners, where he'd wait for me.

Having grown up with incredibly intelligent and well-trained field-trial champion hunting dogs, I have high standards. He never ceased to surprise me, but then he blew my mind one afternoon. He watched intently as I shuffled tarot cards. "What did you come here for, Atlas?"

Huffing, he pawed toward the cards. Amused, I held them out to him and jokingly said, "Want to pick one?" He leaned forward as my jaw got wider and wider. Ever so gently, using just his sticky upper lip, he tugged a card all the way out from the deck, until the moment before it would have fallen. "Letting Go of Shame" had a *black-and-white dog* on it!

I laughed in disbelief. Dogs are shameless, immediately sticking their faces between your legs without reservation. One of the most insidious poisons of our inner realms, shame can be crippling. Of course, this handsome guy, perhaps overly vain in his last incarnation, came through to let go of shame. Perfectly on cue, he leaned down to lick his balls.

"Nice. So what about this wolf thing between you and me?" I pulled the card this time, and there was a girl with *another dog!* The only two cards in the entire deck. This one was "Remember Your Power." I couldn't believe the synchronicities. As if pulling tarot cards with a dog wasn't magikal enough, it was time to be shamelessly, authentically myself. I'd felt so alone in the gifts and abilities people feared or envied; I'd always dreamed of being safe to celebrate them. Let us all learn from animals how to own who we are.

☾

Original stories, spiritual practices, and survival skills came from coyotes or bears like Ursa and Polaris, elephants like Ganesh, or the serpent awakening Eve. As I unravel the subtle yet instinctive, mysterious art of animal communication, it continuously astounds me how clearly *they* understand *us*. The problem lies in *our* understanding of *them*. Animals intentionally convey energy, body language, and eye contact—obviously communicating. Just as with Earth, we've forgotten how to listen.

Genuinely, out of all the unbelievably magikal things that happen in my life, telepathic communication with animals takes the cake! It is the most heartwarming, full fantasy-turned-reality *tangible* experience. It fundamentally shifts your interactions with them for the rest of your life, affirming how real magik and superpowers are in the most delightful way, bringing childlike wonder and awe to a whole new level!

Yet we deny the consciousness of the vast majority of sentient species, dominating and enslaving them, clipping their actual and proverbial wings. Keeping them in small cages, literally and figuratively, valued only as commodities. Which no one, including humans, responds to well. If we ate humans at the rate we consume animals, our population would be extinct in *two-and-a-half weeks*!

We must shift our treatment of animals, Earth, and ourselves. Representing our spiritual Nature, primal power, and oneness with all things and each other, we used to coexist and adapt alongside one another. Learning from animals and *plants* in their natural habitats is crucial, not just for youth but for conservation efforts and the overall balance of our world. This primordial bond must be repaired.

INNER ANIMALS

Like the masculine and feminine, we all have animalistic behaviors that mirror aspects of human society, relational dynamics, and survival instincts. We *all* have aggression, possessiveness, the overwhelming desire to mate, fierce independence, and territoriality; we believe in the optimal function of cohesive packs for accomplishment; and we revel in feline sensuality, delight, and comfort. Reactions like jumping at loud noises, or small sounds on dark nights putting us on high alert, are born from the instinctual reptilian brain.

Directly communicating or embodying creatures' lessons and attributes generates primal wisdom. Eagles' highest flight represents spiritual communion everywhere they inhabit. Rabbits have ultimate creative power, yet risk drawing in that which they fear. Have you ever howled at the moon or with a wolf in real life? It awakens something within us. I've gotten *unexplainably* high from resonating with wolves as their haunting cries ring out. Souls calling for expressing truth and fervent yearnings.

She created us all to learn from people like Jane Goodall, David Attenborough, and Steve Irwin. Dr. Goodall dedicated her life to understanding our relationship with chimpanzees and bonobos, our most genetically similar species. The Earth teaches to never take more than we need, and if we returned to this instinctual behavior, we would all be better off.

We are all animals here on this planet, but they, when left to their own devices, all figure out how to function symbiotically together. It is only when *we* disrupt their ecosystems that things get out of balance. We encroach upon and destroy their habitat for development and agriculture, so they predate on our pets or livestock. Then we viciously attack them, when in truth, this is *their* land and always was. We play God on this planet with no concern for inflicting genocide upon others in a way that wouldn't even be possible in the rest of the animal kingdom.

With receptivity beyond external communication, animals engage with us to unveil a dialogue with creation, revealing our own intricacies to see and heal our magikal essence. Exploring animals' reflection and enhancement of our connection to Mother and Father Nature uncovers new dimensions of our wildness and primal impulses. Forging this intimate and reciprocal relationship opens the doorway to replenish what was lost.

When you reflect on what you've learned about yourself through these chapters, what animal's energy do you think would benefit your evolution most? Maybe you need more predatory pursuit of purpose, or more communal orientation like high-functioning herds. Maybe you need to be more peaceful like vultures, sacred in Tibet for their karmalessness. They kill nothing, only alchemize life that has already ended.

Acknowledging and respecting animal magik beyond those we consider special or interesting influences our interactions with, consumption of, and effect on them.

Witnessing wild natural habitats, like the Serengeti's grazing elephants and giraffes, Alaskan grizzlies, Norwegian reindeer, or whales in endless oceans, it's hard to fathom causing them harm. Yet, such practices happen en masse *every day*. Whaling has *no actual remaining commercial use* and is basically a sadistic sport. Despite its barbarism, it's still legal and driving some of the most intelligent beings on Earth to extinction. Just as all human lives matter, so too do all animals.

Our bonds with creatures, from lions to fish, range from living respectfully in proximity to sharing a bed every night. Taming your inner lioness or discovering the depths of your inner shark establishes trust in your wild nature's primal parts, mirrored through such companions.

Entire fields of study of biomimicry engender the congruence of engineering and architecture with Nature by following Nature's lead. Camouflage is designed to blend creatures into their environment, playing a pivotal role in maintaining and propagating vegetation. Other creatures assert their presence, displaying lavish adornment or marking territory as kings and queens of their domain. I look up the symbolism of every animal I encounter—they each have a message.

Nocturnal navigation of darkness, lightness of flight, and serpentine fluidity all reflect our desires. However, there's a crucial ethical consideration when it comes to animal companions, especially birds. Birds are meant to *fly*, the *one* gift humans envy above all others. Clipping their wings is a form of tyranny and *mutilation*. As spiritual beings, if we want a bird, we must allow it to soar through the sky, embracing the natural ability we will never possess. If you haven't seen that guy who paraglides with his vulture, you must watch it. They fly all over together; it's astounding! Allowing a bird its freedom invites you to learn how to merge with its consciousness, vicariously experiencing the magik of flight through its eyes, sailing above the land.

Permitting animals to exist *in* their nature supports us being true to our own. This reciprocal exchange is a symbiotic relationship that frees our wildness. Respecting Earth honors their sacredness. What we do to them, we do to ourselves. Embody your animism—howl like Wolf, soar like Owl, roar like Lion, stand like Trees. More than poetic metaphors, this microcosmic macrocosm is our spiritual reality.

AN ELEPHANT NEVER FORGETS

In Tanzania, one of my all-time favorite places, our incredibly eloquent, knowledgeable guide, Steve, studied wildlife conservation and tourism at university. His parents were farmers near Mount Kilimanjaro, and he brought children on safaris to experience the magik of their country's wildlife.

With passion and enthusiasm, he emphasized the need to protect and hold such unique, precious lands sacred, highlighting the importance of reconnecting younger generations with animals, especially considering how urbanization and colonization have distanced us from their spiritual importance and our responsibility to care for the planet.

Innately, children know how to live harmoniously. Many viral videos depict devastated kids bursting into tears when they find out that eating meat means that animals have been killed, and that "pork" and "beef" really means cows and pigs . We use such euphemisms to detach ourselves from the lives taken for our own. Kids are *taught* that animals are intruders on "our" land, but they *know* this was always the animals' land.

Stories of people rescuing animals and witnessing their extraordinary gratitude or acknowledgment are deeply moving. A viral video of a dog in Gaza burying her deceased puppy displays a touchingly profound level of consciousness. She digs a hole and gently covers the puppy with dirt, just as we return our lost loved ones to Earth.

When elephants lose a baby or herd member, they hold a funeral mourning process. These behaviors highlight how much closer we are to animals than we acknowledge. Visiting wild natural habitats, respecting them, and learning from their behaviors is vital for children, conservation, and the sustenance of life on Earth.

One of my most cherished animal experiences occurred when I was 14, on an elephant trek in Thailand. My father took my brother and me to a sanctuary that rescued elephants from the logging industry and gave people humane opportunities to interact with the gentle giants.

Sauntering elephants take your breath away. Their sun-dried skin covered in red clay looks like cracked surfaces of empty lake beds. Long, black eyelashes surround tiny but infinitely aware onyx eyes. Precious moments of connection with them stay with you forever. Exuding knowing contentment, wise old grandmothers have sassiness second only to sacred human elderhood, while babies are incredibly playful and curious. I've witnessed an elephant in a moment of upset, trumpeting and running around messing with everyone else in his band—a good reminder that emotional release is necessary for all of us.

Riding elephants without chairs (seats hurt them) was still acceptable then, but bathing them in the river was one of the most remarkable experiences of my life. These elephants, captured for use as logging equipment, showed incredible interactive behavior. They playfully squirted water, trumpeted, and offered their feet as stepstools for hard-to-reach ear scrubbing.

Every day meant new missions with our pachyderm partners. A botched poaching attempt left one with a gaping wound and sliver of tusk remaining. We searched high and low across mountains and valleys, foraging for a specific flower, and administered the tea treatment with a Super Soaker into the infected cavity. You can feel the loving dedication of "Mahuts," elephant caretakers.

Each morning they adventured to fill up with flora, and before dusk we tracked their wooden bells to bring them back to camp. We watched them mating with tenderness, ferocity, and the epitome of big dick energy. Interacting with such rare, exquisite creatures was powerful testimony to the resplendence of revering and rescuing rather than enslaving animals.

When Nature is untamed like in the foothills of Kilimanjaro, plants for every ailment or malady are available year-round. We roamed waterfalls and valleys, riparian river canyons and lush grasslands. Our Maasai guide shared his grandmother's wisdom of every shrub, bush, vine, and tree's different use and process: "Tea for gout; paste for skin irritations; this quinine cures malaria."

We also witnessed giraffes' peculiarly long-necked alien appearance, leopards battling cobras for tree territory while eating baby zebra, and happy hippos lounging in muddy cuddle puddles. Seeing cheetahs chasing antelope at top speed, being so close we could hear blood slurping, was completely different than watching them on TV. It was the definition of awe.

PRIMAL URGES

Africa is our home. We *all* originated there. Touching the holiest ground, humanity's primordial part of the planet, is utterly otherworldly. The saturated sepia soil's pulsation is palpable. Our DNA feels inherently alive.

Ethiopia's ancient temples and the Serengeti's mystically diverse landscapes and iconic wildlife, which have been unchanged for 5 million years, are Gardens of Eden. Yet the Nile has been concretized to its very banks, annihilating any greenery or wildlife that once thrived in Egypt's wide delta that hydrated this dry desert region. Funny how poorly we could treat our Motherland. Gripped by overzealous colonizers and Western power, the African continent is actually *14 times* larger than depicted on maps—the Roman Empire employed inaccurate illustrations as a tactic to disempower Africans despite their physical prowess compared to invaders.

We've inflicted abhorrent poverty and enslavement upon this continent full of some of the richest and most fertile and abundant soil. That's why Britain and France colonized them for their labor force and mass factory farming. And now Earth's most unique and last-remaining mega fauna are fighting extinction just like the bygone creatures of the ocean, as well as in America, where colonizers decimated species as industry expanded. Thousands of wolves and grizzly bears in Upstate New York, millions of bison on the Great Plains—the largest North American mammals were mostly exterminated.

Massive African hippos, elephants, rhinos, and giraffes make bison look like garden-variety Guernseys. The energetic field is different at our origin. These magikal, mostly untouched places didn't require pyramids; they have Kilimanjaro. Nature is effervescent without us changing or obstructing her beauty. Our every step is upon and within the Goddess's temple. Some tribes still sit beneath baobab trees receiving God's messages, observing clouds, and picking up scents on the wind. Until European invasion in the late 1400s, indigenous people relied on the same animals as leopards did.

Watching herds of elephants march across the Serengeti forces a recollection of how magikal and powerful we once were—and can be again. We *are* wild Nature, with trees millions of years old, Pride Rock formations rising over the horizon, and shaded groves of lazily lounging lions.

Again, travel and personal development are the only things you can buy that make you richer. Adventuring where your favorite (or spirit) animal originates is so inspiring. I've looked forward to seeing wild tigers all my life.

On my second trip to Thailand, peacocks, which resplendently represent masculine devotion, renewal, growth, luck, and fortune, surrounded my villa. Peacocks' tailfeathers symbolize beauty and luxury, and shed to regrow each year, preparing them to impress their mates. Associated with self-confidence, expression, and masculine royalty, they were a perfect sign after ending my relationship.

Each moment these spirits cross our path signals, "Pay attention." Whether on safari or home with pets, the depth of animal consciousness reveals lessons to teach us. We remember the sacredness of all beings when we open our hearts and minds to their power. Whether directly communicating or symbolically interacting, open your eyes to the erudite reflections their rich emotional lives offer; expand your own union with oneness.

Paying homage to Mother and Father Nature, we recognize animals' rightful respect. We would not have survived without them. Honoring their maternal nurturing and paternal provision reminds us of our intrinsic connection to Nature and our responsibility for stewardship. Staples for our survival throughout all time deserve appreciation. Yes, we are the top of the food chain, but it wouldn't have any other links without them.

Like the elements, animal treatment mirrors treatment of ourselves. Hurting, disregarding, or disrespecting Nature's animals or denying their intelligence denies our own instinctive insight. Like plants, animals have roamed Earth far longer than us. Returning them to the thrones of our hearts as sacred collaborators integrates ritual for magikal living. No matter how technologically advanced or civilized we believe we are, we are *animals*, albeit very different beasts. So let your inner lion roar and eagle soar, and thank them all, especially those animals you consume for protein, for all the gifts they bring to us.

THE CARNIVORE QUESTION

I grew up in the country, my dad is an avid hunter and fisherman. But when I learned about factory-farm industries, I couldn't participate in or support the majority of our food system. I refused to ingest vibrations of agonizingly painful brutality into my body. I was unwilling to eat such detrimental chemicals, pesticides, and cruelty.

Preaching reverence to the animal kingdom, you might expect a vegan tirade—sorry to disappoint. After almost 15 years of vegetarian, or plant-based, lifestyle, my body begged for omnivory. It took many medical professionals to get me eating meat again, but I finally listened, and support ranchers doing it the way we have for thousands of years.

Before a castle retreat in Scotland, I spent a few days in dragon territory, chasing waterfalls in Wales. After a long day singing beneath one of the most spectacular cascades I'd ever seen, I sat down for a meal, feeling the magik of the land I'd been drawn to by dragons themselves. The menu was classically English, with few vegetarian options. At every previous retreat we had plant-based menus. We'd sing to cows in the fields who immediately came trotting over. Cows love music. We got kisses from their soft, wet noses and thick curly tongues. They were so sentient, so connected; we lovingly petted them and had profound interactions with them.

So I asked the waiter about the origin of the beef. Still not accustomed to the idea of eating it, I hoped he'd give me a great excuse to order something else because it had been trucked in from elsewhere.

He pointed out the window and said in his lilting accent, "D'ye see dat hill? Dose are dem right dere."

Testing my luck, I shot back, "What about the butcher?"

"Oh, he lives right in dat wee white house at the bottom of the road dere. Brings 'em straight up to us. For a feed animal s'about as good as ye can get."

My resolve deteriorated. I'd hoped for an excuse to keep avoiding my new prescription. It was surreal. The rolling hills, dark lake, enchanting waterfalls, and autumn colors—the cows freely enjoyed existence in that beautiful landscape.

With my life's personal and professional commitment to sustainability, I still couldn't just become a constant and unconscious carnivore. So when my plate arrived, I thought about every cow who has come when I sang. Their sweet, wet snouts, long tongues, and playful curiosity. I imagined petting the soft, shaggy coats of the roaming Highland cattle, feeling their furry faces, scratching behind their ears, and expressing gratitude for their sacrifice throughout human history. I thanked them for their service, acknowledging the evolution and symbiotic relationship we've had with them for thousands of years. I wept, thanking the entire species.

The steak grew cold during my 10-minute meditation blessing, but it was still the best bite of beef I've ever had. I was astounded at how viscerally I could taste the magik I'd poured onto it, adding a whole new level of rich vibrancy. It was a ceremony, a moment of being grateful and acknowledging the sacrificial gift of sustenance that animals provide.

I have continued to consume as we're meant to: humanely, regeneratively, and with conscious conscientiousness, using animal communication in prayer blessings as I'm fueled by their grace.

Instead of nourishment with sunshine and Earth's bountiful vegetables and minerals, these days children are stuffed with sugar hidden in every processed snack, sauce, and beverage. Margarine and American cheese are one molecule away from *plastic*!

Genetically modified "foods" and other GMOs are made with petrochemicals and poisonous dyes, causing health conditions from the body's utter inability to recognize these mutations. We can do, and have always done, better. The trad wives have one thing right: Food is better from scratch. It's time to remember our ancestral ways aligned with land's spiritual wisdom.

When I first started spending more time in Austin, Texas, my conscious friends shocked me by shopping only at Whole Foods. I'm all for the company's *original* intention, but Amazon (who owns it now) doesn't need any more of our money. *Farmers do.*

"Where can I find duck eggs and gluten-free sourdough?"

"Sorry, girl, this isn't California."

I refused to believe it. I found a co-op *immediately*. A neighborhood artisanal grocer, Royal Blue Spyglass, carried freshly baked gluten-free sourdough. Triumphantly overjoyed, I got raw goat milk and duck eggs from Human, a Persian engineer turned Texan regenerative farmer. I love supporting people who care to do it right.

Ditch large chains for local food cooperatives! They're community-owned and stock the same products.

I know my farmers—they supply 95 percent of my food. It takes a little more time, but less than growing wheat, milling flour, and baking bread yourself! I love my weekly Farmers Market Witchual. My cat refuses storebought chicken, but scarfs it down from our local source. Pay the farmer now or the doctor later—you decide.

Each magnificent, constitutional planetary element is woven into you. Your home and your body—more than living *on* Earth, we're made *of* it. Now we can respond in turn. Your body and Earth will thank you.

Conscious consumption is an imperative to being conscious individuals. Our spiritual path *must* transcend the trap of modern convenience driven by greed, scarcity, fear, and unworthiness. We are obligated to devotional service, dutifully reciprocating the bountiful nourishment bestowed upon us, nourishing Her in return. Our survival depends on necessary reciprocity.

Polluting waters or ravaging forests harms external *and internal* environments, impacting our vibrational physicality. Let us walk mindfully and courageously, treading lightly on native grasses, reducing ecological footprints, and tending to water within and all around. Humanity is urgently reminded to synergistically align our actions, lifestyle, consumption, and creation with Nature's regenerative rhythms and cycles, learning from plants and animals how to live in right relationship.

Whether through plant medicines, gardening, or Nature, this energetic embrace is your greatest resource for healing and releasing stored trauma. Recognizing your wild archetypal landscapes will grant you unlimited opportunities for reclaiming power, beauty, joy, fulfillment, transformation, and access to magik's infinite wellspring.

Witnessing anima(ls) in our habits and behaviors, we emulate them to evoke more of what we desire and less of what we don't. Reawaken to the World Soul, dear reader. By being both the garden and gardener of the Earthly Spirit, we're rewarded with primordial tranquility, benefiting us physically, enriching us spiritually, and creating homes that are true sanctuaries for the soul.

✦ ✦ REFLECTION ✦ ✦
Elemental Examination

This is a deep one! Using the elements is one of my greatest hacks for manifestation that no one talks about. These answers will be your North Star to the life you want to lead and the rituals that will get you there, so please take the time to thoroughly explore this exercise. Then make a plan of action with your responses and stick to it!

1. First, think about your primal parts, your strongest sensibilities.

   Are you a visual, auditory, or kinesthetic learner?

   Which are your keenest senses?

   What animals share that honed vision, clear hearing, or physical prowess?

   Do you relish in serpentine hip movement while dancing or making love? Play and frolic in the ocean like a dolphin? Long to soar through the skies like an eagle?

   What aspects of feline sensuality or canine loyalty resonate with you?

   Are your sixth or seventh senses heightened, always alerting you where you are directionally the way migratory flocks are drawn by Earth's electromagnetic energy?

   What species would you link or associate with your gifts?

Nature's infinite metaphors, our most ancient, primordial language, reveal the smoothest course forward through diverse iterations of beauty reflected in our own wild (woman) archetypes. Some of us are mermaids who love the sea; others are mountain mavens, forest creatures, or desert dwellers. Each ecosystem, understory, and medicinal plant does what it needs to survive, offering evolutionary wisdom to the cauldron of collective consciousness.

Earth represents our body, health, relationships, career, finances, and material reality. Water is our emotions, subconscious, creativity, sexuality, memory, adaptability, and pleasure. Fire is transformation, motivation, drive, will, action, orientation, strength, power, and capacity to shine. Air represents our minds, expression, intellect, consciousness, voice and communication, perspective, and imagination.

We need every unique version for the multidimensional whole. The greatest gift is reclaiming what safety in the multifaceted, infinitely prismatic spectrum of passion and power authentically looks like for you. Then the fear of showing up as yourself disappears, and you are unstoppable.

2. Now, consider the greatest challenge or frustration you're currently dealing with.

   Which element is it associated with?

   What is the medicine or remedy for this issue in the elemental world?

Here are some examples:

Are you going through a breakup (relationships are ruled by Earth), and the loss is overwhelming? You can't see through the storm of what once was falling away. Your tears fall like rain (waters are emotions), your heart broken open; the pain is excruciating.

How does Nature remedy such wounds?

She needs rain to a certain extent, for resilient regenerative healing, time, and new growth. Seek supportive resources; take tender care of yourself; cry as much as you need to. Eventually, strive to rebuild inner stability from your crumbled foundations. Let everything you've learned inspire new artistry and embodied wisdom tempered over time.

Maybe you've had a dream on the back burner far too long? You're pretending to be a candle rather than the shining sun. Do you need the winds of change to clear your mind's belief systems and internal and external communication? Have you avoided taking action? Do you need a wildfire of passion to alter the very landscape inside you?

Maybe you have felt sexually or creatively shut down; the coursing waters of pleasure and flow have been dammed or stagnant.

What way might you find to chart your own course around this obstacle?

If you're being overly stubborn or stuck in your ways, could a little earthquake shake things up?

Have you let the tornado take hold of you, using your words against others, being unkind? Or are you suffocating from never having let yourself speak your mind freely?

Are you longing for a refreshing breeze of acceptance and celebration for all your hard work to caress your face, providing momentary respite in the scorching heat that's brought you to burnout?

3. Find your journal, get comfortable, and take a few minutes to write down even brief responses to the following questions. Allow any other guidance or insight to bubble up along with them. Then, read over what you've written before continuing.

Earth

What is the greatest challenge in my Earthly realm?

How do I relate to my body? How would I like to?

How do I operate with money? How would I like to?

How confident do I feel in my purpose or career? How confident would I like to be?

How is my physical environment: my home, office, vehicle, or other places where I spend time?

What kind of home do I want to live in?

How close or far am I from spending my time and life as I would like to?

How do I engage in relationships? What could I do differently?

What is my community and social life like?

What do I want to experience in friendships?

What do I need to feel supported?

Water

What am I here to birth into this world?

Do I feel safe to do so?

How do I want to create?

When do I feel most in flow? How do I block this experience?

How do I experience my sexuality?

How do I want to generate intimacy? To make love? To fuck?

How do I relate to my emotions? Do I allow them to flow freely or dam them up?

What stories arise when I experience big feelings, and how do I respond to them?

Do I let myself dream big and imagine more?

How adaptable am I?

Do I listen to my intuition or more often find myself regretting it when I ignore it?

Fire

How action oriented am I?

How willing to change and transform?

What actions do I take to do so?

How do I treat myself when my energy or productivity is low?

Do I feel worthy of shining my light?

How do I share my brilliance with others?

In what ways do I feel strong?

In what ways do I feel weak?

What is my relationship with burnout?

Do I let myself be a gentle candlelight or expect myself to always be the shining sun?

How do I rest?

How driven am I to accomplish what I feel like I came to Earth for?

Air

How do I think and speak about myself?

What do I believe about who I am?

How do I respond to myself during challenges?

Am I good at communicating my truth?

How strong is my imagination?

Do I let myself believe in its possibilities?

Do I have a clear vision for myself and my future?

When I feel confused or uninspired, how do I interpret that? What do I make that mean about myself?

How has my programming created my external experience of life?

Do I create my own opinion and belief system about the world and my surroundings or rely on the opinions of others or what I was told as a child?

How can you use the magik of Earth, Water, Fire, and Air to walk forward out of old habits into new ones? For example, as a Gemini, archetypally known as the Divine messenger, I needed the foundational element of Earth to truly step into my message. Now I get to use my gift of transmission to speak on behalf of Nature. Her stability keeps me grounded, directed, and healthy.

Use wind's wisdom intentionally to clarify how to plant new seeds and shift your mind. Sit down with this issue at the forefront of your consciousness and breathe deeply. Just six deep breaths transform your inner state and regulate your nervous system.

If you are numbing emotions, take it to the waters. Scream and exorcize it out in the ocean (one of my personal favorite Witchuals). Take a healing bath with the time and space to let yourself really feel.

When we're overly concerned with building and consistency (the masculine aspect of Earth), the womb water's wisdom will call to us:

"More pleasure or play, please!"

"More silence, stillness, reflection, and rest."

Energetic sensuality and fluidity ask us to surrender, trust, and flow. What will it take to maintain balance for you? Establishing a deep connection to Earth by living in the country, working with Her cycles and seasons, trading fruit instead of cryptocurrency?

Distraction is a defense mechanism against hidden challenges. We can get caught up in the day to day and let our whole lives slip away. Explore what needs to evolve in your life, where you're out of alignment. If your job, partnership, community, location, or anything else have been gnawing at you, draining your energy, it's time to let go, or do something different.

MICROWITCHUALS

If you haven't yet forged a relationship with an animal, explore primal expression within your body. The easiest Earth rituals are spending quiet time with Her. Sing or speak your praise, prayers, and appreciation.

* Lie on the ground or beneath a tree as long as you can without distractions, absorbing Her consciousness. Observe swaying branches, and take in as much sensual information as possible.

    Turn face down, womb and heart on the earth. Send roots to connect with what's beneath you. Stay as long as possible. Make sound; let your body be your guide.

Artfully extend your awareness, expanding real and imaginary sensory perceptions. Tune in to the myriad of life forms and natural processes occurring in your surroundings.

Begin by focusing on the audible landscape. How many bird songs and calls can you hear? How do the leaves sound rustling? Is there water burbling nearby? What can you smell? What can you feel on your skin?

Fill life into what you hear and don't. Sense the microorganisms beneath the soil. Imagine busy ants, worms, and vast mycelial networks connecting underground worlds. Stretch your sensory muscles to plug into the pulsing, endless web of life.

Recognize the interconnectedness of all living things and your place within this intricate ecosystem. Extend your awareness, perceiving the world not as a backdrop but a living, breathing entity we are part of.

* Sustainable living means taking control of everything brought into your home. Guilt and shame are most toxic, but chemicals that inhibit our bodies' regulation system impact mental and physical health too. Take charge of your cleaning and body products! It's fun, empowering, revitalizing, and reduces environmental impact, as it heals and reclaims sovereignty. Home rituals are about more than maintaining living space. Reducing chemicals and plastic pays homage to Her bountiful purity while saving money!

* Lie down and fill your bones with your breath. Even if you're indoors or several stories up, visualize strong, stable stone beneath the grass, mud, or concrete between you and the ground. Connecting with Earth's energy, feel your bones as if they are your favorite mountain range, surrounded by the most nourishing, lush soil environment (your muscles).

* Visualize rocks as "stone people"; feel trees' sentience; anthropomorphize Nature's sensual aliveness; learn from His steadfast stability. Tap into a deep well of solid, reliable tranquility, anchoring yourself in Nature's nurturing embrace.

Animal Communication

* To initiate animal communication, even with a pet at home, breathe slowly, opening yourself to their energy. Imagine *your* field expanding to encapsulate them too as a copper-colored cord flows from your heart to theirs, a direct channel between you.

    Consider what messages you wish to receive or convey. Visualize a door opening from you to them or vice versa. Hold a specific *image* of what you want to communicate, a walk or playful interaction, and transmit it from your mind to theirs. Actively send your intention visually through a picture or as a feeling; see it arriving in their mind's eye.

    Be patiently open. Sit still, breathe calmly, and listen. Keep practicing!

* I envelop my cats with heart energy and warm love. Imagine your spherical energetic field getting bigger and bigger until it surrounds them; they almost always come closer.

* Cats have extensive vocabulary, and dogs have animated facial expressions. Track your pets' specific requests or responses, when they're saying "Mom!" versus asking questions or having desires.

CHAPTER 6

"Sleighing" the Dragon

Legendary dragons inhabit every major ancient civilization. Romans and Mayans both rose to power in the 600s CE, long before trading tales across oceans. These unique societies, and many others unconnected throughout history, all have stories of dragons. How could that be if they never existed?

Flying creatures' hollow bones require very specific conditions to fossilize. But even if these conditions weren't met and there are no fossils to prove dragons' existence, millennia of *myth* eclipses absent *physical* evidence. Earthly wisdom keepers symbolizing magik, rebirth, spiritual or supernatural gifts and abilities, Divinity, and treasure since time immemorial, dragons share intentional extinction, persecution, and imprisonment sagas with women, witches, and priestesses. Villainized by Christianity, these warrior guardian angels inherently reflect our own mystical nature.

What sparked the patriarchy's punitive, shadowy greed, rampant abuse, and fearful power purge? We know the church "found and confiscated" millions of dollars' worth (billions today) of gold and gems, plundering "new worlds." Many saints were made so for slaying dragons (depicted as guarding hordes of treasure). What if these villainous colonizing crusaders rewarded their minions for violent thievery and pillaging dragons' tomes and caves?

What if gold and jewels were mere bonuses on the real treasure absconded? Supernatural, medicinal benefits from animals have been a part of traditional pharmacology worldwide. An elephant is killed for ivory every 15 minutes. Rhinos, tigers, and pangolin are all endangered because of supposed support for virility. In ancient stories, dragon scales imparted said supernatural gifts.

Could dragons have been a lethal weapon for the dark forces' world domination? Was the first persecutor violently vengeful from rejection by a powerful priestess? Did he question his worth after the Goddess incarnate denied him Her Divine beauty, sexuality, and pleasure?

Malleus Maleficarum, the treatise on "Hammering Witches," written in the 1400s by Heinrich Kramer, a Catholic priest, was the second most published book after the Bible as printing became commonplace. It detailed ludicrous factors for detecting witches, heinous (and illegal even then) torture practices, and encouraged brutality of all kinds after Kramer accused a woman of witchcraft by arguing against her "sexual promiscuity"—without any evidence of foul play. The jury found her innocent. His humiliation and outrage lead to the torture and murder of millions.

Forcing citizens to pay for their connection with God, religious middlemen accused benevolent leaders of the evil they themselves committed. Unlike those who suppress them in his name, Jesus loved and uplifted women. He spoke reverently of them. Only mental sickness or deep pain could motivate our world's dominant, tyrannical subjugation of feminine nobility's loving reverence for Earth and Her people. Thinking that oracles, queens, and creators of beauty, magik, and *all of life* were the *problem* rather than the *solution* is absurd.

Religion taught us to fear our power, spiritual gifts, individuality, mysticism, and primordial essence—to slay witches and dragons, the central pillars of lore and magik. Our reluctance mirrors the historical reality the European indigenous pagans faced. Openly identifying as the village healer or wise woman led to death. Fear of our magik is an instinctual survival mechanism with factual roots embedded in our psyche for millennia.

Rather than slaying dragons, "sleighing" (or riding) them requires the alchemical power of *actual* heroes. Real, high-value men support and celebrate women. Only those *afraid* of true power strip others of theirs.

Sleighing the dragon is scary because shadows are epigenetically imprinted. But studies by UC Berkeley, the Mayo Clinic, Yale, and other institutions show that healing pent-up, suppressed emotions and rewiring trauma is the greatest way to achieve happiness and fulfillment. When we do, we regulate reactions, defuse internal battles, and mine diamonds from the farthest reaches of our souls.

Wallowing on pain's surface misses the jewels that can be mined beneath the pain by going *all the way* in. Stretch your comfort zone's edges. Rather than denying grief, surrender to it—sob and wail, surf waves of sadness, and accept "bad" feelings as purely releasing hurt.

Undertaking this bravest work mends ruptured hearts, rewriting new narratives from damaging delusions. Ancestral trauma and generational karma require *someone* to transform patterns. You're here because, in your family, it's *you*.

Dragons and fairies aren't mere fantasies. Fairy tales keep our legacy of divinely powerful godliness alive, passed down in whispers—the vehicle for teaching and safeguarding magik. Your inner child's magikal enchantment doesn't *have* to be literal—symbolically embrace dragon's alchemical and spiritual prowess. For us romantasy girlies, if you're lacking motivation or procrastinating try telling yourself, "A dragon would never choose you . . ." If that doesn't get you up and at 'em I don't know what will!

Maybe *your* fairy tale is more sci-fi. That's great—all mythical stories represent self-discovery.

In my legendary fairy tale, I'm a Goddess-guided, dragon-riding heroine. My magikal relationships with humans and animals, the rare miracle of my business, books, community, lifestyle, and adventures, are my dreams come true, luxurious fantasies in pleasure of all kinds. I wrote this chapter in Thailand surrounded by the dragon guides and guardians I cherish, on doorways, in temple and cave entrances, holding grand staircases, and on endless carved statuary. Sleighing dragon magik is certainly working for me, and I know it will do the same for you.

THE UNTREASURED TREASURE

Today, with natural resources and lives privatized, people are commodities. You'd think governments and global leadership would strive to care for rather than poison and exploit us, but c'est la vie.

Your body, mind, and spirit are your most valuable assets. To stop being pillaged and reclaim your sovereign power, you *have* to be "selfish," because you are the only person you can control. Your healing can trigger projections from people who haven't been brave enough to do their own. Focusing on others easily distracts us from working on ourselves.

Studying the Law of Correspondence, the aforementioned foundation of *IntuWitchin*, changed the world around me by changing my *inner* world. Suffering around us reflects suffering within us. We change our future by changing our present. Laying down the sword that was sabotaging and cutting me down helped me release external battles.

Establishing robust, sovereign inner authority grants the kind of power that makes us largely impervious to external dominion. The autonomy of living off the earth, healing ourselves, and bartering with neighbors was an unacceptable threat to absolute rule because we didn't require anything external Mother Nature hadn't already provided. Personal growth evolutionarily advances our entire species and planet beyond individual benefit, but most humans are too afraid to do it. Courageously walking ourselves home to our *true nature* makes us a guiding light for others coming home to themselves, and we are all so lost right now. Let us be fierce dragons standing for what's right. When patriarchal forces try to push you down, rise anyway.

You are the untreasured treasure.

"SLEIGHING" THE DRAGON ☾

I *saw* a dragon once. On a mystical full moon night, right before my birthday, I gazed up at her luminous glow rising in the rosy dusk when a giant black silhouette crossed her face. A long, elegant neck stretched across the milky orb, and suddenly, a massive wing unfolded beneath. Stark and defined against the incandescent backdrop, the dragon soared gracefully across the night sky. Its long tail trailed behind and, as quickly as it had appeared, was invisible again. Sheer ecstasy coursed through me—I couldn't contain the thrill bursting my heart open. Every cell in my body was scintillated, and I thought I might explode.

The next day, awestruck and amazed, I bumped into Theresa Bullard, my initiator into the Modern Mystery School. After I shared my experience, she explained dragons' ability to bend light: "The moon is already reflected; of course the refraction allowed you to see her. Black dragons are cosmic, the great creators from the void." So nonchalant and matter of fact, her words immediately rang true. In *Pete's Dragon*, a 2016 remake of a beloved '70s children's movie, Elliot's light-bending invisibility is real dragon magik at play

Later, in a redwood forest, drawn to a special fallen tree that remarkably resembled a reclining dragon, I caressed the contours of her resting form and asked the dragon spirit its name. To my astonishment, it responded: "Anora. I am the black dragon."

Even though I'm *so* into all of this, I still have plenty of moments of doubt, brushing off messages my soul knows as truth.

Okay, girl, now a dead tree is the dragon you saw . . .

But an even more surreal turn eliminated any remaining hesitation. "Randomly," someone gifted me a black Beanie Baby dragon. I already have four blue ones. I looked at the name tag, and feeling faint, I understood the ladies of yore in that moment, although their fainting was mostly caused by suffocating corsets. The TY tag said, Anora. Shrieking, I almost hyperventilated and lost consciousness.

Anora ensured I hadn't needed a shred of suspicion. A tangible talisman of my encounter with the holiest, blessed dragon crossing the moon that unforgettable night is always with me.

Pre-Christianity, dragons brought great fortune. Myths regale the blessed protectors guarding caves, castles, and gleaming hoards, *astride* true heroes. They are still the penultimate totem of abundance, prosperity, and good luck in Chinese mysticism.

Why would heroes turn on them?

Because "historical" narrative is controlled by those who execute its legends and heroes.

Again, the Vatican, despite funding endless crusades, supposedly only generates income through tithings/donations. Idolizing dragonslayers throughout history, they have more than just exorbitant wealth hoarded in their vaults, kept from those they claim to serve and who need it most. Beneath the modern parking lot the church stores 53 *miles* of archives containing correspondence from world leaders, royal families, and nearly every remaining ancient mystical and alchemical text, keeping unimaginable secrets of true history hidden from us.

Sadly, corrupt captains currently navigate our global ship. Chasing money, status, or superiority misplaces our collective focus, ensnaring us in individualistic pursuits and material accumulation. We're conditioned to suppress our vast potential, supernatural abilities, and innate inclinations to connect with God or liberate love when they are the surest, clearest path.

Fear is the number one suppressant of every bodily system. Yet the greatest treasures come from wielding it to fuel our fire, riding the dragon into the darkness we're most afraid of. When we sojourn into the soul's uncharted territories, we trust fall into the Universal embrace. Learning to alchemize our trials into triumphs cultivates our confidence to take risks, and resilience when they don't work out.

Without proper support and aftercare for the abusive atrocities we've endured, traumatized people plow us head-first into spiritual dystopia—the blind leading the blind. In fact, our eyes see only an *infinitesimal* range on the spectrum of light, 0.0035 percent, to be precise. That's how much of "reality" we're capable of viewing. So opening our inner and spiritual eyes to wider possibilities—of dragons or invisible, energetic realms—helps us envision a brighter future.

Magik, precisely what our ancestors lauded dragons for, is the true treasure. What if we protected and cultivated our shared riches? We could craft a world where magik isn't just a distant tale, nor a fun idea for children, but a palpable force architecting our reality. We must make self-care nonnegotiable to maintain unshakeable trust within ourselves and the Universe. We need to be vigilant with self-talk, especially during frustrating moments, responding as we would to our inner children. After all, they're the ones feeling disheartened. Dragon sleighers are guardians of true wealth for our inner children and all those who inherit it. We can steward spiritual and financial fortune to build regenerative resource solutions and effect change for the benefit of all.

Watching magik become real in my life slayed the terror of success that had me hiding, playing small, and letting *others'* projected fears dictate my choices. I grabbed my worries by the reins and tamed their tired tale. I am big; I am a dragon, a force of nature. I can't let people's shame or projections slay me. Becoming my own dragon, I unfurl my wings and soar.

Redefine what motivates your own choices. Synergize and harness your communal strengths and gifts to lead with wisdom rather than wounding. Dismantle society's oppressive systems from your internal functions. Rather than holding back, harness the fierce power coursing through you to confront your fears and unlock the chains on your supernatural energy.

SLEIGH SIGNALS

You know it's time to sleigh when you're ready to rise out of current circumstances that are beneath you. Here are some key indicators that dragons are charioting treasure troves your way:

- You're fed up with one or more elements of your life. Make one transformative action from this place.

- That pattern you still haven't figured out gnaws at you. When did your inner child adopt it?

- You're inspired to heal your trauma—even though it's intimidating, there's a thrill of excitement. Connect with who you'll be on the other side!

- Your soul yearns to disrupt the status quo. "This can't be all there is." It isn't!

- You question your routine and everyday existence.

- You're constantly searching for deeper meaning, more magik, and answers.

- You see angel numbers, notice synchronicities, and keep having "No way!" moments.

- Money and opportunities "coincidentally" fall in your lap.

- Your sensitivity to the world's writhing turmoil, inequality, and hardship is heightened. Overwhelmed by the noise, you feel compelled to do something. Headlines stir storms in you; injustice cries for you to make a difference.

- You attract people with a shared commitment to psychological advancement.

- You're seeing dragons (or will soon). They pop up on tattoos, on a show, on a truck passing by, or in conversation. Or dragons call you ethereally.

Nothing clearly signals "Dragons, I'm ready for you!" quite like facing off with your shadows.

TEAMWORK MAKES THE DREAM WORK

Dragons operate in sisterhood, like brotherhoods of warrior knights. "All for one and one for all" over "every man for himself." Society opposes establishing relationship teams of primordial creative forces like our original councils. As Andrew Carnegie said, "Success has to be given away in order to keep. He who helps the greatest number of others to succeed is himself the greatest success."

Humanity *needs* collaborative spirit. Joy and achievement love company, just like misery! Millennials are all pining for homesteads and communities because that's our tribal imperative. People who encourage your growth rather than stifle it, who cheer you on, call you forward, and comfortingly reassure you when you stumble, *accelerate* your healing.

When we know we're worthy of community that we truly love and admire, we can intertwine creative efforts with shared pursuit, building bonds beyond all others. Could you professionally, romantically, or creatively collaborate with friends?

Dragons can get excited about treasure—elated to share and bestow precious gifts upon others, sometimes to our detriment. I wrote a book, read my own Audible, and got featured on national media, yet I didn't do much to celebrate myself because I hadn't been surrounded by parents or partners who acknowledged major milestones. Accomplishment is great, but it's practically meaningless with no one to share it with.

In the final phases of completing this manuscript, I called in the big wands. Weekly bodywork, acupuncture, medicine ceremonies, EMDR, family constellations, yoni massage, workouts, trauma healing, and astrology or psychic guidance *always* made me feel better, but there was nothing more medicinal than sisterly love, snuggles, and giggles. The comfort of supportive community, along with leaning in to the *discomfort* of setting aside my to-do list to let them hold me brought physical, tangible changes to my health, heart, and soul. Their loving reminders illuminated a pattern I hadn't previously known to work on.

Having intimate, spiritual allies is precious. If you don't have any, set intentions to find them and follow the breadcrumbs you're shown to cool sound baths, moon circles, parties, or retreats.

Travel to places you've always dreamed to visit, even close to your hometown. (Or come to one of my castle retreats!) If a place or people bring you down, change your circumstances, move! You are your soul squad's team captain. Mentally recruit on the tenets of motivation, play, appreciation, trust, and courage to manifest the one that takes you to life's championship.

THE INNER VOLCANO

Anger is a volcanic eruption that can sometimes leave a wake of devastating death and destruction. But over time, volcanoes can create paradise—Hawaii, Fiji, the Philippines, Azores, and Galapagos are all volcanic islands. In every mythology, Goddesses exhibit wrath, reflecting Nature's ferocity. In the animal kingdom, standing up for ourselves or our kin is our wildest nature.

After eruptions, cool breezes (calm thoughts), nourishing waters (peaceful, healing emotions), and seeds sprout new life (new habits, relationships, or purpose). Released anger becomes beautiful. We can't suppress it, but we must be mindful how we express it. My life has become my own volcanic paradise, and yours can too.

Tapestries depicting dragons don't show ferocious, evil beings but familiars being of service and inspiring awe. Exhibiting power has led to ostracizing persecution—like witches to be burned, conditioning us to ignore and control the force within.

Since childhood I would sob inconsolably for "no reason," unknowingly sensing the unbearable weight of pain and suffering on Earth I came to help alleviate.

My mom would ask, "Why are you crying?"

"I don't know; I'm just sad!" I'd wail.

"Well, choose something to cry about."

"Puppies and kitties in the pound," "Trees being cut down," or "That homeless lady," I'd say.

"SLEIGHING" THE DRAGON ☽

Overwhelmed by how we treated Earth and fellow creatures, eventually my sadness felt futile. As societal violence reached a fever pitch, my magikal childhood imaginings were destroyed by middle school cliques and teenage torment.

Without healthy outlets, my rage stewed beneath the surface since puberty. Inherited ancestrally from my father, I modeled his volatility and simultaneously responded to my mother's emotional repression. I was clueless where to put *any* feelings. Being too joyful or confident made people competitive, attempting to shut me down. Being too sad repelled them. I hated how deeply I felt the tragedies of life that so many experienced daily. Though too young to understand, I disdained my visceral, unexplainable anguish at my perceived shortcomings—"What's wrong with me?!"

With nowhere safe, I was ashamed of my differences from my peers. Confusion at their lack of awareness or concern morphed into agonizing self-loathing. My borderline debilitating empathy in an unsafe Muggle world was a recipe ripe for rage.

This pattern led to horrible romantic choices who could never hold or love me in all that I am. Debilitated by doubt in the Divine, my path, and the point of life (which doesn't exactly transform fear of failure), I wasn't working toward becoming who I'd always known I was meant to be. I let myself be disempowered and disrespected, enraged at my bad decisions and how I continually sacrificed my own needs to give too much to others. Nothing makes us angrier than hiding from our true power and potential.

It was time to sleigh the dragon.

After years of monastic spiritual rigor, things were heading toward happily ever after with myself. Until I unabashedly exited the broom closet as a witch. I'd dealt with so much trauma-informed behavior, but this public reclamation rattled my repressed rage's cage with a vengeance. I had reached new heights, tapping into a mission and movement far beyond personal endeavor or exploits. For the first time, I could seriously invest in creative projects, real estate, mentorship, or business expenses. I'd been bullied and misunderstood my whole life, worried I'd fail. I was quite literally living in a whole new world.

The flames from every pyre that burned a wise woman alive ignited inside me. "I'm more myself than I've ever been! I'm making more money; I feel happier and more fulfilled than I ever have; my friendships and community are deeper and more magikal than I ever imagined. What is going on? How can I feel so many things I thought I'd escaped and overcome?"

Then the 2020 COVID pandemic shut the world down, and most of humanity stayed stuck indoors, disconnected from Earth and one another. I was blessedly nestled in Nature with community that remained connected. But by the middle of 2021, my sympathetic nature ferociously returned to torment me. I was outraged at the forces of internalized patriarchy controlling our minds with fear narratives, isolating already lonely and at-risk people. Little did I know I was watching them play out far closer to home than I could see.

I'd tried to leave a relationship several times in our first 18 months together but somehow never mustered the courage to actually walk away. Coupled with collective fury for the state of humanity and antiquated propaganda minimizing women and minorities, a volcano stirred within me. The world and my peers had tried to suppress my power by keeping me small and meek—they said women like me are intimidating, too much, intense, too big. And I had let someone in, closer than any person had been to me before, who unconsciously felt the same.

We disagreed on the most valuable forms of treasure. As a feminine crusader, I wanted to enjoy my abundance, see the world I love so much, and celebrate the trove I'd toiled to accumulate. I needed someone to ecstatically revel in life's riches with me. Seeking deeper intimacy felt burdensome, so I shrunk for acceptance, abandoning myself to avoid rejection. I tired of the battle to be heard but was blindly plagued by unworthiness, sacrificing myself and the profoundly special blessing it is to be loved by my devotional service. I was so disheartened. It was time for a fight I'd been denying was mine.

Finally, the chains I'd been shackled in through years of people pleasing were unlocked. While we should never accept abuse, experiencing it can, in some cases of profound resilience, lead us to seek peace and strength through adversity. Underneath all the magik,

I was motivated by what made me mad. Furious at myself for being too afraid to leave, I began erupting uncontrollably with rage.

When we uncoupled, the heartache from compounded disappointment in myself ignited a fury within me to respond with the best medicine I know. I faced every pattern I was repulsed by that had kept me imprisoned in the constricting confines of his patriarchal worldview and expectations of a woman. I didn't come here to be "agreeable" or less successful. Our relationship inspired me to release rage's claws in my back once and for all.

The instant I took full responsibility for the way I'd let anger infiltrate my mind, relinquishing its right to call shots or motivate any aspect of my life, *USA Today* called. They wanted to interview me about the rage rituals designed to release the very pain I'd finally transcended.

That feature and its viral video led to a media frenzy with Fox News, the *Today* show, *Fortune* magazine, and many more wanting to understand the cathartic benefits of this sacredly profane practice.

They caused such a stir in the Muggle world because religious rites (in the public eye) resemble silent, stagnant piousness directed at something outside ourselves rather than within. That's why I design my retreats with so much active, cathartic movement. We have to reclaim that which actually imbues our lives with lasting transformation.

It was not lost on me that when I finally chose to ride the dragon of this volcanic emotion within me, that national press recognition and professional paradise inevitably arrived. Stepping outside familiarity, expanding your comfort zone, surpassing previous expectations, and achieving big dreams will add new layers of growth once your soul is prepared for them.

CONFRONTING THE FEAR OF MAGIK

Fearing this power has a myriad of consequences, from staying in unhealthy relationships to illness and disease caused by stored pain in the body. If I weren't afraid of my magik, I imagine I'd be levitating, teleporting, and have real dragons. I dream that in this lifetime, I will actually fly across an ocean seated between their wings. When we feel unsafe to share the most wondrous, God-given part of ourselves, we extinguish the light of our souls.

Adapting our behavior to avoid abandonment, rather than sleighing that dragon, keeps us in hiding, preventing the people ready to soar alongside us from finding us. Sacrificing our needs depletes our inner resources rather than honoring them and accumulating the treasures of confidence, self-trust, and true loyalty. Being afraid of our magik causes us harm, whether mental, physical, or spiritual. Courageously stepping into our magik is the most surefire way to change the world.

Ask yourself:

Am I afraid of my own magik?
How does that impact my life on a daily basis?
What would I be doing differently if I were absolutely unconcerned about what others would think?
What am I most afraid of with this choice, risk, or opportunity? How am I navigating it?
How is the behavior that was role-modeled to me in childhood showing up now?
What would the most bold and audacious version of myself do?
How could I sleigh that dragon, even a little bit today?

There are many methods and Witchuals for overcoming fear. Practicing presence involves focusing on the moment by using your breath, surroundings, or sensations to combat anxieties about the future or worry about past regrets.

Simply tracking the physical *feelings* of fear can reduce it significantly and instantaneously. *Where is it in your body? Is it heavy or dense, prickly or sticky? Does it have a color, etc.?*

Breathing techniques like box breath (in for four counts, hold for four, out for four, hold empty for four, for at least eight cycles) activate your parasympathetic nervous system, signaling to your brain that you are safe. Singing has the same effect.

Somatic release and movement like shaking and dancing (while out in Nature is my personal favorite) release stored physical tension and generate happy hormones like dopamine, oxytocin, and serotonin, which counteract cortisol, the stress hormone created by fear. Of course if this is chronic fear or paralysis you're experiencing, working with a coach or therapist to shift your mindset reduces the emotional charge beneath the overwhelming emotion. Going to therapy can reprogram your subconscious beliefs by helping you address root causes in your childhood, unpack your trauma, and then develop coping mechanisms.

What some might call "exorcisms" are just intentional releases of emotion, whether on our own or with a practitioner or facilitator holding space. Sleighing the dragon can mean imparting lessons in an empowered, structured way, or accepting your mistakes, owning your experience, taking responsibility for ignoring your IntuWitchin's guidance, and offering safe passage to the anger that follows. Choose your favorites from the spiritual buffet.

Researchers at Yale, Johns Hopkins, and many other institutions have scientifically proven that so-called exorcisms *are* demons escaping our body—just not like we've been programmed to think. They are brazen triumphs over painful traumas that make us ashamed, the diabolical voices of criticism, and stagnant harm being released from within.

Low-grade, consistent anger or sadness wires your brain to believe it is normal. Whereas going full force into your emotions, in a safely held way, actually helps heal them. I'm a big fan of exorcisms! Intentional screaming, raging, and abandoning whatever has convinced you to hold back emotionally purges the darkness whose daily degradation can *feel* demonic. People who've been abused feel afraid and mistrusting of letting out this pain once and for all with good reason. Some emotions are fiercely instinctual, intense reactions to loss or threats against what we hold dear; some are lessons delivered through others. A lioness's wrath protects her cubs.

Most people don't make the effort to understand their underlying discomfort or confusion. Ask questions and face the answers.

Every uplevel and all the dreams I've made reality have certainly brought up tons of fear for me.

When emotions take you for a ride, ask yourself:
What part of me feels unsafe right now?
How can I hold myself and have compassion for my experience without negatively impacting another person?
How can I offer myself the care I need most right now?

Regulating your nervous system, getting it back to homeostasis, can be the most helpful and nurturing thing to do.

FORTIFYING OUR FORTRESS AND OPENING THE DRAWBRIDGE

Your inner fortress—from old French for "strong place"—is fortified by strength, the courage to heal, and inspired action that transforms your mind into a safe, trustworthy, high-functioning haven and psychospiritual landscape. This stability allows your inner child to thrive and play with reckless abandon.

As the body is the home of the spirit, the house is the home of the body. I think of myself as a castle built upon a strong Earthly foundation of beauty, magik, and connection to Nature. Wandering endless enchanted forests, indulging in lavish feasts, and enjoying extravagant balls—everyone is invited to partake in the magik. We're constantly learning, but we also have so much fun, riding horses through mystical meadows whooping in celebration of the fruits of my labor.

Historically, most castles were contained within stone walls beyond the grounds. Similarly, without good, strong boundaries, anyone could come in and take advantage (of me in general, my kindness and generous hospitality—the time, effort, and money I've put into making it so special and spectacular) or even cause damage and destruction. I'm not alone in having unknowingly trusted and allowed one too many maliciously intended people into my queendom. So I've built better fortresses, *fort*ified with discernment, clear values, high standards, and higher vibes.

Now, in my education, I don't believe in protection magik. Explicitly warding off evil implies that it's out to get you, *paying it* attention attracts it more easily. Sure, my gate-guarding knights are not to be messed with, and I've got a big moat, dragons circling, and archers poised and ready on every turret. But my drawbridge is open and welcoming—until I should be otherwise.

People we allow into our sanctuary who hurt us often mirror abusive parents, teachers, or influential adult figures' familiar behavior, elucidating misbeliefs that we deserve mistreatment, or we're only loved, worthy, or worthwhile if we fix people. Comfortingly acknowledge the pain with an "I see you," then confront it head-on. We must master it lovingly, with acceptance, and behave the opposite of our disempowered pattern. Transforming responses to people and toxic situations, consciously using pain for power, is true alchemy.

Imagine your robustly secure fortress with a dragon handling protection. Remember, beyond mythical guardianship, dragons symbolize our confidence and strength through strengthened *boundaries,* like invisible shields. No one crosses into your sacred space without express invitation, and those allowed in only bring value or care.

Secure empowerment allows you to filter who enters your castle grounds. When you know who you are, and what tendencies you have to acquiesce to others, you hold people to a standard of positive, uplifting nurturance, ensuring interactions enrich and respect you. If they can't honor the role offered in *your* show, they are politely told to "Exit stage left."

Selective admittance isn't about excluding others but fulfilling your (and your inner child's) needs for safety and trust with people who honor and enhance your highest self. In Witchual, to set the energetic space, we often visualize or proclaim a circle. Think of it like a vase for the blossoms of your magikal working. My circle casting chant is, "Only love shall enter in; only love shall emerge from within." We can hold anything in that safe, magikal space, but only love will leave it.

When we shift from being reactive to proactive, our improved emotional and psychological well-being turns surviving into thriving, and victimhood of our past into mastery of our future. Majestic dragon guardians are eager to reconnect with the humans who remember them fondly. Invoke dragons of ancient myth's spiritual or psychic surgery, guardianship, fierce power, and alchemy. Summon their magnificent vigor and primordial knowledge to create wonders and enact change in your life. You are the castle and the precious jewels it guards.

ARMORED SKIN

A quintessential aspect of dragon energy is having thick skin. When those external fortress walls are resilient, they deflect projections. Only that which you know is untrue or someone else's issue can roll off your back, but this requires deep work and self-knowledge. If you're afraid they're right or their comments might be true, that's *information* for what else you're ready to work through. When we're rooted in *our* truth, others' mounting attacks are futile. They can say all they want without affecting us.

Imagine yourself as impenetrable: When negativity or criticism is aimed at you, it bounces off. Those metaphorical arrows and barbs cannot penetrate your formidable shield. You cultivate dragon skin through deep awareness of your wounding, trauma, core essence, and capacity to act from that wisdom. When negative beliefs arise, you do something about them.

The chicken-or-the-egg dilemma of authenticity is which comes first?

The media's bombardment of distortions has the world starving for truth. Cultivating crucial inner authority, your truth becomes your guiding North Star, your compass. Follow whatever feels right in your heart. It won't lead you astray. Truth can act as a fortress or a boundary—and, simultaneously, an opening or gateway to deeper understanding and connection. When you're dishonest about where wounding informs your behavior, you create lack, a rift between the wounded child and wise adult. When you are authentic and someone gets triggered by you, that's *their* responsibility. If you're acting from woundedness and trigger someone else, *that* is yours.

Integrity is an amalgamation of honesty and wholeness. Acknowledging that our wounds and struggles are not deficiencies is honesty. Maturely accepting the parts of us we cannot change, and doing our best to change the things we can, is innate wholeness. People know what to expect and can hold us accountable, and we are in right relationship with ourselves and God. If we act differently than we want to (by people pleasing or sacrificing needs), or we say we'll do one thing but choose another, we are out of integrity. When we know and trust who we are, genuinely relying on our own powerful majesty and authenticity, it's as if we're wearing a suit of armor that keeps us *in* integrity.

I learned a lot about integrity in my breakup. I was so frustrated, but I eventually found compassion, remembering my pain when I believed I had to hide who I was. Sharing my hardships with others was harrowing before I realized the depths of my magik, created safety, and fell in love with my true self, overjoyed that I was courageous enough to let her shine. I judged myself so hard internally. I know what it's like to feel unworthy to show up as your full self, especially when you don't even know how.

When you are authentic, you're unfuckwithable. Your dragon spirit unfolds—not from ego but pure courageous confidence. Imagine possessing a dragon's fierce abilities, such as physical and spiritual flight, breathing fire, and being shielded by armored scales. If we all felt that indomitableness, not from arrogance but from integrated empowerment, nothing would deter us from our greatest dreams coming true. That's what it's like to just be yourself.

The dragon and the mythical phoenix represent rebirth: Whether I fall, break, or even perish, I rise again, reborn. Living with this conviction, you remain steadfast, adaptable, and eternally resilient, even in the face of adversity, willing to do whatever it takes to stand up for your truth, what you believe in, and magik itself. When wounds no longer have power over you, no one can say anything you haven't already heard, acknowledged, and taken responsibility for.

I did this countless times at the beginning of my journey.

When I first started sharing on social media, I was doing livestreams for big pages on Facebook. As I got more popular, I started having trolls of all kinds attacking and attempting to distract me. They would call me ugly, question my intelligence; they pulled out all the stops, but their barbs never hooked me. Instead, I would name whatever they called out and say with compassion: "I feel for you deeply, that you would be in so much pain to feel like you need to attack me from behind your keyboard, someone must have told you you're ugly, stupid, unworthy, and so you're trying to project that onto me in an effort to alleviate your hurt. I'm so sorry that no one made you feel special, I've been there, and luckily now I love myself enough to reject and reflect your opinions, you can do the same but it's going to take a long hard look in the mirror..."

Rather than ignoring them, I gave them what they wanted, attention. But I did it in the opposite way that people usually deal with trolls, which is defending or avoiding. I kid you not, *every single time*, I got a message from them later apologizing and thanking me, and to this day some of them are still my biggest fans.

A powerful male friend, who was obviously triggered and throwing daggers at anything he could pick apart about who I was, let me have it one day. Rather than argue, I stood calmly and listened. When he paused to take a breath, I acknowledged the part he spoke into: "I see how you could experience me that way."

For every complaint, I explained with tough tenderness the wound or belief that informed my behavior, and its attempt to stand up for or defend my inner child. Eventually, he had nothing left. He was shocked. I left the house and came back a few hours later, where he proceeded to bow before me, kiss my feet, and beg for my forgiveness. He ended up cradling me in his arms, apologizing and saying that women like me needed to be revered for the royalty we are rather than cut down, shamed, or belittled.

Alchemy. Dragon power, again and again.

As you step into it, you may find more frequent opportunities to sleigh from various avenues. You are a force of nature with dragon skin. Let nothing prevent you from moving forward, guided by your truth.

Having thick skin doesn't mean losing your sensitivity. There is a fine line between wearing armor and remaining open and tender. Be conscientious of the tiny humans inside you and others; speak kindly and compassionately. You can be tough and soft, firm yet gentle. This vital equilibrium protects you without closing off your ability to experience and express compassion and empathy. Be patient, but take no shit.

Power manifests in varied forms. Soft power's gentle influence can be just as effective—if not more so—than fierce power in many situations. Relentless willingness to face adversity head-on is invaluable, but there are times when bracing for impact isn't the best approach. Sometimes, defusing tension and conflict without confrontation leads to more desirable outcomes.

Almost every decision you make, every interaction, is an opportunity to choose how you wield your power. When you have a complaint for your boss, for instance, what's your desired outcome? One of my team members asked for a raise by laying out her timeline, responsibilities, desires, and needs clearly with space to respond and negotiate. Because of her presentation, I immediately gave her what she wanted—it was a no brainer.

If your partner refuses to do the work, maybe a firmer approach is required. Calmly stating, "I love you. I don't want to force you to do anything that isn't right for you. But I have to honor my needs; I am a queen (or king), and I want to be with someone who values me enough to want to grow together. It's okay if you don't, but I'm willing to walk away." Lovingly firm boundaries are not an ultimatum; they are the guards at your gate. If someone shouldn't be in your castle grounds, they are escorted out.

At a party a few years ago, I walked out of a photo booth and some random guy grabbed my ass, not casually. I immediately turned around and said, "What the fuck?" He pretended he didn't know what I was talking about, but I refused to let it slide. I didn't have a gigantic partner to defend me at the time, so I was my own knight in shining armor. I got other men involved, and he was asked to apologize and leave. Especially as women, we have to be willing to fight for our own honor when no one else will.

Will you slay the challenges or be slain by them? Rise up or fall? Make good choices or succumb to detrimental ones? In every confrontational situation, you choose to stand for what is right or inadvertently perpetuate the problem.

Easy choices, hard life; hard choices, easy life—remember? We have been programmed to react instinctively in ways that may not serve our higher selves. Mastering the dragon means responding rather than reacting, choosing your battles wisely, and employing the right leverage at the right time. Mastery is more than small adjustments; it's radically evolving, thriving in your inner world, constantly overcoming tests of strength and integrity, rippling resilience out into the Universe.

BEAMING THE BEACON

Loneliness and isolation can plague those standing tall in their power. Most of us discover our gifts on our own or only through the lens of others before we've fully grasped what's different about us or are ready to share it. Many of my clients' potent psychic or premonitory gifts were misunderstood in childhood to the extent that they were heavily medicated or even institutionalized. Yet they persevered, even when they were pharmaceutically numbed or labeled outlandish, delusional, or crazy. They kept opening their hearts and trusting its magik.

Rising and being visible inspires awe that motivates others to believe they can do it too. That is the essence of true power.

Society is depressed because we're convinced we're not Divine. But you can choose how you play the human game, finding beauty, magik, and abundance everywhere you look. People didn't even have hot water until 50 years ago; we are living like royalty compared to all of history!

Your healing journey—with spiritual medicines like ayahuasca or psilocybin, talk therapy, dance, or self-exploration—will be as unique as your trauma. The treasures you seek in your shadow and the dragon safeguarding them will differ from everyone else's. Remember, this process can be subtle and tranquil. Simply sitting with your fear of loneliness, rejection, failure, or connection can be enlightening.

Shadows manifest physically in eruptive or contractive ways. If we ignore our body and spirit's communicated needs, life has a way of forcing our response. To mitigate disease and injury, listen attentively to these signals and act accordingly.

What gems might you uncover or cultivate within your shadow? What would alchemy look like for you?

When your body urges you to stand up and stretch, do it. When you feel that mental or physical nudge for Witchual or spiritual practice, go for it. Yours might be as simple as lighting a candle, going for a full-moon hike (my monthly tradition), journaling, taking a bath, pulling tarot cards, or joining your local yoga studio for a ceremony. Dance, cry, run, sing, rest, laugh, scream, build, burn—embrace inspiration as it comes. Sleighing the dragon incorporates intentional energetic precision into your routine and ritual, even when things get messy.

Despite the church's effort to obliterate it, dragon essence remains unbroken. Just as no one and nothing can take away authentic integrity. We may not see dragons as frequently as we'd like, but that hasn't stopped them from playing major roles in our favorite stories. Beacons of uniquely potent magik, they prove that even the strongest beings can face downfall yet never be fully erased. Truly powerful beings take infinite forms but arise from the same source. Authenticity serves something greater: that which created everything. The Universe never pretends to be anything other than it is. How could it, and why should it? Shining the light of God as only you can, being authentically yourself, brings the dragon's spirit and scaled hide alive within you.

THE INNER TRINITY

Another profound dragon teaching imparts the anomalous integration of the three middle chakras, or energy centers, into a singular vortex. Referred to as the "HeartWomb," heart, solar plexus, and sacral chakras fuel creation with the power of love. Energized by the power source between them, the appreciation of our heart breathes life into the fires of our motivation, generating power and creative vibrancy.

The sun inside us, our solar plexus's drive and autonomous authority, asks for our fullest capacity, while the heart expands our intimate gratitude. Someone once told me, "The heart can't break; it's a waterfall." The solar plexus shining beaming rainbow light through prismatic mist carried on the winds pooling in your womb.

The world dictatorial administration had dragons slain, quantifying completely contradictorily to the HeartWomb, breeding discontent and scarcity. Totalitarians feared the transformative power of love and unity's threat to their structures of coveted control. No one needs billions of dollars if they are creating from love.

Imagine how different life would be if all we made and built was fueled by love instead of greed, hatred, or abuse! We'd spread rather than hoard money to help all those who could benefit (without sacrificing any lifestyle, pleasure, or delight).

Global leadership could rule from giving rather than taking, enhancement rather than diminishment, reverence rather than destruction of Earth's beauty and precious people. Sleighing the dragon changes the very systems dominating our world. Harmoniously empowered abundance contributes to the world's fortunate future. Dragons guard this treasure, attempting to help us re-create it through loving communities, collaborations, and collective competency. The courage of the dragon HeartWomb frees us from the dictatorial regime's propaganda, and offers a feminine form of orchestration that feels magikal for us all to live our legendary lives.

The HeartWomb's essence asks, *If you knew you could create anything, free from scarcity and fear, how would you courageously wield your personal power—your voice, choices, and actions?*

Riding the dragon embraces our inner child's magikal resilience and fearless curiosity. Keeping mystical realms alive, guarding our core essence and potential, honoring this connection, we restore our authenticity, unlocking an inspired, purposeful, enchanted life.

The most profound magik we wield is rediscovered within our fearless childlike spirit and dragon's heartful wisdom. The legacies of undaunted dragon-sleighing heroes remind us of the cost and *pricelessness* of truth.

MICROWITCHUALS

Journal Prompts

What do you love and cherish about yourself and your life?
What do you reject about yourself?
Where are you inadequately serving or nourishing yourselves or Earth?
Does your business hurt or harm you, others, or the planet?
How can you maintain balance between work and play?
Can you recognize the conscious vibration of scarcity?
Where are you operating from unworthiness?
How does feeling not good enough influence your spending?

Raging Release Ritual

This experience is meant to heal, not retraumatize you. Before beginning, find a resource to connect with if you get overwhelmed. This can be the blue sky, a part of your body, a particular tree, an element, or anything that will help ground and regulate you. I use the mantra "I am in the hand of the Goddess" or the Nature around me. (You can simplify this process by beating pillows to heavy metal at home, but I prefer the full protocol in Nature.)

Find a place in Nature (or your backyard) where you're not harming anything, such as a patch of empty dirt or a gravel path.

Gather Goldilocks rage wands (sticks). Not too long, short, thick, or thin—*just right* for a good thrashing.

Travel through all the moments you were mad, felt unsafe, or were unable to express or protect yourself. Reflect on everything you've held back or suppressed—words, tears, anger, or other emotions.

Swing your arms and shake to get energy moving while taking deep breaths and releasing a sound on the exhale.

Set a timer for a minimum of 20 minutes. (Or keep going until you can't continue.)

Begin in slow motion, like you're moving through honey, tracking the sensations that arise in your body as you swing the stick without any force. This helps regulate your nervous system for the movements that will come. Let yourself feel what your body presents.

Then state your feelings out loud activating your voice. "Right now I feel frustrated . . . scared . . . stuck!" Whatever is true.

Whenever you feel that deeper emotional well, grab your wands and go to town!

* Whether you are a painter, dancer, singer, or speaker, use art to forge and bring a dragon to life. Knit a winged beanie, carve a sculpture, make a headdress, draw, or create a talisman as a tangible representation.

* **Badass Morning Affirmations:** Looking into your eyes in the mirror, give yourself an Oscar-winning pep talk to fire you all the way up.

    "Today, I embrace my inner dragon [choose your archetype and adjectives]. I am bold, wise, and fearless. I am free to live my authentic truth." Set a powerful tone, reinforcing strength and sovereignty, and ask periodically, "What would a dragon/queen/hero do?" Let your actions be guided by those frequencies.

* **Sleigh Your Dragon:** Consider a challenge you've been avoiding. A hard conversation, sharing something vulnerable online, asking for help and support, or setting a boundary for your fortress. Handle it. Use all your tools; be the heroic archetype of your fairy tale and complete the loop so it's not draining your life force.

"SLEIGHING" THE DRAGON ☾

* **Embody the Dragon:** Close your eyes and invoke the image of yourself upon, or transforming into, a dragon. Feel your powerful freedom soaring high above wondrous landscapes—enchanted forests, towering mountains, or vast seas. Zoom out from challenges with graceful acceptance.

  Let her take your vessel for a whirl, moving united with sweeping wings or feline and serpentine languidity. Be moved by how you would dance *for* her. Not imitating, but allowing that presence and essence to infuse your movements, liberating you from limiting constraints.

  Or visualize the dragon merging with you in stillness. How would your body feel being 10 (or 100) times bigger? Sense the weight of your wings. What do your scales look like? How would she move?

* **Evening Tale of Transformation:** End your day journaling in the style of a mythic tale where you as, or with, your dragon overcome obstacles on a legendary quest. How did you face the day's challenges? Draw parallels to mystic dragons who guard treasures, navigate mazes, or seek enlightenment. Reinforce your triumph and connect everyday experiences to epic adventure.

* The purest dragon ritual is just showing up fully as your fiercest, most fabulous self. Share a truth you've held back. Wear that outfit you've been saving for the "perfect" occasion that never comes. Ask your partner to fulfill a fantasy with you!

  Invoke dragons, asking them to show themselves. Journal about your gratitude for your life's treasured abundance, courageous expression, and greatest wisdom you would impart upon another. Weaving dragons into daily routines inspires new sleighing habits. Their transformative power, elemental mastery, wisdom, and sacred treasure guarding reconnect us with the unbridled imagination and boldness of childhood too often tamed by adult reservations and fears.

CHAPTER 7

The Circle of Life

Sweet, ripe, juicy peach, or crisp watermelon drips down your hands. A gentle breeze caresses your face as you slurp the lusciousness of summer from Earth's splendid nectars. Giggling, your friends make the same mess of their delicacies. Sticky and satisfied, you jump into cool, clear rivers or lakes, basking in endless golden sunlight that never seems to fade. Days stretch into balmy twilights, stars shimmer in the indigo sky, and fire crackles as you roast hot dogs or marshmallows, gathered to sing or share blessings of this season.

Then fiery leaves astound you. Fallen, they crunch beneath your feet, the air carrying its first whispers of refreshing chill, as you walk arm in arm in warm companionship with someone you love. Comforting, spiced scents waft with satisfying anticipation in every breath. A hearty stew greets you in your cozy home, with apple pie for dessert. There's merriment to be made. Gratefully, you gather around the hearth, feeling the shifting seasonal preparation to brave the coming storms.

Waking to a winter wonderland covered in billowing blankets of white snow, sunlight glistens off sparkling stars of crystalline perfection. The world beneath becomes a mystery, the preeminent purity like a dream of endless possibilities. Stoking the fire, a warm mug in your hands, you're enchanted by perfect stillness. Bundle up. Your breath fogs while wandering this mysterious landscape, familiar yet entirely new. The frozen fractals have come to stay.

Build a snowman, carve angels in pristine powder, and throw snowballs squealing with delight. Gather garlands of evergreen boughs and deck your halls; get engrossed in books, rousing games, or quiet contemplation as festive tree lights glow. Holiday music wraps you in a nostalgic embrace.

Out the window everything is green again, reborn. Your blossoming unfurls like the yawning wildflowers' blooming open faces. Every verdant shade of vibrant neons and deep-emerald greens glisten in the luminescent sunlight as sprouts and saplings emerge. The fragrant blooms waft their perfume through your nose, scenting aliveness, sun, and rain's petrichor.

Bunnies nibble your garden groves; birds tend nests of soft blue shells; speckled fawns on spindly legs follow gentle mothers, curious but cautious. Your hands are soft from sowing seeds of new life in the soil. Crunching on crisp veggies, paradisiacal picnics are reminiscent of all we share.

Every season's perfect days offer their own sacred frequency and unique magik. Whether you're amid the granite boulders of the Rocky Mountains or the Seychelles, the jungles of the Amazon or Polynesia, each diverse Earthly landscape's breathgiving beauty travels through some or all the seasons with initiatory invitations.

Which is your favorite? Which offers you the most medicine? Which do you resist or rush through on your way to the next?

Color magik comes from subconscious, primordial divination from Nature's communication. Flora and fauna inspire crafts, altars, and decoration for hearth and home. Halls are decked with boughs of holly because its bold red berries bravely show fruit through blizzarding snow! Change your internal landscape or honor the external one by invoking specific energies in altars, candles, clothing, and home decor (more about this in "The Imperial Secrets of Adornment").

Colors evoke emotion; they mirror and influence your inner states and intentions like seasons. Harness them to mold your environment to reflect your dreams and desires. They're crafting your day-to-day experience whether you realize it or not!

Deliberately invoke autumn's transformative pulse by infusing your wardrobe with fiery hues. Red with gold jewelry for reaping abundance from your efforts, appreciating gifts, and harvesting energy any time of year. Donning indigo blue and white conjures winter's restorative, contemplative, tranquil stillness, summoning inner peace and replenishment.

OH HOLY NIGHT

Originally, seasonal celebrations centered around available food. For example, pumpkin pie and jack-o'-lanterns come from harvest staples that sustained indigenous Americans through many long winters. They last for months when nothing else grows! Chickens slow or stop laying eggs altogether in winter but restart in spring, when rabbits give birth also. Our Easter *bunnies* are another natural resurrection. Ostara (Easter's Celtic origin) was the Goddess of Fertility.

Diamonds, the most "valuable" resources, made by the densest pressure, are mined from deep within the earth, just as hardship often teaches us. Persephone, the queen of the underworld, descends into darkness for half the year, taking vibrant life with her into hibernation. She emerges only when the blossoms are ready to be reborn, carrying the fragrant flowers upon her robes as she rises from Earthly depths, charioting the wisdom gleaned from treasures lurking in shadow. Perfectly illustrating Nature's magik and how we too can become our most beautifully magikal selves from facing desolate darkness.

Significant solar or lunar alignment rests at the heart of nearly every holiday, or holy day. Religions shifted the narratives to transform ancient Earthly stories into dogmatic allegory, but our observances remain deeply rooted in Nature's cycles. After Winter Solstice (December 20 or 21), the sun's *re*birth became the "Son's" birth and Christmas. Easter originally celebrated Earth in Springtime, resurrecting its verdant life and fertility rather than His return.

Prior to the Gregorian calendar, we synchronized our souls and internal clocks with the Universe's grand timepiece. Adaptation to standardized schedules intentionally discouraged Earth-based living.

There are 13 moon cycles (month = moon cycle) per year, directly correlated with menstruation. Thirteen was a sacred number, holy to the Goddess, hence becoming associated with negativity and superstition. Jesus selected his 12 apostles, equivalent to the zodiac signs, 13 including him, like the original cycles of the moon. With 13 months instead of 12, each would begin on Monday and end Sunday, have 28 days, exactly four weeks rather than four-ish, and be perfectly aligned with the moon. Just sayin'.

Our months' names display dissonant, mislabeled prefixes. Beginning haphazardly, the year ends with incorrect structure. March, the zodiacal and Lunar New Year, was originally the first month named for Mars, the God of war, marching forward! Summer's unrelated words are namesakes. Juno is Rome's Mother Goddess. July and August, honoring Julius and Augustus Caesar, were added arbitrarily. Then, *Sept-* means "7" but is the 9th month, *Oct-* means "8" but is 10th, *Nov-* is "9" but is 11th, and *Dec-* means "10" but is 12th, further proving our sense of time and holy days are entirely made up.

Our ancestors lived by Nature's cycles, not indiscriminate numerical assignments. Golden Age civilizations were often built on energetic ley lines, and many sacred sites precisely orient to the sun's celestial magik, testifying the importance of alignment.

Strip malls or subdivisions (named after the original terrain like Cedar Creek Estates or Rolling River Commons) were built atop precious wetlands and wildlife habitats as well as ancient worship sites, often destroyed in the name of the church. Rich traditional celebrations of planetary evolution harmonized our species with our environment, honoring our place here and cherishing ourselves as extensions of Her.

WHEEL OF TIME

Each High Holy pagan Sabbat—Samhain, Yule, Imbolc, Ostara, Beltane (or Bealtaine), Litha, Lughnasadh, and Mabon—has seasonal significance. Observing and maintaining customary roots or reinterpreting heritage practices connects us with *timeless* traditions, renews spiritual connection, and reminds us Earth is what really matters. We exchange consumerist and consumptive cultural programming for Her holiness.

Samhain, Día de Muertos, and our modern interpretation of Halloween is the only cross quarter day celebration that withstood the test of time and honors fallen spirits like autumn leaves. More than hallmark holidays, they're meaningful portents. Yule became Christmas, celebrating the birth of the Son instead of the returning Sun. Ostara has become Easter, the resurrection of Jesus rather than the verdant Earth. The rest have been lost to antiquity in most of the modern world.

From Stonehenge to the Great Pyramids, we've revered and received undeniable energy and solar power that endures today, infiltrating our cellular memory and reconnecting us to ancient Goddess worshipping lineages. Her presence vibrates in every atmospheric particle where people have prayed to and ritualized Her for millennia.

Our original calendar, the Wheel of the Year, marks changes through solstices, equinoxes, and their midpoints, offering contemplation, appreciation, reflection, and greater intimacy with Nature's cycles.

Solstices and Equinoxes

Yule—Winter Solstice: height of winter, shortest day, longest night
    Acknowledge darkness's lessons learned from hardship.
    Assess the year, gathering insight in quiet, reflective stillness.
    Celebrate solar rebirth, symbolizing hope and light returning.
    Evergreens inspire enduring life amid the cold.
    Colors: white, silver, brown, blue, red, and green mirroring the muted landscape

Litha—Summer Solstice: height of summer, longest day, shortest night
    Embody exuberant playfulness, festivities, adventure, and life's fullness.
    Celebrate life's abundant fruitfulness with bonfires, feasts, and fun.

Shine your brilliant, radiant light.
Be powerful and bold.
Revel in penultimate celestial energy.
Colors: sky blue, sunny gold, bright colors, neons, and rich emerald green

Ostara—Spring Equinox: balance between night and day returns
Herald rebirth and renewal—as Nature awakens, so do we.
Celebrate the joy of surviving desolation.
Use insights gained to initiate new projects and relationships.
Honor resilience and embarkation.
See where flowers bloom and vibrant new life abounds.
Colors: pastels of spring—green, pink, yellow, and purple

Mabon—Autumn Equinox: balance between day and night's darkness
Winter's impetus begins the cycle.
Reap final fruits and harvests.
Reflect with gratitude on labors and lessons learned.
Prepare for the coming cold.
Descend into the crepuscular half of the year.
Use your wisdom to help plan for the next chapter.
Colors: orange, gold, yellow, and red

Cross Quarters

Between solstices and equinoxes, many cultures have traditions and integral festivities with their own unique characteristics and celebrations.

Imbolc, Maha Shivaratri, and Chinese (Lunar) New Year: February 1-ish
Imbolc translates to "in the belly."
Earth stirs before awakening, preparing to burst into fertile spring.
Welcome new purification and anticipation energy with candles and spring cleaning.

Adorn your altars with white and green, representing possibility and growth.

Traditional foods include dairy and seeds.

Beltaine: May 1-ish

A celebration of fertility and abundance.

Herald summer's arrival with maypoles and merry revelry for life and love.

Traditionally, jumping over bonfires ensured fecundity for fields and females.

Decorate your altars with bright flowers, greens, pinks, and yellows reflecting life's lushness.

Foods are decadent and plentiful, such as sweets and dairy, symbolizing richness.

Lammas—Lughnasadh: August 1-ish

The first of three harvest festivals, associated with grain.

Share summer's abundance with thanks.

Bake bread from the first grain harvests.

Feasts salute communal success.

Gold, yellow, and green represent sunlight and vegetation.

Altars have grain stalks, bread, and the first harvest's seasonal produce.

Samhain: "Witch's new year"

The harvest's completion—winter is coming.

A liminal time for divination when the veil to the otherworld is thinnest.

Warm days give way to cold.

Complete inventory to ensure everything is arranged for dark days ahead.

Honor ancestors and loved ones, acknowledging death is part of life.

Like orchards' fallen fruit, we compost leaves to feed our future.

Adorn your altars with black, orange, autumn leaves and sustenance offerings to the deceased.

There are global festivities on sacred sites and temples you can visit to honor Nature's holy days in conscious community. If you can travel, go. Now. When my financial status was "scarcity," I used Google Flights as divination to see where the cheapest tickets would take me. Goddess guided where I was meant to go. The exact destinations I desired reached all-time-low prices, and I bought them immediately to hit the road.

These festivities provide unique opportunities to reflect on corresponding spiritual transitions within us and the world, easily aligning our lives with celestial cycles and Nature's melody.

Harnessing their energies fosters growth, gratitude, and endless evolution. Figure out what magik means to you and where you love to pray. Get yourself on an airplane to a place you've always dreamed of seeing. If money feels scary, take the leap, work the system, get a credit card or loan. Seek out the healing of these holy sanctuaries, and the miracles you'll find will astound you.

FOLLOW THE FEELING

We know the world's wonders, but our most personally wondrous places may be different. Many of my most mystical moments arose simply from listening to aliveness around me. I highly recommend adventuring to a place that beckons you to celebrate ancient seasonal rituals. In 2019, for instance, Bealtaine, the midpoint between Spring Equinox and Summer Solstice, on Ireland's Hill of Uisneach changed my life. Five years later, I brought back an incredible group of international women to experience it with me, and it had the same effect.

On that first trip, we cast winter's troubles into blazing bonfires upon grassy glens, welcoming summer's fruitful fertility sweetened by warm sun with endless merriment. I approached the massive luminous effigy, mentally gathering all the old ways I was ready to release, and thrust them with all my might into the inferno. (I went on to witness my most massive transformations the following season.)

Then, after exploring the Hill of Tara, another of Ireland's oldest and most sacred sites, we took a spin through the gift shop. All my friends got perfect power pieces. Our guide, Ryan, who wore a jaguar tooth, found a jaguar wand.

"I wish there was a dragon wand," I said beneath my breath. I settled for a beautifully carved but clearly overpriced apple wand, and we headed out for our adventure.

As we were leaving, a man looked at me and said in a lilting Irish accent, "Dat's a nice wand yeh've got there."

"Oh! Thanks. I just got it."

"Pretty expensive, huh?"

"Definitely, I actually wanted—"

"You're meant to have this one." My jaw dropped, and my eyes instantly welled with tears. He'd interrupted me to present a smooth wand with a *dragon* etched on it.

Awestruck and dumbfounded, I managed to say, "How. . . ?"

"I can *see* ye are a dragon. This is meant for you. The runes say, 'I am the dragon.'"

Both giggling and crying in disbelief, I gave him a hug. He went on to bestow many more gifts upon us from fallen wood in the small remaining sacred grove in the enchanted fairy glen.

"You gave me a miracle today and have been so generous," I told him. "Can we do anything to repay your kindness?"

"Well, I've been having trouble with me eyes. I really need them for my carving craft, y'see. I love it so much, but it's getting worse and worse."

My friends and I gathered our hands around his eyes and envisioned them healing.

Five years later, when I returned for Bealtaine, I went back to Hill of Tara. As soon as we pulled up, I felt it in my bones.

He's going to be the first person I see.

I got out of my car slowly, offerings in hand, turned to the right, and there he was. Parked in exactly the same place, in the same car full of treasures, Celtic and pagan statuaries and deities, the Santa Claus of Tara.

I walked up to him immediately. "Hi, Tommy, do you remember me? You gave me a w—"

"Of course, the dragon witch. I saw ye then as I see ye now."

Unbelievable.

"How are your eyes?"

"I never had a problem with them since that day."

I still get teary just thinking about it.

Tommy came and shared a Celtic and Norse pagan ritual at my retreat. Moments with him are some of the most special in my life.

HOPE FROM MY HOMELAND

Though they get some of the least recognition, Holy American lands and monuments of antiquity, destroyed only in the last few hundred years, are some of the most remarkably magnificent ancient worship sites.

The Black Hills, considered the center of the world and birthplace of their people, is the holiest location for Lakota Sioux. Treaty after treaty was signed promising their sacred vision questing site, the mythic home of their Gods, where life originated in their legends, would never be disturbed, mined, or settled upon. Today, we call this place Mount Rushmore, carved with faces of the very immigrants who desecrated the local way of life.

The Yurok and Hupa villages in Northern California where I grew up are over 15,000 years old. The Bearpaw at the corner of the Natinnoh (Trinity) River has been a sacred feminine site for millennia. Their legends, lore, knowledge, and traditions are intrinsically linked to the abundant landscape. Those who tended them for eons are kept on a reservation nearby.

After a float one afternoon, my dad and I hauled his drift boat back onto the trailer. A man came down to collect our fee, and within moments we were deep in conversation. He was a Hupa elder, Enker McCovey, who helped organize their dances and powwows. I had so many questions.

He handed me a delicate, white bald eagle nape feather. I gasped, touched by this gift; eagle feathers are more than auspicious for First Nations people.

"Have you been to our pyramid?" he said. "Come."

THE CIRCLE OF LIFE 🌙

On a majestic plateau overlooking the winding emerald-green water, granite stones covered in ochre lichens and pillowy mosses rose into a perfectly pyramidic peak—a massive rock slab shaped like a bearpaw at its base. The giant palm with toes and claws appears like Bear Gods left gargantuan footprints millions of years ago.

"Our women pray and vision quest here," Enker told us. "Thousands of years we've lived on this riverside hill."

The moment *my* paws touched her giant earthen pads, lightning bolts zinged up my legs. An undeniably radiant, healing vibration emanated from beneath madrone and manzanita. I fell to my knees and laid down, like I have in so many places with Her. The mama bear, their Goddess, revered in many original civilizations for her fierce protectiveness, playful sweetness, and permission to rest. I felt her viscerally welcome me home into Her embrace.

"Do you have dragons?" I asked.

"Of course—our last dragon lived here through the 1700s," he replied matter-of-factly.

Instantly, I burst into tears. He had answered so plainly, nonchalantly, without thinking I was crazy—his kind, knowing gaze reminded me how sane it is to be "insane" by modern standards. It was one of the most validating, affirming, and emotional interactions I've ever had—with a man who had been a stranger only moments before.

"Your daughter is very special," he told my dad.

A Nature lover, but not much of an esotericist, my dad is no stranger to psychedelic journeys. But they were less about actual spiritual liberation of consciousness and more about getting high. He stood wide-eyed, scratching his head, never having witnessed anything like this:

1. with me

2. with someone stone cold sober, and

3. with a "stranger" intimately connected and tuned in to me and what I believed that he'd brushed off as a little too kooky.

Unsure of his role or what to do, he replied, "Yeah . . . I guess she is . . ."

I've had the blessed pleasure of sitting and listening to Enker's stories since that day. During COVID he shared the Hupa prophecy about a mental plague among people who have lost their way, their connection to Nature. Red, white, black, and yellow tribal serpents would divide, battling for freedom on Earth.

I'll remember till my dying day his response when I asked why stories of indigenous people portray them as violent savages. Were the people I love learning about in these pristine places actually warring like white history claims?

He looked me dead in the face and said slowly, "We did not have killing before the white man came. We are a forgiving people. All life is sacred. We thank the salmon and deer we eat, the water we drink. Look around this valley, this river, abundance everywhere. Fish, fruit, animals, there is plenty for everyone, more than enough to share. That's what we did. We worked *tribally*, but our ways were stolen from us when settlers arrived. *They* showed *us* what savagery really means."

That bear pyramid, a sacred site few people know, is one of the most magikal. But Hupa women aren't supposed to pray there anymore, though you can still feel their magik in the brilliant, generous indigenous man striving to return peaceful celebration and tradition home to his land.

Enker is a rare, true leader. He never holds a grudge for what was done to his place and people; he focuses on repairing as much damage as possible, reconnecting to ancient ways. He doesn't blame me for my race or ancestors' actions; he encourages my appreciating the true power of those sacred lands and their original inhabitants.

I understand why many elders act differently though. It's despicable, abhorrent what was done to them. Stolen children, outlawed languages and dances, sovereign people killed en masse like in the witch hunts for oppressors to maintain absolute control, spreading vicious diseases. It's heartbreaking what people in pain do to others. But Enker gives me hope. There is a path forward for humanity, hand in hand.

MIRROR, MIRROR

Seasons whisper secrets—our bodies mirror Earth's orbit through brilliance, growth, decay, and darkness. Each breath rustles Her winds through your lungs' leaves.

We're easily convinced of our unworthiness—imagine how air feels being polluted by exhaust, carbon, chemicals, and its generative sources (forests and oceans, the most beautiful and precious parts of Earthly life) destroyed en masse every day. What if we're "only using 10 percent of our brains" because the other 90 percent has been vehemently polluted? We're desensitized from fighting for Her, forced into ignorant, obedient subservience with only prescribed ritual.

Trees and lungs look alike because She created them to give *and* receive air. Yet we clearcut our planetary lungs, blindly denying their blessing of our *most vital* sustenance. We must lift the veil to innovate new solutions for thriving and surviving.

A redwood study injected them with chemicals like adrenaline to omit hibernation and increase growth. Within one year, millennia--old trees decayed and died from foregoing mandatory rest. We should not be shamed or punished for rest; it is an imperative part of becoming. Winter's heart demands restoration, reset, shedding the past, accepting decay and stillness, preparing for spring's rebirth. Pushing and forcing productivity is unnatural. Whether each morning, or upon lengthy introspection, we need to pause, turn inward, and do deep, reflective work assessing inventory.

As green seedlings sprout, we too are urged to emerge reborn, pollinated with new ideas and projects, fertilizing plans with action.

Summer brings the pinnacle of fruitfulness, thriving celebration for the bounty of labor, revelry, and warm shining. Abundant fields and friendships enjoy vibrant, long days. We have it so easy, but modern conveniences disconnect us from each season's genuine invitations when a tree's shade was your only respite from summer heat! Why seek cool, crystalline waters if we're air-conditioned all day or have a cold plunge? Which is *all* our ancestors had for bathing.

Autumn's arrival encourages deeper community connection, gatherings to share bountiful harvests, give thanks, and nourish each other. Gratefully reflect on your hard work and blessings, preparing for the cycle to begin anew.

Our hormones, style, expression, and nervous systems ebb and flow in internal and external rhythms. Understanding our bodies' needs for rest, hydration, expansion, blooming, and death mirrors Nature's alchemy. One day we need more restoration; another day, we need spring's inspired growth. "Four seasons in one day" doesn't just refer to weather—it captures the dynamic, ever-shifting spirit of *our* nature closely woven with Earth's larger terrestrial tapestry. We require the same things She does. Be inspired by and learn resilience from Her.

Seeds are thrust down into dark soil, emerging satiated by water and coaxed by light, unafraid of winter's barrenness, excited by spring's rebirth, blossoming as summer's bounty, and appreciating autumn's harvest. The living elements can always remind us of sacred reverence for life. We consecrate space with attention to living land beneath our feet.

OUR DEVELOPMENTAL NATURE

Just as Earth goes through Her cycles and seasons, so do our lives. Women's hormonal cycles rise and fall each month, men's each day. As with everything else throughout these pages, we are reflected in Nature.

Our inner rhythms relate to those all around us.

Childhood: Spring

A time of rapid growth and burgeoning potential. Like Earth's fresh awakening bursts of verdant enthusiasm, children experience significant cognitive and physical growth, exploration, and learning. New experience plants seeds for future blossoming.

Moon Cycle: Follicular

* Mirroring spring's rebirth and new beginnings
* Estrogen levels rise, energy increases, like life in Nature
* Physical and mental energy reach their pinnacle, inspiring motivation for projects and activities

Puberty-Prime: Summer

This season governs young adulthood to maturity. It's the longest season for those who have kids later and shortest for those who have them young, so appreciate it while you can! Enjoy Earth's fullest fruiting, flowering, and abundant energy. Significant physical, or biological, transformation; secondary sexual characteristics and menstruation mark major milestones. Vital and exuberant, inner summer awakens rich potential for personal discovery, growth, pollination, and how we celebrate life in connection with others. We find careers and cultivate the sprouting shoots growing in our gardens.

Moon Cycle: Ovulation

* Expression and outward energy
* Vibrant, communicative, sexually scintillated, and connected to desires—paralleling summer's full bloom

Adult/Parenthood: Autumn

During this season, we're raising and nurturing children, or creative babies like books and businesses, and harvesting accumulated knowledge, experiences, and wisdom. Cultivating family, legacy, and personal and communal relationships reaps earlier efforts' rewards as Earth yields her bounty before winter. Inventory what's required to fully enjoy it, grasping opportunities for fulfilling

 WITCHUAL

renewal. Reparenting our inner children synthesizes spring and summer's insight into maturity's "innerstanding."

Moon Cycle: Luteal
- ✳ Harvesting insights from this cycle
- ✳ Finalizing tasks prior to hibernation and hermitude
- ✳ Set yourself up for successful rejuvenation
- ✳ Autumn prepares Earth for winter; prepare for restful retreat

Elderhood: Winter

It's a time to be introspective and conserve energy. Waste no time on people-pleasing—we do only what serves and allows us to serve better. Menopause or comparably significant shifts may happen. Business, busyness, and outward growth become retired contentment and stability. Essential as winter for land restoration, transformative reflection is crucial for passing on special gifts to future generations or descendants. Spend quality time appreciating all we've done, taking it slow and easy.

Moon Cycle: Menstruation
- ✳ We have less energy—during winter's rest and introspection, our bodies shed stardust (losing iron), releasing the uterine lining that our wombs expend so much energy to uphold.
- ✳ Get more sleep and sustenance
- ✳ Be easy, reflect, meditate, and focus on nourishing renewal

My internal seasons have been virtually opposite since celebrating Christmas of 2018 in Australia with the beautiful family of my dear friend Liana. Christmas was Summer Solstice rather than Yule, a gloriously sunny day with golden ribbons and playful rituals.

For several years after, I stayed seasonally Southern Hemispheric. Vividly summery when the world was hibernating, I was energized, social, filled with inspired ideas, manifested like crazy and adventured extensively. During actual summer, especially around my birthday, I turned inward, desiring solitude for personal reassessment, hyperfocused healing, working, or writing. A classic Gemini polar-opposite role reversal.

Seasonally synchronizing your lifestyle internally and externally teaches through change and challenge, engendering authentic connection with Nature. Gather around a campfire or home hearth, lay beneath stars, or let your imagination roam free as you watch the clouds. Befriending Nature—being Her student, collaborator, and devotee—turns environmental interaction into a celebration. You're *supposed to* have rejuvenating periods! Can Her mirror of your existential rhythms let you give yourself a break?

Listen to physical and emotional needs; avoid overjustifying against societal expectations; rest during personal winter; play with summer's activity. Big rebirths are followed by periods of instability as you find your footing. Be patient while you get springtime pep back in your step. Honor *your personal cycle*. Sometimes everything feels perfectly ripe for the picking; other moments ask you to pause.

How can you savor life's recent outcomes or achievements? Relish your rewards!

Ask yourself:

What season am I currently experiencing?

Does where I live support it? Does it encourage and inspire my goals and aspirations? What is it teaching me?

Do its rhythms align with how I feel best nourished? Could another place do so better? (You don't always need to sync with Nature; sometimes you're ensconced in metaphorical winter during summer's peak or bursting with possibility in winter.)

What's falling away to be alchemized while the rest of the world is bustling?

Identify which energy you need to enhance or reduce. Traversing all four seasons in a day requests empowered decisions for restful breaks or afternoon naps when exhausted. Brief "winter" pauses can rejuvenate your energy for a burst of spring or summer later. Accepting all phases of life's inherent cycle—barren and quiet winters, vibrant and luscious summers alike—persevering through lows without judgment, befriending Nature, enlivens your true nature.

BALANCE IN BUSINESS

Earth is ready for an intuitive business cadence that regenerates *holistic* capitalism, rewriting unconscious, outdated consumption forced upon us by captains of industry's overvalued operations.

A new, sustainable business season is on the horizon where cultural imperative requires corporations to be *of* service rather than just *offering* services. Women-run companies get funded because synarchal leadership wins, and accounting for menstruation optimizes productivity. We collaborate, pollinating flowers and planting trees to bear fruit for all.

Conscious leadership is the most important aspect any entrepreneur can devote themselves to. Like soil, societal systems can luckily be remediated too. This is my team, company, and community goal. Products and services were originally designed to *help* customers, not harm, poison, control, or take advantage of them. We can maintain this intention—reconstructing and restructuring our relationship with wealth, consumption, and synergy.

My entrepreneurial journey began with conscious commitment to my growth. Foundational to everything I offered others rather than hustling and working when trauma arose beckoning me to internal transformation, I stopped taking clients until I had integrated what needed healing.

Sales and marketing gurus would never encourage this. "Keep launching!" "You can still be productive!" "You don't have to stop to go!"

Actually, that's denying winter's dormancy—injecting ourselves with adrenaline and forcing burnout. It won't last. Like redwoods, *we* can't sustain that way. Yet this is the constant drive behind the multibillion-dollar coaching industry and business in general. I refused to follow the flock and guide others while reassessing and re-creating a more powerful version of myself that was still wobbling on new legs. I wanted to feel solid and stable, having actualized the new lessons and behavior. To share wisdom, not just knowledge. I'm here to be *that* witch.

Giving your business winter doesn't require off-grid, six month sabbaticals for flourishing spring rebirth. Though taking one after completing this manuscript was necessary for me. Some conscious leaders have daily winter, taking meetings only from 12 to 5 P.M. Mornings are personal time; evenings are with family, no excuses. Others have nonnegotiable three-day weekends. Some take solo thinking days focused on dreaming and visioning what's coming in the next week, quarter, or year.

When I go on retreats, personal development immersions, or write books, I have two options:

1. Batch content, prepare e-mails, posts, and communication ahead of time so I can "keep up" while checking out, *or*

2. Dismiss the algorithm and trust my audience expects me to lead by example and permit myself to take breaks. They want me to be the best version of myself and know I'll be a better teacher on the other side.

The first time I did this with a large account, my winter in summer meant not posting for *six months*. Gasp! The horror?! The month inspiration returned, one cold and snowy December, I was on fire and gained 35,000 followers in 30 days. I effortlessly shared the magik that had fully gestated until the perfect moment to be reborn.

WHEN IT FITS JUST RIGHT

Interacting with each season's liquid emanation—creeks, fog, thunderstorms, and pillowy clouds—offers particular insights to empower the blood running through us. Silent snowfall, rushing rivers and waterfalls, or refreshing rain showers invite *us* to flow through different iterations too, just as varying terrains, flora, fauna, fruits, fungi, and flowers are vivid environmental soul expressions.

Oceans are for healing; mountains are for rising; forests are for growing; waters are for flowing. Individual ecosystems impact us.

Which do you need most? What does yours offer?

Growing up on Northern California's rugged redwood coast, I rarely saw extreme temperatures or snow. Before drastic climate change, it rained *constantly*. Now, though it's much drier and warmer, you still barely break a sweat. I *thrive* in moderate climates—not too hot, not too cold, just right. I love being outside but dislike sweltering, cloying humidity or the inability to expose my skin to sun and Earth. Warm autumn days with chill, cozy nights? Yes. Florida's intense sticky heat or Michigan's biting winter chill? No.

Yet I have fallen in love with snowcapped mountains' harsh "barren" months in Montana and Colorado. Something about majestic, expansive views and glistening snow is magnificent for me. Building fires every morning with enough sun for naked Earth meditations? Bless! I couldn't follow my Californian compulsion to be outside all day and was incredibly productive (book deadlines certainly helped). May brought endless green, whispering aspen leaves, and heat that drove me into refreshing alpine streams. Paradise.

Different environments can be immensely instructive. Illuminating each place's rhythm educates us to work with our own. Quiet stillness speaks volumes, revealing unique lessons only dormancy can teach. People from places where summers are unbearably hot get accustomed to AC, not playing in Nature. Others from cold places avoid winter, seeking islands or tropical rainforests.

How did your childhood environment affect what's best for you?

SEASONAL SANCTUARIES

The traditional seasonal perspective doesn't have to dictate your personal rhythm. Winter's dormancy can be invigorating. I'm *always* productively engaged in work. I let myself do *nothing* during my monthly winter menstruation, but tend toward activity that whole Earthly season. Conversely, summer typically suggests leisurely vacations, more social engagement, and parties. I'm hibernating in dedicated spiritual growth work.

Listening and responding authentically to our needs creates the ritual basis for a personal ethos that reflects who you truly are. Embrace what seasons mean for you, allowing activities—or lack thereof—to fulfill what genuinely serves your evolution. For example, if playing the cello or reading by firelight rejuvenates you, your stool or couch can be an altar, if time upon it is intentional.

Relationships, like Nature, undergo seasons—periods of closeness, connections, and clear understanding can shift into confusing, opaque distance. It's a natural ebb and flow. However, some connections defy this pattern, maintaining a perennial summer of harmony and lightness with rare conflicts.

It's okay to pull away from your family to practice being who you want to be until you're rooted and grounded with unshakeable truth in the face of their opinions. Romantically, internal seasons can affect partnership dynamics, so we must know how to tend to the world around us *and* within us.

Venture out on autumn days, letting trees demonstrate how important it is to let things fall away. Our tears and prayers are leaves letting go to become rich black-gold soil that feeds our future for generations. That's why we call it "fall."

It is *perfectly*, and literally, *natural* to retreat, hibernate, and reflect internally. We are currently navigating an unprecedented societal season as a species. Technology's rapid evolution and social media have transformed our communication and connection, thrusting us into uncharted waters.

Fast-paced, overwhelming expectations for instant replies to messages mean people freak out if you don't respond within minutes.

Only a few years ago, getting in touch was slow; you would leave a message and wait. There was *no* constant contact.

This new era requires adapting and learning to maintain meaningful relationships amid chaotic, limitless distraction and possibility, respecting connection's naturally evolving pace. Nature never rushes, we, too, must pace interactions and expectations, allowing relationships to breathe and flourish in their own time, empowering us to choose what's most significant to honor. If you're uncertain about what to celebrate, turn to solar holy days. Delve into what they summon within and demand *from* you.

From watching weather to holiday decorating, celebrate seasons by witnessing Nature's changes within yourself. Accepting inherent seasons eliminates guilt, shame, and the sense of being wrong—we're aligned with righteousness, cultivating a deep compassion for oneself and all of life. Enhancing this mystical dialogue achieves graceful flow and alignment through inevitable waves of change.

Reverence is the root of true magik. Harness the highest Universal powers; work with the cycles of birth, death, and rebirth. Your life force is sunlight within you. Gravity is the magnetic pull that connects you to the Divine.

We are miracle workers creating heaven on earth, alchemizing human experience. We compost grief to deal with death and rebirth life. Mourn and feel your pain. Put on sad music and move. Write and burn all the things you never said. Build an altar, paint, talk to Earth, pray, or speak to what you've lost.

I'm doing that for Minerva. I sing for her as tears stream down my face. I sing for the time I spent with a man who wasn't right for me.

How can love and beauty fuel your stamina through loss and death?
How do you mourn?
How do you heal?

MICROWITCHUALS

How do you ritually or ceremonially close or complete, or open or inaugurate, a cycle or season? What soothes your spirit in moments of pain? How do you celebrate those of power?

Seasonal Sensory Walk

Connect with the current season. Awaken your senses to surrounding natural transitions.

Choose a dedicated, undisturbed time (golden hour is luxe). Begin walking at a nearby park, forest, or green space that embodies the current season's essence.

Engage your senses individually:

* Observe colors and movement of plants and animals.

* Listen to the crunch of leaves, rustle of wind, or quiet of snow.

* Inhale the air's scent, fragrant with blossoms or crisp with frost.

* Connect texturally with tree bark, cool stones, or warm sunbeams kissing your skin.

* If safe, taste something like a berry or herb; slurp a hanging dewdrop.

Conclude in stillness. Reflect on the season's energy, messages, and invitations for you.

Consciously Release the Past and Set Intentions for the Future

Gather two envelopes, a pen, and two sheets of paper. (*Optional:* Include seasonal symbols or herbs.)

Reflect on the ending season. On a piece of paper, write down lessons you've learned; experiences you've had; and habits, feelings, or situations you're releasing. Place this in one of the envelopes and seal it. (*Optional:* Add a release spell or mantra to the envelope.)

On the second piece of paper, write down your intentions or goals for the new season that's beginning: personal growth, projects to initiate, or qualities you want to develop. Place it in the second envelope.

Add anything to this second envelope that represents the new season's energy (seeds, flower petals for spring, leaves for autumn). Then seal the envelope while visualizing your intentions manifesting. Say, "I open my heart and life to [new beginnings, or any spell that expresses your desires]."

Keep this second envelope in a prominent place where you'll see it often, such as on your altar or pinned to a bulletin board, reminding you of your intentions and physically representing your commitment to growth. (*Optional:* When the season changes again, open the intention envelope, review what you've accomplished or experienced, and prepare for another transition ritual.)

Build a Seasonal Altar

Choose a space you'll see consistently for morning practice or a focal point in your home.

Gather things you already have, elements from Nature like moss, branches, leaves, fruits, and flowers, or go get some secondhand treasures.

Follow your IntuWitchin to arrange and organize, thinking about seasonal colors, waters, and invitations you're honoring or drawing in the frequency of.

Sit before it once you're complete (you can always keep adding) and visualize or journal what this season means for you. Consider changes you'd like to make or goals you'd like to achieve. Leave this on your altar, or write specific affirmations you'll see each time you pass by or sit beside it.

CHAPTER 8

Kitchen Witchery

Warm, cozy kitchens tantalize with tendrils of holiday harvests, festive cakes and cookies, or traditional Sunday roasts wafting through the air. Knead your prayers into sourdough, stir spells with your spoon, or conjure connection in cupcakes, making memories and baking beauty. You can heal your gut, skin, teeth, or bones with magik from the land. Come unlock the original form of magik as we know it: Kitchen Witchery. Since we first captured fire, food roasting over it has drawn us in and brought us together. Kitchen Witchual is ancient, innate, medicinal simplicity.

Have you noticed how people inherently gather in the kitchen at parties? A friend I used to travel with a lot would peek her head in to see me kicked up on countertops, chatting away with someone. "I knew I'd find you in the kitchen, Witch." It's no accident they're almost the same words; the hearth is the heart of any home—where the magik happens. Food and medicine intertwine to heal and nourish us, body and soul.

Though my family had a rollercoaster of emotional challenges, despite our differences, most evenings in my childhood, we gathered for dinner, which was always divine. There weren't many particular practices—after a simple grace of gratitude, we ate together—the ritual to end each night. My parents brought Earth's bounty onto our table. We went to farmers market on Saturdays, shared special treats like jam or duck with neighbors, and bought bulk at our local co-op. "Food is love" was a tangible, classically Italian mantra my whole life.

My dad was a river guide and a hunter. *Preparing* ducks, geese, or pheasants was almost as much a ritual as the chase itself—a spiritual practice of primal nature and original human roots for him. On a stool at the kitchen counter, he'd pluck feathers off beautiful birds our dogs retrieved at breaking dawn in marshy wetlands or fields of grain, butchering them himself for delicious meals. Every time we sat down to eat one of them, he thanked the bird gods for blessing our table.

He learned Kitchen Witchery from the same person I did: his mom, Elva. The only grandparent I grew up with, she was every inch a Kitchen Witch and quite a character. You could feel the love in her pies and at every special holiday dinner. She always had a recipe nearby when baking but relied on kitchen IntuWitchin.

We spent summers and weekends running rivers in rafts or kayaks, cooking freshly caught fish or roasting hot dogs. We expressed sweetness, care, and nurturing in shared meals and were tended to with little treats or remedies that made us feel better. It wasn't fully anti-Western-medicine hippie vibes, but halfway. We still got antibiotics, though I wish we hadn't, but food was part of our medicine too. Mashed bananas for tummy aches, warm olive oil for ear infections, then I took it further in adulthood with apple cider vinegar as my cure-all.

They don't say, "An apple a day keeps the doctor away," for nothing. I've cured strep throat within a day by drinking it straight with cayenne pepper. I'll make pastes with ACV, bentonite clay, hydrogen peroxide, and activated charcoal for poison oak or other skin ailments, or put those same ingredients in a bath to banish a UTI. When I'm sick, I drink them steeped with garlic and lemon. I'm usually better within 24 hours. I've healed so many maladies with deep nourishment, whether love of family or food.

My mom is one of those people who thinks her chefery is nothing special, but she is one of the best cooks I know. Even still, when I try to re-create some of her specialty staples, I fall devastatingly short. I swear this woman has magik fairy dust I just wasn't born with, and I'm a great cook!

When I was 11, she went back to work, and my dad, who had retired early, took over as majority chef again. But no matter who was in charge, you really couldn't go wrong. Olive oil and Meyer lemons, rainbow peppercorns, and big chunky cloves of garlic were all we needed. I could survive on those accoutrements alone. With whole, healthy ingredients, everything was easy and tasted amazing. Everybody wanted to eat at our house because it was the best, hands down.

Investigating my lunch box, friends would ask, "What'd you have for dinner last night?" Unimpressed with daily leftovers, I occasionally rebelled and traded for PB&J's on white bread, which I wasn't allowed to eat at home.

Our food kept us healthy. No sugary cereals, soda, processed, packaged foods or candy except on Halloween or at Grandma's. I have an amazing immune system: I've never had a cavity, braces, glasses, acne, or allergies. From age 7 to 15, I changed from little kid to teenager without visiting the doctor *once*. I remember finally seeing him as puberty was rocking and he was shocked. "Goodness, has it really been this long since I've seen you?"

I shrugged. "I haven't been sick in a while."

Entering the larger world from my small town, seeing people heavily medicated was major culture shock. No one took Ritalin where I grew up, even me, who was hyperactive, intelligent, independent, and outspoken. Naturally, as such an important part of our life, family, love, and health, food became my first professional foray on the spiritual path. I became a chef because I wanted to heal people, and the most magikal life has evolved from that fundamental origin.

ELEMENTAL MAGIK'S ORIGIN

Food is exquisite elemental alchemy, but we've forgotten how easy it is to make healthy food delicious! Soil is the foundational ground upon which we, and our food, grow. Moon phases, seasons, water, and weather all play a role. The precious balance of sunlight, wind, rain, and dirt teaches us about rising from darkness, working collaboratively with our surroundings, surviving and fulfilling our destinies.

We cook with butter, fats, and oils, melting solids into liquids. We eat earth in animal or plant form, all of us filled with water that also boils them. Our saliva enzymes in our stomach digest using the water within. The heat and transformation of fire alters the earth elements. Aromas, scents, and sense of awe we inhale, the air caramelizing and tantalizing us.

We make magik with these elements.

Galas and banquets use food to impress, like the proud culinary expertise of France and Italy. The sensual experience of feasting has become such an enriching part of modern life carried forth in Witchual, enhanced with intention, high vibrational growing practices, and conscious people who provide for us. Gaining higher consciousness improved our meals. For millennia we've salted fish and meat, preserving anything savory and storing salt itself in huge reserves. Minerals contribute another elemental aspect.

We must appreciate the people who tend land, allowing us to thrive, *and* make different choices that ripple through our mental, financial, and spiritual health. It's time to reclaim our sovereignty over these systems. Start small by switching shopping to the farmers market. You don't have to build a full-scale food forest in a weekend, but get inspired by urban farmers who turn backyards into thriving gardens that feed their communities. Begin anywhere in your own food cycle to unravel and discover ways of creating more intention and magik with your sustenance and its sourcing. Do you have a neighbor with chickens or an apple tree? A nearby spring to switch out single-use plastics or a friend who could teach you to make your own sourdough?

If you can feed yourself, you're sovereign. With just you and Nature working together, you don't have to rely on anyone or anything. Instead, you're inviting another layer deeper in relationship with the ultimate teacher, Nature. Learn to work with the plants in how you prepare, grow, or eat them—connect with the elements, forging a bond with the greater forces of creation.

Earth is eternally generative: one plant or tree has millions of seeds and can instantly spring another, rooting right beside its mother. Magik. Our relationship to eating has become unhealthy; we binge in an attempt to feel comfort and safety that is stripped from societal structures. Beyond ancient, it's primordial, instinctual; we've been consuming since we evolved from bacteria. This is why our bodies can go into debilitating stress responses when they feel unsafe from lack of nourishment. Reclaiming our relationship to food—Earth's gift to us, the land's free, abundant resource designed for healing—changes how we function in every way.

The pressing need, burning spiritual desire, and dedicated movement for land-based communities that sustained our species for generations increases every day. Children grow together, responsibility is shared (it takes a village, remember?), food is collaborative, elders are included, and everyone feels held navigating growth's changing complexity. A soothing network of togetherness bolsters success and solace. Permaculture and regenerative agriculture get our hands back in the soil, exposing us to the medicine of mycelial networks and microorganisms.

Becoming a Kitchen Witch is reclaiming autonomy over the pharmaceutical, industrial agriculture and processed food systems. The earth and its reflection in our bodies have been impacted by microplastics, GMOs, and chemical pesticides. We are unhealthy, and our unprecedented disconnection from Nature is wreaking havoc on us.

Kitchen Witchery is a fundamental aspect of our Earthly education. We can rewrite stories and systems through our actions at the hearth. It's as simple as choosing better ingredients or taking time to nourish when we feel "too busy." It's not about singing mantras every time. What and how we learn, where we vote with our resources, and how we collaborate with one another can change the world.

Our food can heal us, hand in hand with spiritual growth. They are two sides of the same coin and are always related.

AS WE GROW

Imagine the first era of elevated consciousness in our species. With food sourcing reliant on luck and good tools, it seems obvious to create ritual and prayer for harvesting and consuming animals. Hunting and gathering were essential cornerstones of our existence. Some Maasai tribes literally drink *only* blood and milk all year. With uncertain access to water, they get most of their hydration from iron-rich blood drained from cows, goats, or antelope.

In Tanzania, I camped with the Hadzabe tribe, whose stories reach back for 50,000 years. On a hunting walk with boys using rudimentary slingshot arrows, I watched a nine-year-old shoot a bird from a tree, fluttering until he grabbed its head and crushed the skull with his teeth.

It was so primal. I found myself a little horrified, but when he returned *strutting* to his mother and the other women with the feathered body strapped to a leather skin on his chest, I snapped out of it. He proudly showed off his victory to the matriarchs with a celebratory shimmy and smile. This skill was once *necessary* for survival—he *should* be proud. It reminded me of the way cats are pleased with themselves when presenting a kill. This is how worthy every catch was of our acknowledgment throughout time.

How many of us even know how to tend to a vegetable patch? I've got a lot of nice houseplants, but I lost my best garden to gophers in 2021 and haven't rebuilt one since. Right at peak ripeness, every day a head of lettuce or bunch of spinach disappeared beneath the ground. In two weeks the whole thing was gone. Carrots, celery, herbs, and flowers—gophers took it all! The rosemary went last. The only things they left were onions, garlic, and shallots. I had no idea that planting their own little patch as an offering protects your raised beds. Win-win for everyone.

Growing food is a lifelong learning journey. Start at whatever pace and place feels best for you. Using your intuition in the kitchen gently shifts the way you eat. At your next meal, feel into what herbs or spices might enhance the flavors; experiment with a new recipe you've never tried. Bless your food before digging in. I am so grateful for the richest, beautiful duck eggs with big runny orange yolks from my farmers. In summer, the ducks are so happy and filled with plump snails who are gorging on the bounty of the season. The eggs taste like they have cheese in them all on their own!

Kitchen Witchery comes alive in even the smallest choices. Simply saying prayers over what your body receives is an essential element. Considering and appreciating the production cycle is an excellent foundation to an incredible ceremony—bless and express gratitude for your food, the hands that grew it, and the land it came from. You can do this with yourself—every day or every once in a while—and with others, at any time. The more consciousness we bring to our consumption, the more magikal and medicinal our food becomes, and the more we bring our desires to life through eating it.

When Matias de Stefano remembered his past lifetimes, the one he felt most connected to was his role leading Earth's Water Guild.

Intrigued, I asked, "What were the other guilds like? What did Earth people do?"

"They knew the cycles of the moon and land, how to grow the food—essentially, the witches. They tended bees, made offerings to fields, and made food into medicine. They say, 'A woman's place is in the kitchen,' because that's where witches brewed their potion remedies. Food, herbs, and plants were all you had to heal you—the original medicine and magik."

He affirmed and confirmed why the kitchen was the impetus to my mission for healing. I was a witch before I even knew it, following my intuition perfectly and synchronistically.

The sacred hearth births medicine, merriment, and nourishment. The kitchen has always been deeply spiritual, of course, as it was women's original role. Wise women in every village brewed roots, stems, and leaves of medicinal plants as panacea elixirs for whatever ailed us. The doctors and pharmacists, healers and wisdom keepers, witches were the ones everyone relied on with plants as our only healing remedies. We knew the cycles of the moon and sun to harvest and brew herbs optimally. Everyone worked together with Earth, in stark contrast to modern stress.

This is why cauldrons have been considered one of the most important tools of witches and their craft for centuries. Before the modern convenience of propane and digital ovens, a cauldron over an open fire cooked the majority of food. That's why every culture has versions of stews and one-pot wonders as commonly favored fare.

The wtch's brew of fairy tale and folklore was prepared by the alchemist in her apothecary, not as a vessel for violence, but of mending and resilience. Today, the cauldron has become more symbolic as a representation of the womb and how we brew the creations we bring to life.

This deep connection to food as medicine has been the work of many lineages. Stregheria—Italian witchcraft—is based in the kitchen. No wonder they're world renowned for their cuisine. You can see Italian grandmas effortlessly whipping up secret remedies with the same knife they use to cook. Their knowledge and skill of potions and remedies have been passed down through generations, each recipe holding the power and wisdom of their ancestors.

Food has been turned, and is being used, against us. Our ancestors ate whole food, because *all* foods were whole foods; that's all they knew or had access to. No one needed to know if it was grass-fed, organic, or non-GMO. Everything, every human, plant, and animal on Earth was grass-fed, organic, and non-GMO until less than a century ago. This is why obesity in humans *and our pets*, who had never eaten garbage additives in their food until today, is such a new and unstudied affliction.

A GLOBAL LANGUAGE

Cultures worldwide have developed unique forms of Kitchen Witchery, each influenced by their local herbal landscapes and spices. North African cuisine is renowned for rich flavors of cumin, coriander, cloves, chilis, fenugreek, and allspice, creating dynamic dishes that have been cherished for thousands of years. Classic culinary specialties carry traditions passed through generations. We once ground all our spices by hand with mortar and pestle. Another great opportunity for casting spells. Modern convenience has stripped intention from our eating habits.

Every Friday, when I lived in Morocco, we had tagines full of fluffy couscous and stewed vegetables. Ethiopians eat sourdough-style, tangy teff pancakes called injera with their hands.

Food teaches us many important lessons, like how important the little things are.

Each member of my family has their own iteration of our infamous Banducci salad. It's a common request at dinner parties, always exclaimed upon with, "Wow, this is the best salad I've ever had," regardless of which one of us threw it together.

I'm heavy on garlic, lemon, and balsamic. My dad on oil and salt. My grandma added parsley, where I thought it should stay a garnish. Now I love just about anything with fresh herbs.

Some things need to take their time. Others are meant to be in and out.

Short ribs want to be low and slow, cooked for eight hours. A good rib-eye wants hot and fast, searing on each side for a matter of minutes before enjoying the dripping juices.

Día de Muertos, the Mexican equivalent to Samhain, the cross-quarter day between autumnal equinox and Winter Solstice, like Halloween was originally. They honor the dead with offerings, altars, and feasting. Special foods like sugar skulls and pan de muerto (bread of the dead) are infused with symbolic ingredients and prepared with deep reverence.

Similarly, lunar moon cakes are an integral part of the Mid-Autumn Festival in Chinese culture, where these delicately crafted cakes symbolize unity and completeness, often shared during the full moon.

Roasting pigs is traditional in various cultures, from Hawaiian luaus to Filipino fiestas. Both groups are descendants of the wayfaring Voyagers who sailed across the Pacific. More than the meal itself, it's about the communal effort and festivities surrounding it. These feasts often mark important life events or seasonal changes.

The three sisters are companion plants that each offer a blessing to the other. In Southern and Midwestern civilizations, corn lifts up the beans, who send nitrogen into the soil for squash, whose big leaves become umbrellas to maintain moisture in the ground. They help each other simply by being themselves.

Dishes that accompany cultural rituals are more than just food; they are deeply embedded in the identity and spiritual fabric of communities. They serve as a bridge to the past, connecting people to their ancestors and the land. Specific grains, holiday traditions, or ecosystems that grow foods nowhere else can, each culinary custom carries a wealth of knowledge, history, and spiritual significance.

Your grandma's specialty food, a homeland delicacy, fills us with wonder when done right. Scents and flavors contain or make memories. In the film *Ratatouille*, the villainous food critic is instantly transported back to his childhood from one bite of the iconic peasant dish the film's named for. Scent is our sense most tied to our brains' memory processing, while taste offers the comfort of nostalgia like nothing else.

Ultimately, the most essential element of Witchual food is seasonal Earth magik, constant in our daily routine and imperative for survival. An opportunity to engage more consciously with the natural world. We find the balance of pleasure and purpose with what we love and what's best for us, like Mother and Father Nature. We can build gorgeous altars using just food, as we'll discuss in the "Imperial Secrets of Adornment." Each particular item brings symbolic significance, adds vitality and vibrance. Pomegranates are like ovaries we can eat and decorate with, becoming her body. We honor our inner children with nostalgic treats and slay the dragon of overconsumption or binge eating when we cook consciously.

Exploring diverse Kitchen Witchery worldwide opens up a realm of possibilities for incorporating ancient wisdom into modern life. Reclaiming our relationship with food recognizes it as a sacred, abundant resource from the land, a deep connection between our culinary practices and spiritual well-being.

OUR PERFECT POTION

Every culture has a morning beverage ritual. I love coffee, but my gut doesn't, and frankly, I don't need it. I have endless natural energy. Some like it black, some with cream and sugar. Others prefer tea (maybe matcha or chai), cacao, or lemon water. A morning potion is age-old for hunters, mothers, and waking centurions standing guard. Whatever our desired feeling or outcome, there's a tonic for it, even an evening glass of milk. No matter what you choose, and how you like it, you start your day with a potion.

I am a morning beverage connoisseur. Sometimes I have three or four: a green collagen booster with herbs, a raw living spirulina water, a coconut cream, peanut butter protein shake, and maybe an Earl Grey tea latte with raw goat milk. I like to get my herbs from Anima Mundi (**animamundiherbals.com**); you can use my code MIA for a discount.

When I'm in the UK, which is quite often for my castle retreats, I drink approximately two-and-a-half cups of tea a day, complying to cultural imperative. But most mornings I love whipping up a thick coconut-cream cacao with rose, vanilla, cardamom, and collagen. This potion has opened hearts in ceremony throughout South and Central America for thousands of years. Sharing it or starting your day with soothing chocolate feels so naughty and fun!

Regardless of its base components, the real power in our morning mugs is the fact that water holds memory. Whatever you're physically infusing into the recipe and alchemy of the ingredients is altered by what you put into it energetically. You can program any water-based beverage with prayers and intentions. Stir in love, joy, happiness, and harmony, opening your heart. Bless the potion as you create it.

Brewing your own tea blends in a French press can create miracles, both from the medicinal benefits of the plants and your belief in their ability to help. Nerve, joint, and tendon healing; digestive soothing; sleep-induction; dream-activation—herbs can do it all. My Chinese medicine doctor, Nadia, makes incredible blends with roots and flowers that work wonders for any ailment! Choose your adventure from our endless plant pharmacopeia, our primordial apothecary of original medicine. Tea can be a ritual, remedy, or luxurious indulgence. Little girls playing tea parties, pouring for everyone in their little cups, is fun *and* one of the oldest rituals on Earth—literally herbs in water.

Connect with a specific desire—you're invoking it with this potion. Love, peace, abundance? Honor the blue lotus petals that grew from the mud beneath lily pads sweetening your dreams. Recognize the beautiful long pods of dried vanilla beans scraped from the sheath into cane alcohol for flavoring your most scrumptious baked goods. Vanilla is universally appealing as a unisex smell that every gender is attracted to, considered one of the ultimate aphrodisiacs. Rose reminds us to stop and enjoy their sweet smell and the beauty of Nature's majesty. Imbibing and ingesting these beautiful beings in beverages can bring so much nourishing nectar to our lives.

Consider how you're consuming your spell:

* Are you rushing, or do you take your time?

* Is that a pattern in your life?

* Are you intentional or not?

* Have you been longing to touch the sacred but feel like it evades you?

* Do you really experience the flavor or just chug it down?

* How else might you benefit from a little more luxurious appreciation?

* Has your body been asking you to slow down?

If you receive your potion as medicine, it can heal and grant you the benefits—you decide.

MISUSE OF MEDICINE

Undeniably, modern medicine can save us in many emergency situations that would have ended our lives in the past. However, outside the ER, it is not designed as healthcare but *sick*care. Instead of prescribing pills derived from petrochemicals for suppressing negative symptoms, we should address their root causes. Let's reseed our inner gardens to grow strong gut microbiomes and digestive systems with the power of the sun inside and above.

When you speak to indigenous tribe members, they often say it was the plants themselves who guided the people in how to make them medicinally. "They told us to dry this one on the full moon, mix these two together this way, and cook that for two weeks . . ." There are many alternative treatments that have been brewed in cauldrons across the globe for millennia. Plant medicines like ayahuasca, whose entheogenic effects and healing benefits are some of the oldest potions known to humankind, and some of the greatest to emerge from Kitchen Witchery.

John D. Rockefeller discovered in the early 20th century that petrochemicals could be used to create medicine. Before this discovery, natural medicine was *all we had*. Once Rockefeller realized he could add chemical compounds into *crude oil* for "medicine," he used his wealth and influence to promote pharmaceutical pills and completely discredited natural medicine worldwide, changing traditional remedies into "quackery" peddled by "snake oil salesman." Sound familiar? It's always the guys pointing fingers!

Reclaiming our sacred relationship with sustenance is imperative, because society is becoming increasingly toxic for us: microplastics and hormones in the water, pollutants in the air, petrochemicals turned to pharmaceuticals, EMFs, and fluorescent light all threaten our wellness. We're getting sicker, and food is the foundation of health—the easiest combatant to global systemic poisons.

Funny how a main pillar of the patriarchy is projecting onto someone else the exact evil they're perpetuating in the world? The origin of gaslighting. Rockefeller's propaganda campaigns led to the widespread use of pharmaceutical drugs, marginalizing the medicine our species has evolved with since the beginning of time. Now, many children are forcibly medicated with antipsychotic prescriptions to quell incredible psychic gifts. Clear visions, prophetic dreams, or the ability to read people's thoughts are unfortunately mislabeled as mental illnesses or even demonic possession.

The loss of natural medicine is part of the Witch Wound, where people have been stripped of their knowledge of how to heal themselves—the most ancient wisdom on Earth. In indigenous traditions, plants are our older brothers and sisters because they have evolved for millions of years on the planet, far longer than us.

We speak to the trees, like Grandmother Willow in *Pocahontas*, the ents in *Lord of the Rings*, and my personal favorite character in *Guardians of the Galaxy*, Groot. I share the same intimate connection with Grandmother Redwoods. I feel the trees I grew up surrounded by singing to and teaching me. Reclaiming this relationship with Nature and the elements, claiming authority as parents of children is crucial. We can learn from kids. They know how to talk to animals and plant spirits who can teach us the best way to use their herbal powers for supplementing and enhancing our natural gifts. It's never too late to form this relationship, which can begin with each morning's pick-me-up potion, or those we choose late at night.

POISON OR POTION?

Personally, I don't resonate with alcohol; it tastes like drinking poison for a reason. I love its usefulness in creating tinctures and tonics, a vessel *for medicine*. But for me, it never feels beneficial to ingest straight.

Many people take alcohol too far. It's mis- or overused, becoming poison if not consumed mindfully. The real poison isn't as much in the substances as in the demons residing inside your mind that make you reach for something to rely on or numb them, which I find alcohol to be a doorway to. Its influence has harmed many families, perhaps more so than any other substance due to its accessibility.

People who succumb to substance abuse justify it. While most common afflictions like alcoholism, cocaine, or heroin addiction were originally derived from plants, those spirits know it's *your* responsibility to use *them* responsibly. Today, it's the chemical compounds that really harm us, like methamphetamines, pharmaceutical pills, and addictive additives in cigarettes. The "powers" that be know these compounds are *lethal*, yet do nothing to halt their production, advertising propaganda to keep us hooked.

Cannabis is a holy plant, revered for thousands of years. There are mantras to it, rituals that honor its spirit. Mushrooms are an incredible balancing act between poison and antidote. Some can kill you instantly, yet turkey tail and chaga are proven to cure cancer. Lion's mane benefits the brain, and psilocybin changes neural pathways, fostering new connections and insights.

The history of these plants spans tens of thousands of years. Mushrooms are not quite human, not quite animal, not quite plant, but have influenced us profoundly. They exist beneath us, under the ground, everywhere. Santa Claus and his flying reindeer originate from Scandinavian mushroom shamans whose presents (the red and white *Amanita muscaria* toadstools) popped up beneath the evergreen trees to offer their gifts of wisdom. Mushrooms can send their spores as high as *50 miles* into the sky to interact with the atmosphere and generate rain clouds to bring hydration down upon the exact places where they live. Now that's the kind of weather modification I can get down with. Some people believe mushrooms are an alien technology planted here to awaken humanity; they are so much older than humanity itself. A constant, global reminder of the medicine of the earth, showcasing both the supernatural and natural powers of plants and herbs. Mushrooms, in many ways, symbolize the reach and inherent power of Nature.

SACREDLY SUSTAINABLE CONSUMPTION

Training his breath to swim deep beneath the surface, my dad would pluck meaty, gorgeous, abalone from underwater ocean coves. He dug them from their colorful shells, sliced them up, then drenched them in lemon, butter, and garlic. Abalone are sweet and tender, with incredibly nutritious meat. Considered one of Japan's utmost delicacies, in America, we know them best for the gorgeous rainbow homes we use as sacred objects for smudging herbs and precious gifts.

We hunted, foraged, and gathered since the beginning of time, until the modern introduction of factory farming, massive food and plastic waste, overconsumption, and genetic modification. Returning to ancient practices teaches us food and plants are not only medicine but also a way to express kindness and gratitude to the earth.

In 2022, the stress of growing my business and shrinking in my relationship wreaked havoc on my gut. Over the course of three months, my digestive issues became severe. Every holistic nutritionist, regenerative medicine doctor, and naturopath said the same thing: "You have to start eating meat."

As this would be a significant departure from my vegetarian diet of more than 10 years (with infrequent exceptions of ethically sourced wild game), I refused. "That's not who I am; I don't support that industry. My lifestyle, values, and brand all oppose carnivory."

I tried going gluten-free, eliminated anything processed. Nothing helped.

"Can I just eat chicken?" (I'm not a huge fan of chickens.)

"No, you need minerals from red meat."

Eventually, despite my reluctance, I heeded their advice. My body's needs were paramount; ignoring them was no longer an option. So I approached the shift with intention and respect for the animals I would consume.

GO BIG OR GO HOME

Naturally, as an extremist, I couldn't casually start buying beef at the grocery store. I wanted to be truly connected to the process of life offering itself for my own. So when I was invited to a bison harvest in southern Wyoming, I knew this was the only way I'd feel right about returning to omnivory.

It was one of the most emotional and sacred rituals of my life.

The buffalo, Gus, was running with his herd when he was taken down with one shot. We surrounded him, petting his massive head and curly beard; touching his hooves, wet nose, and beautiful face. We sang, danced, drummed, placed tobacco prayers upon him, made offerings, and shed tears—many in my case. It was a moving experience for all of us, including our Lakota brothers who had done it several times before. I cried so much and so hard. "Primal" barely begins to describe it. We took a life; it was cellularly sentimental.

An angelic little boy wrapped his arms around me as I wept. Precious tenderness in the future of masculinity I will remember forever.

Not a bit went to waste. Gus's hide was stripped; his organs and blood were collected and freeze-dried for supplements. We sliced his meat to eat fresh, passed the heart among us still pulsing with electromagnetic life force, and everyone took a bite. The liver and testicles were some of the most delicious meat I'd ever tasted.

Touched by how good it was raw, my body had never responded to sustenance like this before. Despite that, I still couldn't help but wish Gus would have stayed alive, running with his herd. So I praised his offering to my healing. His bones became the richest, most gelatinous broth, and we each brought home 50 pounds of steaks. Gus fed us for almost a year.

After viscerally understanding the process, I felt like I'd been initiated into carnivory in integrity. Participating in such a sacred ritual helped me empirically understand the profound relationship we have with animals, who offer their lives for our sustenance.

When I eat meat, I think about the creature itself, offering a blessing for its sacrifice. The first burgers we ate from Gus were orgasmic, the richest we'd ever tasted, and we spoke his name in thanks every time we consumed him.

I still don't order meat from restaurants in the United States, but now I feel in right relationship with eating it. I only buy from specific, regenerative farmers who are healing their land with livestock grazing. These animals are tended to with care and love, killed quickly and humanely, and live as they are meant to. It feels wonderful to give my money to people who aren't just taking the easy route but doing it right!

If more meat eaters got more intimately involved in the process, our farming and agriculture industry would evolve rapidly. We could change the world in a matter of years. Cows can fertilize the land, move freely, heal and remediate soil. By returning to ways we lived for eons, eating what roamed nearby rather than what was placed on Styrofoam from across oceans, we would be healthier mentally, physically, and spiritually.

Experiment with new ways of relating to your food; start now! What can you store to make it last by preserving, pickling, or canning?

Explore ways to make what you have into something else. Banana peels make great indoor plant fertilizer. Watermelon rinds are hydrating treats for horses. Avocado pits make gorgeous pink dye. When you have lemon peels, dry them, turn them into tea or lemon juice, or add to a spice blend. I highly recommend checking out Alessandro Vitale, also known as "Spicy Moustache" (@spicymoustache on Instagram), for inspiration—this low-waste, urban gardener is full of bright ideas!

You can still use your food as medicine if you buy it in plastic packages at the grocery store; it just takes a little more effort to recharge the vital energy that's been lost. Going plastic-free, talking to the butcher, and doing it right is a whole other ballgame, but it's so commendable! Try your best; support and meet local farmers, get to know them, talk to them, go to farmers market every week. Do the absolute best you can. Pay the farmer now, instead of the doctor later.

Kitchen Witchery isn't just culinary cooking expertise; it's about reclaiming our ancient relationship with food, Nature, and the elements. The true magik lies beyond flavors in the love, intention, and consciousness with which it is prepared and consumed.

This is an opportunity to honor the plants, animals, and mineral elements that sustain us, recognizing the sacredness in every meal. By mindfully approaching cooking with gratitude and reverence, we transform the act of eating into a deeply nourishing and healing experience, for ourselves and the planet.

With open hearts, grateful spirits, and a commitment to healing ourselves and the world around us, let us remember the wisdom of our ancestors. When we know the plants as our older brothers and sisters, we can reclaim the power of food as medicine and magik. Embracing this daily ritual cultivates a deep respect for the food we eat, the hands that grow it, and the beings who sacrifice so we may survive.

MICROWITCHUALS

* Join a local Community Supported Agriculture (CSA) garden or farm share. You can volunteer and get your hands dirty or just pick up bountiful harvests.

* Go to the farmers market! Try whipping up a new meal with all the goodies you find. Support *local* growers who are doing it right. Meet the people who grow native, seasonal sustenance. Or, at the grocery store, thank the farmers and land who grow everything. Envision the places nonnative foods originated. Tropical islands' mango trees, Maine forests of blueberries. Research where your favorite foods grow.

- ✳ Eat only what naturally grows each season.

- ✳ Use your Kitchen IntuWitchin for flavoring or charge up your spices with this MicroWitchual:

  - **Sacred Spice Offering:** Select a variety of your favorite spices and herbs, focusing on what resonates.

    Place each spice in a small bowl or dish; arrange in a circle or other meaningful shape. Light a candle in the center.

    Offer a silent prayer as you charge them with intentions for abundance, health, or whatever feels true, and then enjoy the magik they bring to your cooking.

  - **Elemental Blessings:** Before cooking, acknowledge the elements you're using: earth, air, fire, and water.

    As you prepare each ingredient, reflect on its elemental expression. For example, earth for vegetables, air for aromas, fire as heat, and water for liquids.

    Thank the elements for their gifts and ask for their continued support.

☾

Simply thanking your food and farmers is the easiest and most accessible Kitchen Witchual. You can also create special feasts or celebratory meals for holy days or at new and full moons.

- ✳ **The Moonlit Harvest:** On the night of a full moon, prepare a simple meal using ingredients from your garden or local farmers market.

  Set a table outdoors under the light of the moon or near a window where the moonlight can shine in.

As you eat, reflect on your journey last month—and the food's—from seed to harvest to plate.

Offer prayers to the moon, connecting with the archetype of the zodiac it's in. Give gratitude for its guidance through the darkness and for the abundance of the earth.

Leave a small portion of the meal on a spirit plate as an offering to the earth, returning the nutrients to the soil as a symbol of reciprocity and appreciation.

CHAPTER 9

The Imperial Secrets of Adornment

You *are* the temple, the sacred site, the altar—your home houses your body, as your body houses your spirit. Decorative devotion to the deity within illustrates your soul's essence upon your skin. Worship warm weather or send a chill down the spine; strut your stuff looking as majestic as you feel. In your sanctuary, take the command position, and greet every opportunity like the leader you were born to be.

Adornment is the art of us—tattoos, jewelry, makeup, hair, car, wall and bedding colors, visionary paintings—whatever awakens or honors our Divinity. Priestesses used to meditatively paint themselves, akin to South Pacific shamanic tattooing—we have always utilized embellishment to bless and celebrate who we are. Mindfully, appreciatively, and passionately adorning our inner temple confidently motivates us to strengthen and honor our bodies, the most necessary element of our destiny.

Your life is what your eyes and senses experience as your dreams, made manifest. So, how do you want it to look? To feel? Who do you want to be? We have been programmed to be less, not to shine, not to stand out. But when you surround yourself with what you desire to be, you're reminded of who you are, even in moments you forget. Your best self looks back at you, convincing you to blaze brilliantly every day.

Adornment is about more than just looking good. It's about expressing love to yourself, affirming and broadcasting your true essence, from your morning coffee mug to living room crystals and outfit for farmers market. You're creating a life that mirrors your inner beauty and values, turning everyday objects and choices into expressions of your deepest self. Adornment isn't merely aesthetic; it's a way of living that embraces and enhances your magikal journey.

The original altar, your body, is the primordial personal and seasonal transformation site. Once you understand its language, you can take its precisely requested pathway—whether more creative expression, or quiet contemplation. Building an altar in the home of your spirit extends your inner state to transform the world around you.

Invoke summer sexiness with vibrant colors to capture its exhilarating energy. Build altars aligned with current or seasonal weather; sweltering sunny days reflecting aspirations and aiding manifestation's fruitfulness. Honor prevailing elements, incorporating items that draw in what you seek—safety, growth, or resilience, serving as focal points for prayer and petition.

When you travel or are out and about, remember you are the temple, the walking altar. I always bring a little something with me, like a dragon figurine or a crystal for my nightstand. Sometimes, I make an altar out of my jewelry, arranging it in a mandala wherever I am. This small act of creating sacred space, even on the go, helps maintain connection to adornment, no matter where I am, carrying a piece of home, of my magikal self everywhere. Reminding me I am always my sacred space.

Embrace your authenticity through every aspect of your life, from the car you drive to the clothes you wear to the rituals you perform. Align your external expression with your inner essence, and watch the world around you transform. By honoring your body, creating intentionally, and dressing for the life you want, every day becomes a Witchual of self-love.

And remember . . .

That which you have adorned for is already yours.

THE ICONIC WITCH'S HAT

In 2019, two months before I moved into the first house I Feng Shuied, I met a gorgeous Persian priestess at Burning Man. She wore a big, black, felted witch's hat—I immediately knew we were supposed to be friends. We ventured out the final night, and I was utterly entranced, trailing the conical lighthouse as we wove through massive crowds. That iconic spire served as a beacon guiding me through seas of people. I was totally sober, but it was psychedelic, as if many other lifetimes converged in that moment.

She was a masterful seductress, enchantress, Goddess, and queen. She crowned me with this twilight halo, and the moment I put it on felt like being reunited with a missing piece of me. Like my antenna had been reattached. This was the adornment I'd searched for all my life.

"This is the magician's hat I've been waiting for."

We did a photo shoot in the dust that final dusk before venturing out, and those were the first viral posts on my account. When I returned to regularly scheduled programming of me living my life, nobody gave a shit. It didn't matter how cool the background, pose, or location was—from that moment on, the people had spoken.

"No witch hat? Not interested."

I was bamboozled. "Wow. Okay, people like it as much as I do."

I'd earned my hat. It felt so deeply right and true for me, like I was whole. I started feeling naked without it, and I wore it pretty much everywhere—grocery stores, events, airplanes. I became "the girl with the witch hat."

Everywhere I went I got asked, "You're that witch girl on Instagram?"

It me.

People resonated with it because, unlike those shown in the media, I was a friendly, intelligent, pretty witch. Wearing this notorious symbol of evil took a lot of courage, and that bravery inspired people. My own bold reclamation was a statement to the magik so many were missing. Professor Minerva McGonagall got to wear it in *Harry Potter*, but she's the only non-villain we've ever seen rocking one. All of a sudden there I was, like young Minerva channeling her wise, mystical vibe. People loved it.

Within a few months, COVID shut the world down, and I wanted to help. A friend suggested I do a "How to Be a Modern Witch" course. She said, "People want to learn about their magik. They're waking up. They want to know about your practice."

Thus, Witch School was born, which hit six figures in its first 90 days. I looked back over the last few years, even 10 months before, when I'd been living hand to mouth. Every big client I signed, it was like the money disappeared instantly. A few years prior I had none at all and spent the last dollar in my bank account over and over again. Everything had changed, seemingly all of a sudden.

Which inspired me to do a course using spiritual healing, balancing masculine and feminine energies and utilizing Feng Shui to help people manifest money magikally—aptly named "Witchy Rich."

Now, many thousands of people have been through those programs, accessing magik and abundance in their lives. With ritual, ceremony, interpersonal alchemy, and awareness of how the world communicates its messages and we can respond in kind, my entire world transformed. This chapter was one of the most pivotal parts of that journey. Of course, I did a *lot* of rituals, healing, new-moon intention setting, and endless spiritual growth work to support it. But home and personal adornment are two of the least-discussed manifestation methods that have brought me the most magikal blessings.

No perfectly synchronistic person showing up with an opportunity, shared wisdom, or place to stay in a foreign country happened in a cubicle, building someone else's dream. That's why I know we don't have to do what everyone else tells us we're supposed to, following the typical nine-to-five slog. I didn't learn any of these things doing what society expected. My IntuWitchin led me every step of the way. The only hard part is actually listening once you learn how.

Once you're willing to believe that voice is actually trying to help and show you where you're meant to go, be, and do, nothing can stop you. The magik of these Imperial Secrets of Adornment brought me to where I am and allowed life to reflect so much magik back to me. I know it will be the same for you.

CURATING YOUR CLOSET: ILLUSTRATING IDENTITY

When choosing your outfit each morning, what words capture the essence you're going for? Some days I want to feel "magikal" or "witchy" alternating between more formal and mature Professor McGonagall looks, whimsical Fairy Godmother vibes, and sexier *The Craft* or *Practical Magic* kind of witches. Other days I want to embody more queenly regality or my tantric Goddess. Declaring your identity can be dynamic, changing to influence or reflect how you feel.

Knowing when to introduce new pieces to your wardrobe and when to let others go is a constant ebb and flow. We all have sentimental items, those that make us feel our best, and others we hide behind. Consider the intention behind your clothes. How do they make you feel? I cherish cozy cashmere sweaters I've picked up secondhand, for instance. Some are hoodies that might not be the height of fashion, but they're snuggly, keep me toasty and comfortable, and are my staples for airplane travel and throughout winter.

When it comes to fabrics, there are too many words that are just euphemisms for plastic: nylon, polyester, vinyl, rayon, viscose, Spandex, Lycra, elastane, acrylic, polypropylene, Gore-Tex, and fleece (which was originally from animals but no longer), among others. They are made from petrochemicals (yes, fossil fuels, aka *oil again*, yuck), and are one of the main contributors to destruction of our physical health and that of Earth. These materials disrupt our entire endocrine and hormonal system; put microplastics in the water, soil, and our skin; and can be easily exchanged for natural fabrics like cotton, linen, hemp, bamboo, wool, and peace silk.

Traditionally, silk is made by silkworms spinning their delicate threads in Mulberry bushes then being boiled alive in their cocoons before they become spectacularly beautiful moths. They're not worms. Would we treat them differently if we called them caterpillars? Moths are just nocturnal butterflies. It takes *412 pounds of cocoons* to create less than two pounds of silk fiber we use in clothing. It's heartbreaking. Thank Goddess now there is a fabric called peace silk that allows the moths to fully mature before harvesting, then using their cast-off cocoon rather than boiling them alive. Now, even rose petals can be turned into a silken fabric.

This is the same reason I buy only vintage fur. Animals were tortured, often electrified, to strip them of their pelts. Buying new fur contributes to the gross domestic product of the industry and communicates to those companies to continue their atrocious practices. But secondhand honors those animals, continuing their use for warmth, and supports a small, sustainable business. The beauty of Nature brings ancient art into the modern day, and it is up to us to respectfully and sustainably empower our choices to stand up for what's right *and* be who we really are.

While writing *Witchual,* I mended some cashmere sweatpants myself, which I've generally taken to the tailor. The time, money, and energy I saved *paled* in comparison to my sense of accomplishment. My grandma would have swelled with pride that I remembered her basic sewing lessons.

"Wow! I did it!" I was so impressed by a task that would likely have been several hours of my weekly routine not long ago. Endless generations' survival before *hot water, central heating, and Gore-Tex boots* seems unfathomable! Imagine having to shear your sheep, spin your yarn, knit your cloth, *and* sew your sweaters, just to exist!

Bringing these ways of life home is a sustainable, familial bonding experience.

Make finding clothes that truly reflect you a Witchual. Set out on a Sunday to visit thrift stores or antique markets. Find pieces that make your wardrobe feel like an expression of your authentic essence. Think of it as finding a costume for the character you want to play in the movie of your life—your You-niform.

SHOPPING AND SWAPPING

I try to get rid of one thing for every new (to me) item I bring in from my favorite vintage shops. When shopping online, especially secondhand, it can be unpredictable. That's why one of my absolute favorite wardrobe-refreshing activities is a clothing swap. It's a fun, sustainable way to rejuvenate your style and play dress-up with your friends. I've found some of my all-time most beloved pieces in my collection from my girls' castoffs. One woman's trash is another's treasure!

A beautiful cycle of renewal—what's outdated or overused to one person becomes an exciting addition to another. I've seen incredible transformations where items I've grown tired of find new life with a friend, and vice versa. Hosting a clothing swap isn't just about updating your wardrobe; it's about exchanging energies and stories, making each piece more special. I'll get things tailored to fit me even better, and especially if they were free from a swap; it's such a small price to pay for perfection!

As you can tell, I'm beyond passionate about secondhand adornment. I furnished my entire 6,500-square-foot house from flea markets and consignment apps. It was no small feat, but it made me feel so accomplished and of service to my holy mother. More on this momentarily.

When you're shopping, rather than trying to fill an emotional void of validation within, contemplate your intention. Will they be the kind of shorts you climb Kilimanjaro in? Is this a dress you'd wear on the first date with the man of your dreams?

Glamour magik isn't just about dressing for the life you want; it's about embodying the life you're stepping into. Every piece of clothing can be a declaration of your intentions and desires.

Our spiritual work reinforces our belief in ourselves. Adornment helps you convince your mind to believe in yourself. This potent physical manifestation of self-acceptance and confidence beams love and magikal presence into the world. See your true self reflected back at you every time you look in the mirror, reinforcing your personal and spiritual growth. It's hard to speak down to a Viking warrior or an Egyptian queen. That's how simple makeup, jewelry, face painting, hairstyles, and wardrobe can be spells all on their own.

WEARING YOUR MAGIC

Growing up, I never saw wild, fully expressed, happy-go-lucky witches! They only existed in my books. I had to become one. I made my motto, "If I wouldn't wear it at Burning Man, I'm not wearing it at all." Cloaks, capes, my witch hat, or crowns instantly invigorate my spirit and make me feel like myself when I see my reflection. Radical self-expression, in which I dress each multidimensional and prismatic facet of my spirit, is a highlight of my life.

Playing the character you want to play, in the story of your life and sanctuary of your home, is so much more fun and feels so much better than conforming to societal expectations!

What could you wear today to feel like the heroine in your legendary life?

I've got mountain pants, but I still wear velvet capes traipsing through mud, because that's what happens in my magikal life. That's who I've chosen to be and the adornment accompanies me throughout.

As the house holds the life you live, the clothes hold the body living it. Let your wardrobe communicate the kind of life you want to lead and show you the reflection of the person who is living it in the mirror. Thrifting is a fantastic way to act it till you attract it and be it till you become it.

The witch hat and my cloaks do that for me. I feel like who I truly am when I wear them—no hiding, no mask. They're not costumes, they're outfits. It's not about the clothes making the person, it's about giving yourself permission to be the person you were destined to be and expressing the power inside you on the outside.

As red velvet floats behind me tromping across misty moors, I am transported to my days in the highlands, living my *Outlander* lifetime. (Anyone else?) I put on a corset and billowing skirt, and I'm a French noble in my chateau, or a Fairy Godmother granting wishes. I've been playing dress-up to *"make believe"* since I was old enough to put clothes on. Why stop now?

As I've said, our imagination is one of the most important factors in creating our reality. So when we look at ourselves in the mirror and see not a costume, but our true nature, it helps us embody that authentic version of ourselves even more. It *makes* us *believe* we are capable of being these empowered, magikal versions of our highest selves. Because we are.

RITUAL ADORNMENT

What transforms dressing into a ritual isn't just the clothes you wear but the presence beneath the process. Whether it's getting ready for an outing, doing each other's hair and makeup, or dressing up for a teaching session or presentation, the act of adorning yourself can be transformative. It's not just about looking good; it's about feeling powerful, confident, and inspired in your identity. When you dress with intention, you're not just preparing for an event; you're invoking the energy you want to carry and project, turning every moment you step out into a reaffirmation of your strength and magik.

Whether you're running errands or meeting friends, adornment shapes your interactions profoundly because it illustrates your inner world externally. Once, on my way to a party, dressed extravagantly in lingerie with a flowing skirt, an ornate orchid flower crown and thigh-high boots, I cast an invisibility spell on myself. I walked into a grocery store and despite my striking appearance, I moved through utterly unseen, with people looking right through me—it was uncanny.

As I paraded down the aisles without a second glance my way, I thought to myself, *Holy shit, the spell is working!* My shift in certainty broke the spell *immediately*, and all of a sudden, three different people complimented my regalia.

The power of dressing your true nature is transformative, especially in social settings. I've met some of my most cherished friends while unapologetically embracing my witchy self with lacy black dresses, my witch hat, and not a stitch of makeup. Our connections blossom naturally, perhaps unexpectedly, rooted in authentic expression.

Get all dressed up and go be yourself somewhere. Whether it's a movie theatre or local café, let your essence shine. If you don't have the gear, visit your local thrift shop and find something that feels inspiring. Sometimes just stepping out as your most authentic self can be transformative.

GLAMOR MAGIK: HISTORICAL, MYSTICAL ALLURE

Glamour magik, a practice steeped in mystique and allure, has been a fascinating aspect of witchcraft and esoteric traditions throughout history. Its roots can be traced back to the ancient world, where magicians and sorcerers used illusions and mesmerization to alter perceptions and bend reality to their will. The term *glamour* originated from Scottish *gramarye*, which referred to magikal enchantments and the art of casting spells that made the ordinary appear extraordinary.

Historically, glamour magik was often seen as a form of deception or trickery, used to disguise, bewitch, or enchant. With beauty bloggers using makeup to become completely different people, you can certainly see why. In medieval times, it was believed that witches and wizards used glamour to change their appearance or make themselves invisible. This mystical art was not only about altering how one was seen but also about influencing the beholder's eyes and mind, making it a powerful tool for manipulation and seduction.

As the centuries progressed, glamour conceptually evolved, particularly with the rising romantic movement and burgeoning worlds of 20th century fashion and cinema. Here, glamour took on a more visible and accessible form. Hollywood actresses and public figures harnessed its power to captivate audiences, not through spells, but through the artful combination of attire, adornment, and attitude.

I have found real glamour isn't about what you project onto someone else, but what you believe to be true. At a festival, I cast glamour over a cooler full of precious mocktails. There was so much alcohol everywhere; my friends and I wanted our refreshing, sparkly beverages, but they weren't allowed through the gates.

We carried the cooler in, and a security guard called out, "You can't bring that in here!"

"It's empty!" I yelled back and kept walking without skipping a beat. He didn't say another word and just waved us past.

I believed I was going to be back at our glamping site sipping my restorative tonics without any issues, and made it so. Sure, you could call it lying, but I wasn't hurting anyone; I just transmitted my belief of the outcome onto my external reality to make it real.

Such instances show that your certainty can indeed manipulate reality, but it's crucial to remember we should never use glamour magik to influence other people directly. This is a key ethical boundary, much like the makeup dilemma, where too often it becomes a mask we hide behind.

The true spell of glamour magik is in the authenticity of our expression, the authority it offers us, and the intent behind it.

At Meow Wolf in Denver, I encountered someone who epitomized this principle. She had her head shaved except for two tiny tufts gelled into bright red horns, paired with wild white contacts that left only the pupils visible. Her studded goth outfit made her look like a ninja imprisoned in space. Her look screamed, "This is who I am," and it was absolutely liberating.

That's the true glamour magik—shedding our societal masks and reveling in our authentic selves, remembering who you really are and embodying something greater. Taking care of your body with food and physical activity applies internal glamour. Are you nourishing yourself from the inside out? Practicing yoga, dancing, playing, swimming, or lifting weights? Aligning your physical self with the life you want to live? True beauty starts as an inside job, radiating outward.

Some of my most fabulous friends are garden queens, rocking adorable farmer outfits. They are so genuinely themselves, it's ridiculous—in the best way. To me, they are like forest gnomes, and I adore seeing them in their element.

When we exude this comfort with being ourselves, it radiates out into our environment like an agreement with reality.

Adornment, whether within ourselves, our homes, or gardens, is about bringing our natural essence to life and remaining faithful to it, shedding any contradictions to this authenticity. What we are meant to be loyal to is our genuine self-expression—anything else has to go. This is the heart of true adornment: not the clothes we wear, but the authentic spirit we bring to every aspect of our lives.

THE VEHICLE OF YOUR SOUL

Similar to your home, the way your body is the vehicle for your spirit, your car is the vehicle of your body. Transportation is an extension of you, carrying your body around town.

At the beginning of 2020, a Range Rover was my dream car, a symbol I'd made it. After much deliberation, I finally got one. Two weeks later, COVID hit, and that overpriced grocery grabber sat in the driveway for months, only used once a week to restock the fridge.

It felt ridiculous, and I realized it didn't truly represent who I am. It had terrible gas mileage, was more about projecting power, and I was constantly worried about scratching it. Just an all-around inefficient vehicle for me. You can take the girl out of the country, but you can't take the country out of the girl, so I got a truck.

I immediately felt so much more at home in it. She reflects who I am—outdoorsy, sexy, and powerful. I got out of her on a hike one day, and this man said, "Well there's nothing more American than a hot broad in a full-sized pickup truck." I laughed hysterically. I love how people get out of my way, I can make my own biodiesel from old fry oil, and I can help out whenever my friends need to move. Each car upgrade brought me closer to a vehicle that truly mirrored my essence.

My first truck was black on black, but since the Range Rover was in my name, we put the truck in my ex's (big mistake). When we split, he kept her. I called the dealership and got an upgrade sight unseen, but when I went to drive her off the lot, I realized the nicer bells and whistles came with chrome trim. It wasn't what I wanted, but I'd already signed the paperwork. On our first drive, I got out and looked at the chrome around the windows with a little frustration, grumbling to myself that this was more like a grandpa truck. I swear, she side-eyed me and said, "Bitch, I'm the Silver Lining!"

Relating to life with animism really makes everything around you come alive. Now, of course, that is her name, Silver Lining.

Think about how your car represents who you are. I'm physically petite; having a big rig energetically expresses externally the way I feel on the inside. It's never what anyone expects me to drive, but it's the best I've ever felt while doing so. I notice my ego behind the wheel of a luxury vehicle. We're so programmed to be concerned with status, I can feel my head inflating. But I was in a friends' Fiat once, and I just felt constricted. It was too tiny for my spirit, while she loves being able to zip in and out of any parking spot. Like everything else we've discussed, what's right for you?

ANCIENT ADORNMENT

The Imperial Secrets of Adornment were once closely guarded, spoken in hushed whispers in kings', priestesses', and oracles' chambers. They exert influence and transform the macrocosm with our microcosm, or vice versa. Empires worldwide used colors, textiles, tapestries, natural materials, and clothing to signify status or higher Divine order. The Zhou dynasty, China's longest ruling hereditary monarchy, maintained power for 790 years using Feng Shui, aligning elemental energetic frequencies for specific intentions. Knowing Earth reflected heaven, and all of Nature was interconnected, they subjugated knowledge that could empower civilians.

Drawing from China's dynastic Imperial Secrets kept hidden from "commoners," along with practices from Greece and India, finally, this wisdom has been disseminated for our benefit. Energy is manipulated with specific shapes, structural, and architectural elements. These include Roman columns, stupas, and pyramids (all intentionally symbolic shapes), as well as images, strategic furniture placement, and physical additions—water, fountains, flowers, or crystals.

Combining the Law of Correspondence, Feng Shui, color, and sympathy magik (something used to represent another), the Imperial Secrets of Adornment physically display purposeful prayers upon or around us, harmonizing our homes with our hopes. Golden hues communicate radiant abundance, seeds, or fruits, sweetness, growth, possibility, and bounty.

Elevating our choices and expression into powerful tools of worship and acknowledgment optimizes spiritual alignment in temples, harvests bounty in gardens, and commands power in throne rooms.

It influentially proclaims, "This is who I am, what I desire, and what I am here to create!"

I have decorated homes to manifest partnership, prosperity, and wild dreams, and to hold enriching, safe experiences for my community to feel accepted, supported, and inspired. Create whatever you wish. Life is our reality's canvas, and we are the artists. Make yours a masterpiece.

Most importantly, beyond material possessions, adornment is an opportunity to honor our communion with Nature, the ultimate secret humanity has largely forgotten. Tending to our inner forests, meadows, and waterfalls is profoundly transformative. You wouldn't dump all your trash into a crystal-clear stream—you would jump in gleefully or sit peacefully. The more conscientious of my waste, earthly impact, and footprint I am, the more life rewards me.

Nature's gifts are cornerstones of ritual adornment. Receiving an eagle or macaw feather is one of the highest blessings in indigenous North and South American traditions, respectively, symbolizing utmost respect and a deep connection to spirit. I have been blessed with both *by the sacred creatures themselves* and always find special displays for them. We use crystals, shells, hides, rattles, drums, and feathers as more than decorative tokens; they invoke and evoke spiritual presence.

How many bougie homes these days are minimalist white with massive crystals and plants everywhere? The loss of architectural character and craftsmanship in naked goddesses with cascading cornucopias of pomegranates and floral crown moldings is one of the great tragedies of modernity. I wish Gothic spires and heavenly scenes were still seen everywhere. But some people prefer a cold atmosphere, unknowingly using winter's barren and mysterious purity. They have to bring some Nature magik in to make it feel livable.

ELEMENTAL MAPPING

Taoist Feng Shui's principle elemental pillars, and some examples I used to invoke them, are:

- Earth: stability, knowledge, relationships, health, and wellness
    Crystals, an apothecary, and landscape photographs or paintings

- Wood: growth, birth, vitality, strength, family, and lineage
    Natural fibers (peace silk, cotton, flax or linen), antique wooden furniture, plants

- Water: spirituality, flow, and career
    Fountains, waterfall or river photos, reflective or mirrored surfaces

- Fire: passion, wealth, and fame
    Candles, red light, salt lamps, clean mantle altars

- Metal: beauty, efficiency, organization, and analysis
    Gold frames, statuary, etched brass coffee tables

Devise dream decor DIY projects with a Pinterest board. Whichever area you desire to enhance should become the central focus, and the rest will create balanced support. Wallpaper or a single painted surface brings a room to life. Images or the presence of water invite new opportunities. Red ignites passion and abundance.

My friend Dakota architected my temple bed chamber by narrowing down my top three images, asking, "What's your favorite part of each?"

"Colors, dangling vines, wood with draping fabric."

A regal lace and silk chiffon canopy drapes across curly willow branches representing rebirth, flexibility, and vitality. An altar itself, my bed's custom crystal-grid cubbies hold obelisks (phallic) on the right (masculine) side, and spheres on the left (feminine) side for clear psychic and spiritual vision, sweet dreams, love, and alchemy. Everything is symmetrical and balanced. A partnership or love altar always adorns the mantle or wall facing the foot of the bed for harmonious synergy of relational union.

After I applied the principles for love and prosperity, I met my former partner 30 days later and quadrupled my income. The emerald-and-gold theme, water in the abundance corner, crystal grids, and circular couch for eternal community support *worked*!

What resonates with you?

Some Feng Shui color associations don't make sense to me; organizing elemental placement was most helpful. Particular walls are best for creativity—I cozied up productively when I sat against them. A "command position" grants supremacy and aligns you with your purpose, creative inspiration, and mastery over your dominion. Rather than having my antique desk overlooking the expansive view like I wanted, it felt more regal and authoritative in the center of the room. I was blown away by the difference when I filmed content, taught, or knocked to-do's off my list.

It's important to also create a ritualistic bathroom as the place of spiritual and physical cleansing. Luxuriate in a tub lined with shells and candles. Hang fresh eucalyptus branches from your showerhead. Tropical plants like being moist and salt lamp nightlights keep a cozy glow.

Keeping living room floors soft ensures that they're welcoming communal gathering spaces. I have a massive (secondhand) sheepskin and velvet pillow cuddle puddle in my secondary living room, and people always gravitate there rather than the main space with cloud couches on hardwood floors. An epic flea-market find, my giant vintage Venus emerging from the ocean painting adds to the lounging Goddess vibe.

At the heart of the home, the kitchen, I have a little altar by the stove, keep the counters clear of clutter, and ensure there are always fresh flowers. Hanging herbs or art beautifies and enriches the cooking process.

Entryways and doorways are crucial for inviting energy in. Unobstructed paths, the first Feng Shui rule, are essential for attracting luck and blessings. Decorative elements like cat figurines (or real cats) and lanterns can set the tone right out the gate.

Altars welcome dreams and visions as you do guests and blessings. At your front entryway or centrally located in common spaces, keep your desires anchored where you see them consistently.

Each adaptation enhances the aesthetic and vibe of your home but also aligns your living space with your spiritual and emotional needs.

FINDING INSPIRATION AND INTENTION FOR YOUR HOME

We can draw ornamental inspiration from every corner of the world and human history. What culture's adornment do you love most? The baubles, bangles, and bright colors of India? The soft, hand-spun, naturally dyed textiles of the countryside? Draping diaphanous fabrics like Greek Goddesses?

Personally, I resonate deeply with medieval aesthetics—OG Gothic French, medieval Italian frescoes, and the grandeur of British castles. My imagination is captivated by old-world style. When I walk through the streets of Paris, I can't help but mourn the loss of gargoyles and opulent fountains with elaborate scenes depicting devotion to the Divine in pert breasts, cherubs about to release their love arrows, and bountiful beasts or cascading vines. How have we so digressed to plain, straight lines in black and white?

Although I yearn for more ornate surroundings, I haven't found an authentic castle in L.A. to live in yet. Until I own my own palace and can fully embrace that aesthetic, I bring magik into my homes in other ways, architecting as many Hogwarts vibes as possible. In my Ravenclaw common room, I have plush indigo velvet cloud couches, and an artist sprinkled golden diamond stars across the deep blue wall for me. It looks like fairy dust sprung from a magik wand.

My desk is hundreds of years old, and the silk balloon chair you might know from my YouTube set is a genuine remnant of a bygone era.

I got my love of design from the warm, rustic mountain chalet I was raised in. My mother, an excellent decorator, infused our home with endless color, contributing to my love for vibrant hues and farmhouse comfort. Devoid of a single white surface (except the porcelain sinks and toilets), rustic fixtures, reclaimed redwood timbers, and copper trimmings were warm and welcoming. Like a feminine hunting lodge. The sterility of all-white environments tends to make me a little nervous. Like I'm going to mess something up rather than cozily sink into enjoying them.

My family's house just has a glow about it. Rich, peachy oranges, sunny yellows, and golden-russet sponged walls make it feel cheerful and comfortable no matter the season, though we're all partial to decking the halls for the holidays and trimming the tree with Christmas carols jamming. A roaring fire in the rock-hewn hearth crackled almost every night, for which we gathered each stone by hand from the surrounding six rivers in Humboldt County.

We'd walk down the backyard trail to a field of horses, complete with apple trees and bags of carrots to spoil them. Then past a pumpkin patch to the babbling woodland brook. I hope I get to raise my kids in that house.

Ask yourself:

> *What kind of places make me feel most comfortable?*
> *What places on Earth inspire me?*
> *What do I want to feel in my own home or another's?*

You can create your most mystical setting. A hobbit house den, an enchanted fairy bedroom, a dragon lair sex dungeon, whatever you're into! Following trends is just the influence of manufacturers and the capitalist machine constantly convincing you to consume more. When you cultivate your own look, you are the creator. You're in charge. We're often afraid of standing out or looking different, but that's the point. Walking into a house that feels like any other staged setup just never feels the same as one with a character that's truly authentic to the person who lives there.

IMPLEMENTING ADORNMENT WITH INTENTION

Switching up your decor with the seasons or whenever you move into a new space also infuses new energy into your environment. You can change up the entire vibe as you and your expression evolve. I traded my circular couch for velvet Restoration Hardware Cloud

Couches (from Facebook Marketplace, of course), and they were the perfect comfy cocoons for our Ravenclaw common room vibe.

When I blessed my new home, it was an act steeped in meaningful ritual. My Realtor, who is also a cherished sister in our circle, facilitated a house blessing. It was synchronistically perfect—four women and four men gathered for a beautiful ceremony lighting candles, cleansing, and sending wishes.

During an autumn equinox ritual housewarming, we created a crystal grid. I had a collection of medium and small crystals on a tray, and each person chose a crystal, imbued it with a wish, and placed it into the grid. This collective act crafted a bespoke crystal grid that wove intentions and hopes into the very fabric of my home. It was a profoundly special and beautiful manifestation of community and support. While I cherish luxuriating and hosting in my big fancy house, I would happily choose a simple home where Minerva was still with me any day.

Incorporating these small, intentional elements into your home doesn't need to be grandiose. Simple additions like a Wishing Tree or a bowl filled with meaningful stones can significantly enhance the spiritual and aesthetic quality of your space. These elements invite you to infuse every corner with personal meaning and magical intent, transforming your home into a true sanctuary of your essence and aspirations.

What are you filling your home with? Ritual? Celebration? Ceremony?

Or plastic, child labor, and neglect?

How are you adorning the vibrational walls of your sacred space?

The process begins with inquiry and intention. Do you really need what you're considering? Is it truly in alignment with your values and desires?

We often get caught up in the compulsive cycle encouraged by apps and websites designed to make us buy more. However, the key is to consciously observe your needs. For instance, if there's a specific area in your home where you want to place something unique—like an unusual bookshelf or a treasure chest—hold out for a perfect piece that truly speaks to you.

HOUSE OF MIRRORS

Crossing the threshold into your living space, what sensations envelop you?

Clearing clutter ensures that abundance, opportunities, friendship, and blessings have an easy path through your life. All points of access, such as doors, hallways, windows, and entrances should be just that, accessible. It's okay if you have intentional items, like crystals, statues, or plants (which almost always bring more good Chi—the life force energy that runs through everything—into your home), but there shouldn't be any trash, appliances, or disarray. Clutter in general is said to block and stagnate Chi, so getting rid of excess items is always a good idea.

Regular decluttering is a powerful practice. I once hired a personal organizer who helped me eliminate excess from every room, shedding old clothes and unnecessary items tucked away in drawers. It's crucial to let go and donate what you no longer need, especially during significant life changes like moving homes. Each move is an opportunity for expansion—not just physically but energetically, pushing you to embrace a larger, more demanding space without filling it with mere stuff.

This intersection between home and glamour magik brings a common conundrum. Whereas antique furniture was always built to last—hence, castles maintaining armoires and bureaus that are hundreds of years old—IKEA and Amazon products are quite the opposite. We are confronted with the modern dilemma of alluring cheap, mass-produced items designed to *mimic* luxury that disappoint with their fleeting durability and plastic composition.

That's why I always advocate buying secondhand and incorporating timeless pieces—those old, solid wood items that carry earthy energy or sturdy reliability in Feng Shui. These pieces don't just fill a space; they bring in the frequency of embodied dependability, strength, and grounded growth, a solid foundation for you and your home.

Today, by reclaiming the witch, magik, and our sovereignty, we can harness these ancient secrets in fun, sexy, and authentic ways. Honoring the Earth transforms our existence, while also teaching us not to become overly attached to material things. Remember, you are the altar, the temple, the sacred sanctuary. You are worthy of all the beauty on Earth, and that which you have adorned for is already yours.

MICROWITCHUALS

* **Morning Mirror:** Take a moment to visualize your Highest Self. What is the midpoint between you and the infinite divine? Is it angelic, wild, seductive, ceremonial? How can you dress that way? Put on an outfit someone else might consider a costume. Then spend at least 8 to 10 minutes gazing at yourself in the mirror affirming statements that are aligned with this version of you all in present tense.
  "I am so grateful to be living my purpose."
  "I am loving the feeling of being so safe in my full power and expression."
  "I love myself so much; I love my courage, my strength; I am the baddest bitch around."
  Whatever that version of you knows to feel about their awesomeness or experiences in your dream life, say it all!

* Choose a corner of your home to turn into a sacred space. Adorn it with items that hold meaning—crystals, candles, feathers, or personal mementos. Spend a few minutes there each day meditating or simply being present.

* Before you get dressed, set an intention for the day. Choose clothes that reflect how you want to feel—whether it's powerful, joyful, or serene. Transform the act of getting dressed into an intentional self-expression ritual.

* This practice is a favorite (albeit confronting aspect of some of my most important money manifestation rituals). Look around your home and ask, *"What genuinely represents me, and what I want to create in my life? What doesn't?"*

Consider which items you purchased from a state of abundance and which from scarcity. Like the special painting you got on an international adventure versus the cheaper polyester alternative to velvet, or the sheepskin you wanted but didn't feel worthy of. This inventory surpasses assessing possessions to understanding patterning. Reflect on how each item contributes to the energy and aesthetic of your home ensuring your living space authentically illustrates who you are and supports the life you want. We all want the highest vibes possible, right?

* When your clothes don't feel right, get naked. Don't look in the mirror; just feel your body or dance. Place your hands on it lovingly, tune in, give thanks, and send gratitude.

  Ask your body what it needs from you. If the image you see or the reflections you get don't feel right, it's likely a fracture in your own perception. Understand the distinction between weight that's healthy and genuinely yours, and weight that might be an energetic shield or self-sabotage. If you're battling with overeating or obesity, the glamour you seek is in feeling worthy. It's about nurturing your body so it's vibrant, able to bend, hike, dance, and revel in its existence.

  Begin with an intimate ritual: an eye-gazing practice with coconut oil. Cover your body with the oil, stroking it lovingly, and with every caress, say, *"I love you, beautiful."* Look yourself in the eyes as you do this, embracing and holding whatever emotions arise. This practice is a powerful way to connect deeply with yourself and cultivate self-love.

Conclusion

Well, my dear reader, we've reached the end of this leg of our journey together. I so deeply appreciate your perseverance through this prose, requesting that you relate more ritualistically to life and the world around you. How has your world, or at the very least your view of it, changed?

I pray that you have come to see your life, our planet, and her people, with new eyes. That you feel yourself as the holy sanctuary, the vessel for magik, and the reflection of Nature you are divinely designed to be. That Witchual gives you hope—the kind you can feel on a quantum level, throughout space and time. That it brings you back to your inner child, giving you permission to play full-out and enjoy the beautiful blessing of life. That it strengthens your faith—faith in your own power to create change, to have a positive impact on others and our magnificent Mother Earth, and faith in the goodness of our species, which starts with you.

I hope you'll give up Amazon and fast fashion. That you'll support the regeneration of forests, the cleaning of oceans, farmers markets, and vintage clothing and furniture. That you'll give yourself the unabashed freedom to dress up as your own royal, heroic archetype.

Most of all, I hope you come home to yourself, your innate connection to the Divine, and your original, spiritual essence through Witchual. That you let it lead you to your ultimate fulfillment, grandest adventure, and most legendary life. And, of course, that you will continue to adventure with me so I get to see or meet you in a course or at a retreat! I can't do this alone—in order to live in a magikal world, we have to work together, grow together, rise together.

No matter how many spells you cast, the greatest transformation you will ever experience comes from your healing. From learning not to shy away from your shadows, but bravely facing them, listening to what they're trying to communicate to you, and tending to the garden of your body, mind, and spirit. From watching the way your wounding informs your behaviors and doing the work to transform them.

I know it's hard, trust me. I know it's agonizing sometimes. I know how much easier it is to numb out and watch Netflix. But my only regret in life is how many hours I wasted doing just that. I would do anything to get that time back for working on myself and my dreams. Life is a precious gift; that's why we call it the present. There's no more soothing or supportive way to embark on this path of metamorphosis than with sisters and brothers by your side, holding each other in community. Go out and find those who will walk you home, hand in hand, as you do the same for them. Become a forest, a meadow, together.

Viscerally experiencing yourself as the temple in which you worship, the altar at which you pray, is the most holy and divine feeling we could ever wish for in these bodies. It is possible for us in any moment and offers us endless spiritual riches we can attain no other way.

That is the goal and invitation of Witchual: to be so internally wealthy that you magnetize to you everything you could ever possibly desire, to live in communities where we are all fulfilled in every realm of existence. That is why I wrote this book the way I did. Because just the simple act of breathing is a ritual of health and wellness when you bring your attention and intention to it.

I hope that you take this knowledge into your life and turn it into the wisdom that guides you. May you remember that no matter what your story is, you are living your own hero or heroine's journey, and I'm so excited to see what new narrative you can weave with Witchual on your side. Thank you for making this world a better place.

Acknowledgments

My greatest thanks goes to Mother Earth. All the redwood forests, alpine lakes, Rocky Mountain majesty, snowflakes, streams, and rivers who held and inspired me, guided and led me through this Witchualistic life of mine.

To my mom, who welcomed me into her home time and time again when I needed to escape the hustle and bustle of city life and return to my Grandmother Redwoods for respite, recharge, and rejuvenation throughout this manuscript and beyond.

To my teachers, Layla Martin, Dennis Andres, Ally Bogard, Enker McCovey, and Regena Thomashauer, who have shared stories and wisdom that changed me and this path of supporting others.

To my Topanga Tribe and all the sacred sisters who showed up for me when I couldn't show up for myself. Who took quiet nature hikes, sang, self-pleasured, swam in wild waters, housed me and the kitty girl, and held me as I cried when everything I had identified with as I started writing this book was wiped away from my reality so a new, truer life could be reborn from the ashes. We scattered to the wind during the fires in the final moments of this manuscript and yet found ways to stay connected, deepening in love and devotion to the dream of sharing safe land and resources for our children. You are the greatest gifts in my life.

To my agent, Coleen, who believed in me and these projects from the very beginning, and Hay House for letting me make up my own words and share their wisdom with the world.

Thanks to all of the other brave women who have written books—my Goddess, it is a grueling gauntlet. I have been so blessed by the words of Robin Wall Kimmerer, Dr. Sharon Blackie, Sophie Strand, and of course Sarah J. Maas, Penn Cole, and Tamora Pierce, who created worlds of magik for me to escape into when I just couldn't "learn" more and needed a break from personal development and scholarly pursuits. And as always to Northtown Books, my original access point to the fantastical worlds that fundamentally formed who I am.

To my incredible therapist, Rick, who kept me sane throughout the hardest year of my life and helped me see through so many of the subconscious challenges that created it for my growth.

To Jaspre, my ultimate Fairy Godmother and genie in a bottle, who helped me make so many dreams come true. Thank you for seeing me and supporting me when it felt like everything else was falling away. For being the light at the end of my tunnel every time we connected, and for bringing this wild witch's magikal medicine out into the mainstream media. You were absolutely right when you said, "You ain't never had a friend like me."

Which leads me to my strangest acknowledgment:

I want to honor myself. I have never been challenged the way I was through the year-plus of writing *Witchual*.

I was cracked open in every way. I lost both my soulmate fur children—almost two years after losing Minerva, I still just can't understand why she had to be taken from me, other than removing all cords from my relationship. But I have never missed anyone or anything like I miss her. I pray she comes back to me in an undeniable way and we get to continue adventuring together. Then her brother passed, and my five-year relationship ended. I couldn't show up in my business and "sell" myself from a place of such emptiness and overwhelm, so I experienced scarcity for the first time in many years. I was bleeding money without my normally anticipated returns, yet invested more and more into my healing. It's not the kind of advice that's "do as I say, not as I do." This is one place where I can confidently say without a shadow of a doubt that I fully walk my talk. Then I left the palatial estate I had poured hundreds of thousands of dollars into, worked so tirelessly and intentionally to create as the foundation for what I thought was going to be the *best year ever!* And

ACKNOWLEDGMENTS

when I finally made it back to settle in Topanga again, it caught fire 30 days later and I was displaced for months.

I didn't want to write this book anymore when all this happened. I was devastated. I didn't want to do rituals; I felt annihilated, hopeless, and utterly uncertain of how to carry on. Luckily I was contractually obligated to finish it so I maintained the creative force to make it happen.

Sitting in the verdant meadows of Ojai, California, as summer of 2025 approaches, finishing up these final words, I am so grateful this was the one project and necessity that kept me going. I might have just crawled into a hole, but I didn't.

I was initiated through this struggle. Offered an ordeal from the Goddess. It was the worst grief and heartache I have ever experienced. So I want to acknowledge my bravery, perseverance, resilience, and commitment. I see so many people refuse to do the work, who just complain about their circumstances and do nothing to change them. I am not one of those people. I never shied away, I never backed down, I never gave up. I am so grateful for the spirit Goddess put inside me to so courageously continue facing my own inner witch hunter even when I felt like I'd been ultimately defeated. I am proud of the woman I have become, all the shadows I have faced, and the alchemy of that lead into gold.

So I want to remind any of you still reading that you have immense power beyond what you know, what you think is possible. Even in your darkest days you can still keep going.

About the Author

Mia Magik is a world-renowned transformational healer dubbed the "Spiritual Fairy Godmother" by *USA Today* for her ability to make dreams come true. An intuitive advisor and conscious coach for entrepreneurs, actors, athletes, and industry leaders in technology, film, and finance, she also hosts her own travel docuseries.

With training in a myriad of spiritual traditions, Mia is the first witch to bring wild somatic healing work to the mainstream. Her sex magik pleasure practice was featured in the *Los Angeles Times*; her sacred rage ritual was on the *Today* show, *Fortune* magazine, and *Fox News* and a topic of conversation from Joe Rogan to Brett Cooper.

An expert on earth-based spirituality and reintegrating femininity as manifestation methods, she supports transformation of the way we interact with reality to soothe our souls' suffering. Guiding recognition of how your body speaks to you and how to listen to it, trust your inner knowing, and harness the forces of creation, Mia's magik purifies patriarchal wounds so you can live with confidence and purpose, activating your multidimensional gifts.

Mia is an ambassador for ancient wisdom in the modern world as a remedy to our mental and spiritual health crisis. She has facilitated corporate experiences for Redbull, LinkedIn, Forbes, and YPO, empowering thousands to reconnect with their infinite spiritual abilities and reclaim emotional authority and autonomy to live their most magikal life with genuine fulfillment.

Her Academy of Magikal Artistry and acclaimed enchanting retreats, akin to real-life Hogwarts, offer profound experiences of personal transfiguration by connecting to your authentic nature through Nature.

The best-selling author of *IntuWitchin*, she invites us on a journey of collective healing, awakening to fantasy and magik as our birthright, embodying her mission to liberate and inspire through the wisdom of the witch: wise, wild, and free.

Website: **www.miamagik.com**

Hay House Titles of Related Interest

YOU CAN HEAL YOUR LIFE, the movie,
starring Louise Hay & Friends
(available as an online streaming video)
www.hayhouse.co.uk/louise-movie

THE SHIFT, the movie,
starring Dr Wayne W. Dyer
(available as an online streaming video)
www.hayhouse.co.uk/the-shift-movie

Craft Your Own Magic: Reawaken Your Intuition, Understand Magical Correspondences and Create a Meaningful Personal Practice by Cassie Uhl

The Divine Frequency: Harness the Magic of Universal Laws for Transformation, Manifestation and Freedom by Abiola Abrams

Self Source-ery: Come to Your Senses. Trust Your Instincts. Remember Your Magic by Lisa Lister

Remember Your Roots: How to Awaken Your Ancestral Power and Live with Gratitude (A Book Inspired by Mayan Wisdom) by Christine Olivia Hernandez with Syris King-Klem

All of the above are available at your local bookstore,
or may be ordered by contacting Hay House (see next page).

✶ ✵ ✶

We hope you enjoyed this Hay House book. If you'd like to receive our online catalogue featuring additional information on Hay House books and products, please contact:

Hay House UK Ltd
1st Floor, Crawford Corner,
91–93 Baker Street, London W1U 6QQ
Tel: +44 (0)20 3927 7290; www.hayhouse.co.uk

Published in the United States of America by:
Hay House LLC
PO Box 5100, Carlsbad, CA 92018-5100
Tel: (760) 431-7695 or (800) 654-5126
www.hayhouse.com

Published in Australia by:
Hay House Australia Publishing Pty Ltd
18/36 Ralph St., Alexandria NSW 2015
Tel: +61 (02) 9669 4299
www.hayhouse.com.au

Published in India by:
Hay House Publishers (India) Pvt Ltd
Muskaan Complex, Plot No. 3,
B-2, Vasant Kunj, New Delhi 110 070
Tel: +91 11 41761620
www.hayhouse.co.in

Let Your Soul Grow
Experience life-changing transformation – one video at a time – with guidance from the world's leading experts.
www.healyourlifeplus.com

TRANSFORM YOUR DAY—ANYTIME, ANYWHERE

With the **Empower You** Unlimited Audio *App*

> ★★★★★ **Life changing.**
> My fav app on my entire phone, hands down! – Gigi

Unlimited access to the entire Hay House audio library!

You'll get:

- 600+ soul-stirring **audiobooks** to expand your mind
- 1,000+ **meditations** for restful sleep, morning focus, and gentle healing
- Bite-sized audios **under 20 minutes**—perfect for busy days
- **Exclusive talks** you won't find anywhere else
- **Daily affirmations**
- Fresh content added **every week** to fuel your journey

New audios added every week!

> Driving, yard work, and housework have been **transformed!**
> – Ruffles27

Scan the QR code to start listening or visit **hayhouse.com/unlimited**

CONNECT WITH
HAY HOUSE
ONLINE

🌐 hayhouse.co.uk   **f** @hayhouse

📷 @hayhouseuk.   🦋 @hayhouseuk.bsky.social

♪ @hayhouseuk   ▶ @HayHousePresents

> Find out all about our latest books & card decks • Be the first to know about exclusive discounts • Interact with our authors in live broadcasts • Celebrate the cycle of the seasons with us • Watch free videos from your favourite authors • Connect with like-minded souls

'The gateways to wisdom and knowledge are always open.'

Louise Hay